PRAISE FOR *NOT YOUR RES*

"*Not Your Rescue Project* opens up long overdue space for migrant sex workers—who are routinely spoken about, spoken for, and spoken over in service of expanding and entrenching carceral approaches to violence—to speak for themselves. What their experiences and visions make clear is that borders, criminalization, policing, and punishment are the culprits, not the cure, furthering violence and coercion in every sector of the economy, including the sex trades, rather than preventing or interrupting it. The authors' call is clear: migrant sex workers are the experts in their own experiences, they demand simultaneous recognition of their agency and of the intersecting structures of violence that shape their lives, and their leadership is essential to our movements. Required reading for everyone who cares about trafficking, labor rights, and racial, gender, migrant, and economic justice." —**ANDREA J. RITCHIE**, author of *Invisible No More: Police Violence Against Black Women and Women of Color*

"*Not Your Rescue Project* is a powerful indictment of the violence and injustice that Global South migrant sex workers face under the banners of rescue and saviorism. It offers forthright and compelling documentation of the struggles and humanity of such migrants who live and work in Canada and the United States, while providing a searing critique of anti-prostitution, victim-centered approaches, including the anti-human trafficking industry. This is a much-needed book that brings significant depth to a growing trend in global sex worker rights research—a crucial call to action for students, researchers, and activists concerned with migrant, sexuality, and feminist and global worker justice and rights." —**KAMALA KEMPADOO**, Professor Emerita, Social Science, York University

"You will never be the same after reading, studying, teaching, and sharing *Not Your Rescue Project*. Curating personalized interludes, historical analysis, and grassroots movement archiving, this book is a masterpiece composition of survival, self-defense, and liberationist testimonial strategies. Migrant sex workers are truth-tellers, solidarity organizers, community builders, and grounded critical practitioners who are permanently reshaping abolitionist, anti-imperialist, anti-violence, radical feminist, and various other streams of 'left' mobilization. Simultaneously creative, generous, and graceful in its layered invitations to engage in the complex challenges of 'joint struggle,' this foundational text calls on every justice-oriented community to engage with the incomparable radicalism of migrant sex worker praxis." —**DYLAN RODRÍGUEZ**, scholar, teacher, movement collaborator, and Distinguished Professor at the University of California–Riverside

"*Not Your Rescue Project* exposes the right-wing 'rescue' fraud perpetrated by the sex work prohibitionists and their carceral allies by centering the lived experience of migrant sex workers organizing for their own liberation. It is essential reading for anyone interested in pushing back against those who mobilize state violence in the guise of helping vulnerable workers." —**ALEX S. VITALE**, author of *The End of Policing*

"Intellectually trenchant, emotionally affecting, and deeply needed, *Not Your Rescue Project* is absolutely essential reading for anyone involved in social justice, labor activism, human rights, migrant justice, and sex education. For far too long, misconceptions, racism, anti–sex work stigma, and blatant opportunism have shaped legislation and policy on sex work to the severe detriment of those with the most to lose. Elene Lam and Chanelle Gallant set the record straight with powerful analysis and storytelling drawn from many years of solidarity and advocacy work with migrant sex workers, exposing the exploitation and outright deception perpetrated by the so-called anti-human trafficking movement. This is one of the most important books on migrant justice, labor justice, and sex worker rights that I have read in the past decade, and I am so grateful that it exists." —**KAI CHENG THOM**, author of *I Hope We Choose Love*

"Many queer people are familiar with the saying 'We are all in the gutter, but some of us are looking at the stars.' In this rousing book on migrant sex worker struggle, founder of the Butterfly network Elene Lam and organizer Chanelle Gallant demonstrate how the joyful labor of solidarity lifts everyone's gaze to a just and liberated horizon for all, in stark contrast with the prevalent saviorist and humanitarian approaches to sex trafficking. When butterflies get together to extract minerals from a shallow patch of muddy water, it is called a 'puddle club.' *Not Your Rescue Project* opens our eyes to the powerful human 'puddle clubs' all around us, beating their wings for justice and somehow turning the mud slung at them into nourishment. This book makes joining them irresistible." —**SOPHIE LEWIS**, author of *Enemy Feminisms* and *Abolish the Family*

NOT YOUR RESCUE PROJECT

MIGRANT SEX WORKERS
FIGHTING FOR JUSTICE

CHANELLE GALLANT AND ELENE LAM

Haymarket Books
Chicago, Illinois

Published in 2024 by
Haymarket Books
P.O. Box 180165
Chicago, IL 60618
www.haymarketbooks.org

ISBN: 979-8-88890-086-4

Distributed to the trade in the US through Consortium Book Sales
and Distribution (www.cbsd.com) and internationally through
Ingram Publisher Services International (www.ingramcontent.com).

This book was published with the generous support of Lannan
Foundation, Wallace Action Fund, and Marguerite Casey
Foundation.

Special discounts are available for bulk purchases by organizations
and institutions. Please email info@haymarketbooks.org for more
information.

Cover design by Rachel Cohen.

Library of Congress Cataloging-in-Publication data is available.

Entered into digital printing in October 2024.

To migrant sex workers:
your stories, power, and resistance inspire us

CONTENTS

FOREWORD

Harsha Walia

I n 2019, I recall Toronto City Hall officials being completely shaken and surprised when three hundred migrant sex workers descended on City Hall to speak out against a proposed licensing regulation of massage parlors that would have left two thousand low-income, Asian migrant women out of work. While city officials and mainstream media characterized this proposed regulation as a "safety measure to crack down on trafficking," the workers declared they were not trafficking victims and did not need to be rescued. They shared stories identifying the root causes of their marginalization: racism, sexism, capitalism, whorephobia, police raids, deportations, precarious work, and bureaucratic regulation. Marking the first time in Canadian history that so many low-income migrant sex workers asserted their power, these workers organized in Butterfly: Asian and Migrant Sex Workers Support Network collectively shifted the narrative from one of victimhood to resistance.

Elene Lam and Chanelle Gallant's *Not Your Rescue Project* meticulously maps the largely untold mobilizations of groups like Butterfly and offers a sweeping reframing about state violence perpetrated in the name of "rescue." Lam and Gallant forcefully point out, "Migrant sex workers are under assault by the state." Migrant sex workers are caught in a grinding architecture of carceral control: policing, surveillance, sex work laws, immigration enforcement, child protection services, municipal bylaw officers, and anti-trafficking policies. Abolitionists know that such carceral systems increase harm and isolation. Instead, real safety lies in resourcing life-affirming institutions. In the case of migrant sex workers, real safety is generated by organizing to make the conditions of sex work less precarious and the conditions of migration less restrictive. Supporting migrant sex workers is thus a key part of any abolitionist struggle. Every page of this precise and unflinching book is full of movement-based analysis and organizing lessons for enacting such solidarity and safety.

Some of the harshest immigration restrictions today are enacted against migrant sex workers. This is part of a long history. Some of the very first immigration restrictions and border controls in the US were imposed on migrant women who were—or were deemed to be—sex workers. The Page Act of 1875 preceded the more well-known 1882 Chinese Exclusion Act. Playing on white, middle-class, anti-Chinese moral panics about "prostitution" and "opium dens," the act banned Chinese women deemed to be sex workers from entering the country.

Chinese migrant women were also some of the first targets of anti-trafficking laws, under which they were subjected to immigration investigations on whether they were being trafficked "for lewd and immoral purposes." In 1910, the US Congress passed the White Slave Traffic Act to target sex-trafficking rings and to protect white girls from forced prostitution that they were lured into by "foreign immigrant traffickers." This paralleled the state regulation of Black and Indigenous women's sexuality under enslavement and settler colonialism. In Canada, similar legislation aimed at the so-called white slave trade placed restrictions on sex work and was also used to restrict immigration.

Criminalization through anti-trafficking policies allows the state to emerge as the great "rescuer," while leaving migrant sex workers more susceptible to violence and exploitation. Mimicking the "white slave panic" of earlier eras, today's trafficking discourses are framed in the language of "modern-day slavery." This white supremacist saviordom is a gross and glaring appropriation of Black liberation struggles to enable the very thing that abolition is opposed to: increased criminalization and violence. The premise of anti-trafficking laws is that because vulnerable women and girls are "trafficked" against their will, they must be "sent back." Like the oxymoron of feminist jails, these are supposedly "feminist deportations." This state violence *is* gender-based violence. And ironically, this kind of coerced "rescue" seems a lot like actual trafficking. The purpose of anti-trafficking measures, then, is not to support migrant sex workers but to increase policing and to restrict the free movement and labor of migrant women. Why? Because migrant sex workers disrupt the structure of racial colonial modernity: there is the supposed poor racialized trafficked victim, on the one hand, and the empowered autonomous middle-class white woman, on the other. *Not Your Rescue Project* is a rare gem, its pages brimming with the captivating voices of migrant sex workers rejecting this binary and describing their own complex, multidimensional narratives.

The criminalization of sex work and the criminalization of migration are gendered racial regimes that are not coincidental to but rather *completely constituted* through each other. Anti-Asian attacks, such as the 2021 shooting in Atlanta that killed eight people, including six Asian massage workers, stem from a legacy of sexual violence, imperialism, and control of working-class migrant sex workers. In a time of escalating fascism, this book urges us to refuse right-wing, fear-mongering moral panics. Lam and Gallant drive home that the issue we should be concerned with is not trafficking or victim narratives (what they say function as "a concealed form of state violence") but, rather, the control of migration, the criminalization of sex work, the exploitation of labor relations within capitalism, and the circuits of empire that manufacture vulnerability.

Kate Zen, who is quoted in the pages of this path-breaking book, writes, "Asian sex workers today are not responsible for the negative associations of the sex trade; neither are we responsible for the global economic structures that make sex work one of the most highly paid ways for a woman without an education to survive. Changing those economic and social structures does not start with violently silencing sex workers."[1]

Yet many gender essentialists and sex worker–exclusionary feminists (who shamefully call themselves sex work "abolitionists") manipulate feminism to silence sex workers. Contrary to such white supremacist, colonial, bourgeois moralizing masquerading as feminism, we have an incredible living legacy of Black, Marxist, Indigenous, queer and trans, Third World, and abolitionist feminisms that locate sex work within feminist analysis. Sex worker analysis disrupts the cis-heteropatriarchal model of marriage and the nuclear family. Patriarchy relies on privatized, cheapened or often unwaged, feminized labor— what feminists call the social reproduction of labor. Sex work *simultaneously* makes visible *and refuses* the unfree condition of care work and the social reproduction of labor. The Black Women for Wages for Housework group wrote in 1975: "We take on the second job of prostitution—because we are not paid for the first job we all do as women, housework, the job of producing and taking care of everybody so that we all can work and make profits for the Man."[2] One of the pillars upholding gendered oppression *is* the oppression of sex workers, particularly Black, Indigenous, migrant, racialized, trans, working-class sex workers. Put another way, sex work is not inherently exploitative because of patriarchy; rather, patriarchal oppression is possible because of the punitive regulation of sex workers. As Lam and Gallant describe, the stigma around sex work is one of the key ways that women's sexuality and labor power is funneled into the capitalist cishetero-nuclear family model of marriage and unpaid domestic work. Decriminalization of sex work is thus unequivocally a feminist issue.

Migrant sex worker struggles are also central to struggles against gendered racial capitalism. The slogan "Sex work is work" is an affirmation that sex workers belong in left labor struggles! Rather than exceptionalizing it as inherently exploitative, labor activists ought to set sex work alongside other forms of feminized, racialized work made precarious such as domestic work and service work. Like any other association of workers, sex workers don't all need to "love their job" in order to collectively bargain or be respected as workers. Choice within capitalism is constrained for most, and is always racialized, gendered, sexualized, and so on. We must refuse dead-end debates about choice, while affirming the agency and dignity that sex work can provide for many migrant sex workers outside of conventionally disciplined and disabling work under capitalism.

This book is a crucial corrective and antidote to commonplace liberal, carceral, racist, misogynist, transphobic views on migrant sex workers. Lam and Gallant make clear that the vulnerability of migrant sex workers is deliberately *manufactured*. Migrant sex work exists on a spectrum of work that has been made dangerous through stigma, criminalization, moralizing patriarchy, rescue raids, colonial regulation, border controls, wage suppression, and unsafe work conditions. For migrant sex workers, precarious or illegalized immigration status in particular compounds sexual, social, and state violence and drives them further underground.

Migrant sex work, and in fact all migrant work, relies on the border's production of *deportability*. Even though migrant workers labor in the same space as so-called citizen workers, the border is a race-making and labor-suppressing regime that enforces wage differentiation, labor abuse, and social segregation. The precarity and disposability of migrant sex workers is rooted in their status as migrants. The category of *migrant work* is a state-manufactured relation of difference. Ending the vulnerability of and violence against migrant sex workers, then, does not mean more rescue programs, or more surveillance in health care clinics, or more anti-trafficking "red flag" training, or more cops on the block, or more punitive immigration restrictions. Instead, we must demand status for all migrant workers and labor protections for all migrant workers. To support the safety of migrant sex workers, we need the full decriminalization of migration and the abolition of the border.

An irrefutable lesson from this magnificently unsparing book is that migrant sex workers are not victims. Migrant sex work is often *in itself* an act of resistance to racial, gendered, class, and nationalist oppression. And migrant sex worker organizing is not a siloed struggle. Migrant sex workers are at the heart of many of today's struggles: in global class struggles organizing for labor rights; in feminist struggles for bodily autonomy and against carceral, savior rescue feminism; in abolitionist movements fighting against police, prison, and border controls; in migrant justice struggles making the links between criminalization and illegalization.

Lam and Gallant write, "Racialized migrant sex workers and migrant sex worker organizers are not helpless victims. They take up their rightful place at the center of struggles against the multiple overlapping social and economic crises of our time—carceral states and state violence, xenophobia, white supremacy, patriarchy, border securitization and imperialism, racial capitalism, and its catastrophic effects on people and the planet."

The crystal clear and brilliant analysis of this statement—indeed, of the whole book—originates from the authors' decades of community organizing. It is an homage to forms of knowledge production coming from the rigorous and reflective *intellectual labor and life* of social movements. These two tireless, generous, loving, joyful movement organizers (and my teachers) place their constellation of beloved co-conspirators squarely at the center of political analysis.

Not surprisingly, this book does not simply identify the structures we have to dismantle, but daylights migrant sex worker organizing transforming every corner of the world. Migrant sex workers are literally worldmaking: building awe-inspiring networks of community mutual aid and membership organizations; answering the question of "Who keeps us safe?" through sharing extensive safety planning strategies; providing health, educational, legal, and care services to sex workers and their kin, who are often cast out of state and social systems; and evading and defying carceral, capitalist, colonial power at every turn. This is abolitionist imagination as reality. Let me repeat: migrant sex worker organizing is abolitionist imagination as reality: "The world needs migrant sex workers and migrant sex worker organizing—it just doesn't know it yet." May these pages fuel our fires for abolition and revolution in our lifetime.

Harsha Walia
Vancouver, unceded territories of the xʷməθkʷəy̓ə (Musqueam), Sḵwx̱wú7mesh (Squamish), and səlilwətaɬ (Tsleil-Waututh) Nations

March 2024

INTRODUCTION

A RADICAL REFRAMING OF SEX WORK, MIGRATION, AND JUSTICE

We are not dishonourable trash to be cleansed from the city. We are not expendable labourers who can be coerced into the back-breaking, low-paying jobs they think we deserve. We are not helpless trafficking victims in need of rescue. We are human beings who can choose our own path, make our own decisions, and support ourselves with dignity if they'll only let us.
—Open letter from migrant massage and sex workers[1]

For decades, we have been sold a story about migrant sex workers as being nothing more than silent, faceless "rescue projects." Western governments, the cops, immigration control, anti-trafficking nonprofits, the media, and major corporations have constructed migrant sex workers as sex-trafficking victims or "modern slaves"—and themselves as their saviors.[2] *Not Your Rescue Project* is about the ways that this framing has obscured the truth about the real sources of danger in migrant sex workers' lives—state violence perpetrated in the name of "rescue," and social and economic inequality and injustice.

Along with this emphasis on the real injustices in their lives, *Not Your Rescue Project* is just as much about what migrant sex workers are doing in response—how they resist, organize, and fight for justice. In our framing, racialized migrant sex workers and migrant sex worker organizers are not helpless victims. They take up their rightful place at the center of struggles against the multiple overlapping social and economic crises of our time—carceral states and state violence,

1

xenophobia, white supremacy, patriarchy, border securitization and imperialism, racial capitalism, and the catastrophic effects on people and the planet.[3]

We are activists and organizers working toward migrant sex worker justice. Our writing here draws directly from our years of organizing and advocacy with racialized and low-income migrant sex worker communities in Canada, the US, and internationally who have provided us with important grounded experience to help us understand the issues. Much of our work together since 2013 has been through an organization founded by one of this book's authors, Elene Lam, called Butterfly: Asian and Migrant Sex Workers Support Network. Butterfly supports, advocates for, and builds the power of Asian migrant sex workers in Toronto and the wider region. Elene also provides support and training to organizations that work with Asian migrant sex workers and massage parlor workers in the US and globally.

As we have organized together, and built solidarity with other movements, our understanding and critical analyses of these issues have evolved. We have come to see that the root causes of the injustices that migrant sex workers face are systemic. They lie in state borders that trap people and create a hierarchy of disposable, rightless workers; a capitalist economic system that perpetuates and exploits racialized and gendered difference; patriarchal dominance that positions men and the family as the rightful benefactors of women's sexuality and their reproductive labor; and in the carceral state's oppressive apparatuses, such as incarceration and detention, surveillance, policing, and carceral logics that keep these systems of injustice in place. Migrant sex worker justice can only come through the abolition of these systems of inequality and state violence. From abolitionists, we have learned that abolition is not a single event. It is a process of reducing the size, scope, and reach of institutions of state violence, and delegitimizing their logic. It includes important reforms (such as the full decriminalization of sex work and the provision of immigration status for all), but these reforms alone are not enough. Abolition is also about transforming society in such a way that makes obsolete the interlocking systems and institutions that harm migrant sex workers.

The overarching aim of *Not Your Rescue Project* is to build broad political support for migrant sex worker justice among other people who also struggle for justice, peace, and freedom. On their own, migrant sex workers do not have the resources and power to win against the multiple systems of inequality and injustice that they are up against. No single oppressed community can. They need to be part of transformative leftist and feminist movements working to build power.[4]

We've tried to do this in three ways. The first is to disrupt and challenge myths about racialized migrant sex workers and to create space for the complexity of their stories, strength, and resistance. Many people care about migrant sex workers and want to support them. But they often do not understand migrant sex workers' realities and their need for solidarity, not rescue. We set the record straight about who migrant sex workers are—powerful fighters, oppressed workers, survivors who have been displaced by climate disaster, war, and poverty, all of which are fueled by racial capitalism. We share the complex reasons why low-income racialized migrants choose the sex industry, often to resist hyper-exploitative and controlling migrant labor sectors and migration programs.

Second, we challenge the widespread but misguided support for harmful anti-migrant and anti–sex work carceral measures that claim to combat human trafficking. The "modern slavery" moral panic has led many people who care about migrant sex workers to inadvertently work *against* migrant sex worker justice. We show how carceral approaches to migration, sex work, and human trafficking have been the pretext for expanded surveillance and criminalization, police abuse, and border exclusions and expulsions, while obscuring the real social crises facing all of us—massive inequality, poverty, climate disaster, gender-based violence, the white supremacist securitization of borders, and authoritarianism. We reveal how the industry surrounding efforts to combat human trafficking is designed to function as a concealed form of state violence.

Third, we introduce migrant sex worker political analysis and leadership to global movements for racial, social, and economic justice. The world needs migrant sex workers and migrant sex worker organizing—it just doesn't know it yet. Most people think that the laws and narratives surrounding sex work, migration, and human trafficking don't affect them. They may want to help migrant sex workers, but they don't think that migrant sex worker organizing or analysis could offer anything to their lives or their liberation. We disagree. In our view, the concern about modern slavery is a moral panic pretending to be a social justice movement, and it has significantly advanced right-wing agendas that worsen social and economic inequality for all oppressed people. For over two decades, the figure of the sex-trafficked, racialized woman (the "modern slave") has been mobilized to build support for increased carceral state control and measures such as greater police powers and budgets, increased border surveillance and restrictions (including the push for a border wall between the US and Mexico), and police raids on immigrant-run businesses in gentrifying neighborhoods. The modern slavery moral panic is an important part of how the state and the capitalist class hide the violence caused by inequality and injustice and instead blame these problems on poor, racialized migrants and sex workers. We make the case for the important role of migrant sex worker analysis and organizing as a necessary part of resisting the right.

THE TRUTH ABOUT MIGRANT SEX WORKERS

When most people think about migrant sex workers, they think of them not as humans, but as objects of grave moral concern. Not as powerful and capable community members, but as social problems. We have been trained by politicians, the police, media, churches, nonprofits, and a host of rich white academics and feminists to view sex workers from the Global South as silent, helpless "sex slaves," women sold off by their heartless families, kidnapped from their homes by human trafficking gangs and sold into torturous circumstances for the pleasure of depraved men in wealthy countries. They paint a portrait of a young woman who is too ignorant, naive, confused, or brainwashed to fight back, and quietly prays for a hero to rescue her from her traffickers. *New York Times* columnist Pamela Paul's 2023 opinion piece, "What It Means to Call Prostitution 'Sex Work'," exemplifies this. Paul has a platform at one of the most influential publications in the world, and is entirely removed from the experiences of poor, racialized sex workers in the Global South, yet writes with confidence about them as nameless victims. "I first heard the term [*sex work*] in the early '90s while living in Thailand, where I offered to volunteer for an organization aimed at helping local women caught up in prostitution. . . . We all knew many of these girls had been sold into sex slavery by their own desperately poor parents." Paul succinctly captures the main tropes of the modern slavery panic—helpless women, racialized abusers, and the liberated Westerner coming to the rescue.

Across the political spectrum, from radical left to white nationalist right, the specter of migrant sex workers from the Global South and their association with human trafficking or modern slavery looms large. For nearly three decades, the US and Canada have been awash in stories about migrant women and white girls kidnapped by cabals of sex traffickers, who in popular imagination, are assumed to be men of color—"bad hombres," "pimps," "illegal immigrants," "organized crime rings," and "gangs." Such stories form the moral foundation for international campaigns to "fight modern slavery." Vast sums of money have been funneled into various lobby and advocacy groups that claim their mission is to rescue women and crack down on traffickers. In practice, that has not meant addressing any of the causes of violence against women or abuse in the sex industry. As we'll show throughout *Not Your Rescue Project*, an agenda that claims to protect and save women by combating sex trafficking has actually worsened the situation for poor, racialized sex workers. Anti-trafficking measures—promoted as "public safety"—have reduced migrant sex workers' freedoms, rights, and control over their lives while increasing vulnerability to all forms of discrimination, abuse, and violence, including by cops and border agents, partners, clients, bosses, and smugglers. Second, anti-trafficking measures are the justification for state and civilian surveillance, police and immigration control raids, arrests, job loss, seizure/theft of wages, and deportations of migrant sex workers. Third, narratives that claim to "raise awareness" about sex trafficking have instead spread racist depictions of white-dominated institutions (such as police forces and Christian churches) as "crusading" human rights heroes, bravely liberating oppressed women of color from racialized sex traffickers.

A huge gap stands between people's perceptions of migrant sex workers and their actual reality. The modern slavery narrative is a moral panic that creates misinformation about migrant sex workers' varied experiences in the sex industry, frames migrant women as passive, sexually exploited victims of bad men who are implicitly or explicitly racialized. This is a racist, xenophobic distortion of the actual sources of exploitation and violence in their lives—the injustice meted out by the state, the police, and immigration control agents and the unjust society in which migrant sex workers live and work. These false beliefs are so powerful that they dominate *how* we see migrant sex workers, what we see, and what we think can and should be done. Migrant sex workers' agency, labor, and resistance—and also their entire lives, families, and communities—are obscured and distorted. Their involvement in sex work is seen as sex trafficking; when they cross borders, this is seen as forced movement; when they live where they work, they are believed to be held in captivity; when they have an employer or colleagues, they are considered exploited; and when they are arrested by cops, they are seen as being "rescued." The conflation of migrant sex work with sex trafficking is so strong that ordinary features of migrant sex worker life—such as using a hot plate to cook at work, not speaking English, or carrying condoms—have been misidentified as sex-trafficking "red flags" by the police, media, and neighbors.[5] Even when the state employs brutal violence against migrant sex workers, it can still appear to many people as being protective or a helpful "rescue" from worse circumstances. For example, when, the police seize migrant sex workers' wages during a raid and place the workers inside a jail cell at gunpoint, reporters describe the police as having "freed women." And if migrant sex workers who have been arrested do not identify as trafficking victims, the state's narrative flips and they are constructed as illegal immigrants, participating in organized crime. How have the public's ideas about racialized migrant sex workers become so twisted that their being held in a cage by people with guns could be described as freedom? Why are brutality and terror seen as promoting public safety, so long as the abuser is the state? Why is there so little solidarity with migrant sex workers when they face state violence?

State violence against migrant sex workers is severe. Their experiences are similar to those of undocumented migrant workers in Florida, where draconian anti-immigrant laws make it a crime to assist an undocumented migrant, and similar to those who seek abortion in US states that criminalize aiding or abetting abortion.[6] Leftist advocates have characterized the conditions facing undocumented migrant workers and total abortion bans as cruel, unconstitutional, and authoritarian and reacted with outrage and determined organizing.[7] Yet when it comes to migrant sex workers, these same conditions are considered less significant than the specter of human trafficking. Below are some of the ways migrant sex workers are already criminalized in most jurisdictions in the US and Canada, and subject to state and non-state persecution:

- Travel bans. It is not legal to enter either the US or Canada as a temporary migrant for the purposes of working in the sex industry. These travel bans are the first and oldest continuous travel bans in US and Canadian legal history. The ban on migrant sex workers includes anyone who has received the proceeds of prostitution, potentially making migrant sex workers' family members, spouses, and children inadmissible as well.[8]
- Expulsion. A sex work–related arrest or conviction—or even just an investigation—can result in the individual losing their immigration status, being denied permanent residency or stripped of citizenship, or being deported.[9]
- Surveillance, investigations, and raids. Municipal, criminal, and immigration officers openly and covertly use race and sex work as the grounds to target migrant sex workers, leading to their incarceration in prisons and detention centers and their deportation.[10] During investigations and raids,

police routinely seize or steal migrant sex workers' earnings and property, including their savings, jewelry, and phones.[11]

- Criminalization of self-defense, assistance, and support networks. It is illegal to assist a migrant sex worker to safely get across borders or find work, or work safely, even as a friend or family member. Sex workers are criminalized for taking steps that protect their safety from individual violence, such as working with other sex workers and sharing information about bad clients and bad bosses or workplaces.

- Public surveillance. It is dangerous for migrant sex workers to be seen in public because so many civilians have been trained to view them as sex-trafficking victims and report them to the police. The simple act of traveling, going to school or the store, or meeting up with friends can lead to a police or immigration control investigation, which can then lead to further harm such as the loss of employment or eviction from one's home.

- Digital surveillance. It is illegal for websites to host information online that could assist migrant sex workers in their travel or in finding work, including information that would protect their safety. It is also illegal to engage in any digital communication that assists migrant sex workers, such as text messages and social media posts. These laws are similar to those criminalizing the sharing of digital communication about getting or self-managing an abortion.[12]

- Violation of bodily autonomy. The state uses law enforcement and carceral nonprofit agencies to exercise control over migrant sex workers' sexualities and bodies. Migrant sex workers cannot legally make decisions over the kind of sex they have, cannot legally communicate their sexual boundaries, and do not have the right to determine where they live or work.

- Police and municipal officer collaboration with immigration control. Collaboration may involve police contacting

immigration control, bringing immigration control officers into migrant sex work investigations, demanding that
migrant sex workers provide their immigration status, or
detaining workers until they are passed on to immigration
control. This happens even in jurisdictions where collaboration between police and immigration control is not legal.[13]

- Child apprehension and family separation. The state can
  seize children from migrant sex workers because of their
  sex work, and detain and deport parents, separating them
  from their children. Operating from stereotypes and biases,
  the courts frequently characterize sex-working parents as
  criminal, deficient in parenting, or at risk of harming their
  children.

- Abuse by law enforcement. Police, municipal officers, and
  immigration control agents extort sexual services from
  migrant sex workers and sexually assault, threaten, or rob
  them with impunity. Police also report migrant sex workers to their landlords, family members, colleagues, health
  care providers, and schools, leading to further discrimination and eviction.

- Surveillance at the point of care. Many health care and
  social service providers and educators in the US and Canada are encouraged or required to report to the authorities any "red flags" that they believe indicate suspected sex
  trafficking. But these "red flags"—such as working in the
  sex industry and not speaking fluent English—are not indicators of sex trafficking, they are indicators of migrant
  sex work. This turns medical and social service agencies
  into sites of surveillance for migrant sex workers, who risk
  being reported to the police when they seek support.

- Criminalization by association. Under laws that penalize
  "third parties" in the sex industry, sex workers' coworkers
  and managers, including security workers, drivers, business owners, and receptionists, are assumed to be exploiters and can be charged. Sex workers' partners, friends,

neighbors, and family members can also be charged under "third party" laws.[14]

- Mandatory eviction. Commercial and residential landlords cannot knowingly rent a living space or workspace to migrant sex workers, and if they learn that are doing so, they must evict the tenants or face criminal charges.
- Exclusion from labor protections and unionization. Migrants who work for businesses engaged in criminalized activity (like sex work) cannot effectively be protected by labor regulations. They lack the right to fair work practices regarding compensation, hiring, termination, and scheduling, and thus have no recourse to address unfair labor practices such as when contracts or employment laws are violated.[15]
- Exclusion from health and safety protections. Migrant sex workers are prohibited from accessing minimal protections regarding occupational health and safety such as conditions of work venue and equipment, so they cannot hold employers in illegal sex work businesses accountable for unsafe worksites and unsafe work conditions.
- Exclusion from social services. Migrant sex workers cannot access disability, workplace injury, or unemployment benefits, or any other program that supports poor, injured, or disabled workers.[16]
- Exclusion from political and cultural participation. Migrant sex workers have no representation in any level of government and no say in the policies, laws, and regulations that govern their lives. They also have no say in how they are culturally represented. Stories are told *about* them, not by them. These stories dehumanize and demean them and bear little resemblance to the truths of their lives, their communities, and their resistance.
- A climate of dehumanization and contempt. Migrant sex workers are viewed as less than human, "temptations," threats to be eliminated, ignorant and dangerous outsiders, part of organized crime, "illicit," and a danger to children.

This climate of contempt leads to widespread discrimination and also vigilante violence, including murder. In 2021, a young white Christian man—who apparently believed that massage spas were a source of "temptation" he needed to eliminate—shot and killed eight people. Six of those killed were Asian women. In their statement about the shootings, a grassroots collective of Asian sex workers, Red Canary Song, wrote, "Whether or not they were actually sex workers or self-identified under that label, we know that as massage workers, they were subjected to sexualized violence stemming from the hatred of sex workers, Asian women, working-class people, and immigrants."[17]

This list is not exhaustive, but it shows how migrant sex workers are under assault by the state. Migrant sex workers lack most political, economic, social, civil and human rights and freedoms. They cannot legally hold office, open a bank account, get a credit card, or rent an apartment without the risk of arrest. They have no right to privacy, labor protections (including their own wages), association with each other, freedom of movement, bodily autonomy, or citizenship. The state is authorized to secretly surveil them; seize their children, their wages, their bank accounts, and their passports; lock them into a detention facility or prison; and charge their friends and family with criminal and immigration offenses, simply for being in their presence or assisting them.

Compounding and related to this, migrant sex workers are oppressed people who face all the same social and economic injustices as other marginalized people, who are not in the sex industry. Migrant sex workers are also women and LGBTQ+; they are people of color, people who have been pushed out of their homelands by climate change and Western domination. They are migrants forced to engage in unsafe migration, and to live without legal immigration status. They are poor and working-class people who deal with low wages, oppressive and dangerous working conditions, and frequent sexual harassment and abuse in every labor sector they are employed in. They are economically exploited and unprotected workers under capitalism, no matter what industry they work in, because of their low-income, racialized migrant status.

This is why migrant sex workers are oppressed and why they face violence. When the state criminalizes the existence of a marginalized group of people, systematically denies them democratic rights and protections and makes it a crime to assist them, this leads to every form of social and economic harm, whether it is at the hand of a partner, a client, a boss, or a cop. It leads to exclusion from health care, intimate partner violence, abusive or exploitative working conditions, poverty, trauma, illness, and early death. The modern slavery moral panic covers up the real problems—authoritarian state violence and the overlapping economic, social, and climate crises of migrant labor exploitation and abuse; increasing surveillance and carceral control; climate disaster; violence against women; poverty; and border securitization (both the immobilization of millions and the involuntary migration of millions who are forced to move because of crises). It distracts from the real crises facing migrant sex workers and instead blames their problems on migration and sex work, as a justification to criminalize these activities.

AGAINST "MODERN SLAVERY"

Language is an important part of how the state justifies its violence. The terms *modern slavery, sex trafficking,* and *human trafficking* carry a hidden, racist, and anti–sex work agenda to conceal and justify state violence against racialized sex workers. This is why we think it is important to reject these terms and we encourage others to do the same. These are political terms used to define certain activities and certain people as the legitimate targets for state control and punishment. These terms represent a distorted view of the world, where sex work is purposefully differentiated from other work and conflated with violence and exploitation. And where the police, corporations, governments, and the ruling class are the saviors of poor, sexually victimized women of color. This is why we argue that racialized migrant sex workers are not sex-trafficking victims or "modern slaves," *even when they are suffering coercion, exploitation, and abuse in the sex industry*. This not because we think that migrant sex workers are free and empowered workers. It is precisely because we understand how migrant sex workers are socially, legally, economically, and politically oppressed and the discrimination and violence they face, that we reject the concepts of sex trafficking and modern slavery as ways of understanding those problems.

The terms *sex trafficking* and *modern slavery* do similar ideological work as the concept of "crime." Social harms like sexual and physical assault exist, but the term *crime* is not an objective descriptor of those harms. *Crime* conflates harm (like assault) with the survival strategies of the poor (like shoplifting) and defines them both as individual problems committed by bad people who deserve punishment. The idea of "crime" hides social problems like poverty (and those who are responsible for it) while criminalizing the people surviving the problem. The concept of "crime" invents problems too—by labeling undesirable people and behaviors as "criminal." Consider laws that once criminalized Indigenous cultural practices, or homosexuality. The concept of "crime" distorts our understanding of real problems to make some people the legitimate targets of state violence.

Real harms against migrant sex workers exist—problems like exploitation, abuse, and violence. But the terms *sex trafficking* and *modern slavery* don't neutrally describe those problems, they obscure the problem by conflating harms like violence with sex work and migration. Sex work (and migration for sex work) are not themselves harms, or violence, or social problems. People sell sex and migrate because it is useful to them in some way, often because it solves a problem. For example, people use sex work to resist other, more punitive and lower-paying work on farms or in factories; they sell sex because it is paid work that they can keep secret from immigration control so it lets them get across borders undetected by the state, or they sell sex to avoid having to marry a man to escape poverty. In other words, they use migration and sex work to cope with problems like border security, the impoverishment of women (and resulting coercion into heterosexual marriage), and the problem of migrant labor exploitation. When governments frame migrant sex work as modern slavery, it allows them to deflect responsibility off the real problems like violence and exploitation and pretend that controlling and punishing racialized migrant sex workers is for their own good.

We also reject the terms *sex trafficking* and *modern slavery* because of how their use harms other kinds of workers, by normalizing the exploitation, coercion, and abuse that happens outside of the sex industry. The state gets to decide what counts as modern slavery, and it has decided that it does not include corporate wage theft, even when millions of workers are cheated out of money for their labor. Legal definitions of modern slavery do not include the extreme economic coercion that forces poor migrants to take abusive, exploitative jobs for massive corporations that cheat them, bust unions, and lead to serious illnesses and injury. When corporations destroy the climate, pushing people out of their homelands and into unwanted, forced migration, this is not viewed as trafficking. When governments allow widespread sexual violence in jails, prisons, and youth detention centers, they deny that this constitutes sex trafficking. These conditions of exploitation and sexual and physical abuse are not treated as modern slavery or sex trafficking, because they are perpetuated against other marginalized people, at the hand of the capitalist class and protected by the state. The terms *sex trafficking* and *modern slavery* can imply that the exploitation and abuse of workers outside of the sex industry is normal, fair, or insignificant.

The concept of *human trafficking* isn't much better. The legal definitions in the US and Canada are broad and vague, and anti-trafficking nonprofits use the term *human trafficking* to refer to a laundry list of varying activities that once again conflate sex work with a range of social problems—including migrant workers in sweatshops, intimate partner violence against sex workers, rape, child sexual abuse, the transatlantic slave trade, and the purchase and sale of babies for adoption.

This is why, instead of the terms *modern slavery*, *sex trafficking*, or *human trafficking*, we use language that accurately describes the problems facing migrant sex workers and holds the right people and institutions accountable—terms like *police abuse, sexual assault, poor working conditions, workplace discrimination, intimate partner violence,* and *client violence.* Many of the problems sex workers face fall into three types—state violence, intimate partner violence, and poor working conditions. If a sex worker is being forced to work or forced to hand over all their money, it is usually by a partner and thus is a case of intimate partner violence. If a sex worker is being cheated out of their money, it may be at the hand of a bad boss and thus a problem of abusive working conditions, one that is faced by a lot of migrant and undocumented workers. When the police rape sex workers, we call it police violence. If the problem is forced labor, we call it forced labor. When we're honest about the problem, we can identify the institutions and people responsible for the problem and what needs to be done to fix it, and we stop perpetuating the idea that migrant sex work is the problem.

We also recognize and respect that some survivors use the language of sex trafficking, which they have many reasons for adopting. For sex workers, their complex experiences of violence and harm are often not listened to or understood. Using the language of sex trafficking can be the only or best way survivors of violence to get people to take them seriously, access services and support, or be protected against serious criminal charges. We have known many migrant sex workers who were released from police custody without charges (or a deportation order) only because they were willing to identify as human trafficking victims. We have known others who would have had to wait six months to access emergency rape crisis counseling, but could get it immediately if they identified as human trafficking victims. And we have known migrant sex workers who were facing homelessness but could get immediate shelter if they identified as human trafficking victims. Sex workers and survivors didn't build this system. They are not the ones perpetuating or dismissing violence against sex workers or gatekeeping social services. Our fight is not with them. It is with those who have made the sex-trafficking paradigm the only way to think about harm against sex workers, because it serves their interests.

Understanding migrant sex workers means seeing that they are also more than their oppression. When most people imagine migrant sex workers, they rarely think of resourceful immigrant moms in their thirties, forties, and fifties. But this is the norm. Migrant sex workers are parents, grandmothers, aunties, entrepreneurs, small business owners, independent travelers, struggling workers, providers, artists, storytellers, friends, and lovers with full lives and big dreams. And they are powerful. They skillfully resist criminalization, labor exploitation, abuse, and racist exclusion and hostility through community building, self-defense, mutual aid, organizing, and art and culture. They fight for justice, insist on their dignity, protect their safety, claim their freedom, and carve out their own spaces of joy, pleasure, laughter, and connection. They share their stories of strength and resistance, and increasingly, they organize for labor and migration rights and against state violence. Migrant sex workers are freedom fighters, and their resistance is among the longest-standing (yet least recognized) resistance struggles in the US and Canada. Migrant sex workers are the heroes in their own stories. They are no one's rescue project.

Migrant sex workers do not need rescue, but they do need what every oppressed group needs—more power to challenge and change their circumstances. We have witnessed firsthand the power of bringing transformative social justice approaches to migrant sex workers' lives and struggles. But they are too small a community, without enough power and resources to transform their unjust conditions. On their own, migrant sex workers cannot win against the seemingly bottomless resources of Western governments, the police, border security, anti–sex work nonprofits, and conservative Christian organizations set on controlling and punishing them. Migrant sex workers need to be a part of strong, strategic, and united movements for racial, economic, migrant, gender, disability, and climate justice that can eradicate the root causes of inequality and violence. In other words, what they need are not saviors, but comrades in joint struggle for collective liberation.

We have seen increasing support for migrant sex workers from leftists, progressives, and feminists. This is encouraging. But many often fail to understand the root causes of migrant sex workers' problems. The politics of leftists, progressives, and feminists can hugely differ between each other. But many of them share a belief that the systems that harm migrant sex workers, like policing, are necessary, unintentionally harmful, and can be reformed. They believe in reducing the harm of policing by, for example, replacing police officers with social workers during human trafficking investigations. Or they oppose police violence but not policing itself, and believe that better trained police officers could result in less violence against migrant sex workers. But there is no safe version of policing for racialized migrant sex workers. These politics uphold a harmful carceral logic and approaches to sex work and migration. Campaigns for more, or different, or better surveillance and policing to "combat sex trafficking" only make things worse.

Through our organizing in the migrant sex worker movement, we have observed that it is the abolitionists who most quickly understand migrant sex worker issues and become strong allies to migrant sex workers. Abolitionists are the first ones to truly believe migrant sex workers regarding their experiences of state violence through surveillance, policing, and immigration systems. They understand that these systems were built to uphold colonialism and capitalism and can never be the source of safety or justice. They don't have hope that reforms to policing and prisons can help rescue the migrant sex workers; instead, they work with migrant sex workers to build strength *against* these systems. Support and allyship with migrant sex workers is not possible without abolitionist politics.

THE WORLD NEEDS MIGRANT SEX WORKER ORGANIZING

The modern slavery moral panic and false claims about protecting and rescuing sex-trafficked women and children from international organized crime and gangs (which are racially coded as not white) are foundational to right-wing strategy that attacks *all* oppressed communities in the US and Canada. For decades, false claims about protecting and rescuing sex-trafficked women and children have been an incredibly effective way for a wide range of right-wing figures to win broad public support for draconian laws, policies, and narratives that many people might otherwise oppose, if they recognized them as state control and not as public safety measures. For example, laws and policies that criminalize sex workers and migrants, tighten border surveillance and restrictions, increase police and immigration raids and deportations, shut down immigrant businesses in gentrifying neighborhoods, redirect billions of dollars out of communities and into police and border security, distract from the real causes of labor exploitation and dangerous working conditions, and spread a white supremacist narrative that the US and other Western nations are under attack by dangerous outsiders, sexual deviants, and criminal people of color.

When he was president in 2019, Donald Trump repeatedly defended his plan to build a wall between the US and Mexico by claiming that law enforcement was "battling the scourge of human trafficking on our southern border and all across our nation. Much of it comes—in fact, most of it comes . . . from the southern border, which we can stop very easily."[18] Campaigns to defend or increase police budgets and powers frequently refer to taken-for-granted claims about protecting "innocent Americans" from criminal syndicates of sex traffickers. At the height of the global uprisings opposing police violence against Black communities in 2020, the right's pushback included baseless claims that defunding the police would unleash sex traffickers on American society. A *Newsweek* magazine headline exclaimed, "We Need Cops to Catch Sex Traffickers," and the article asked, "One wonders if the leftists seeking to 'defund the police' realize that this reckless capitulation to anarchy would directly benefit pedophiles and sex traffickers who prey upon innocent Americans. Contrary to the claim that the local police are a 'cancer' in our society, the men and women of law enforcement play a critical role in protecting American communities from the scourge of organized crime, including sex trafficking."[19]

We have also seen those in power, including the police and business owners' associations, advance their gentrification agenda by framing police raids on migrant massage businesses (located in a prime development zone) as "cleaning up" the neighborhood and protecting it from sex trafficking. In 2019, community organizers in Seattle were in a pitched battle against massive gentrification plans for Chinatown, including a new ultra-luxury condominium development (starting prices were $1 million per residential unit) and dozens of development projects that would displace working-class immigrant residents. In late February, Seattle police conducted a coordinated series of early-morning, forced-entry raids on eleven Asian massage businesses near the area slated for the condo development. The police closed down the businesses, seized the money that they found on-site (which would have included workers' wages), and described their actions as having "freed" and "rescued" "victimized women." Some media outlets dutifully reported this framing without question, along with the police description of these workplaces as "Chinese organized crime."[20] Other media reports published after the raids suggest to us a more complicated picture. The workers were not held against their will in the establishments, though they did live there, and most days, worked long hours. They earned high wages, which they split with the businesses, but they also faced client violence and controlling, exploitative bosses. According to the Massage Parlor Outreach Project in Seattle, "The women who had been 'rescued' were simply displaced. They lost both their means of living and their housing, as housing was connected to their workplace. Many had their meager cash savings and other belongings confiscated."[21] The developers were able to move ahead and build their projects.

We spoke to a community member of a group that had been conducting outreach in Seattle massage businesses, who explained, "In general, from what I have observed of massage workers, their experiences do not fall neatly into human trafficking, and the anti-trafficking framework is not the way to support workers in exploitative circumstances. What matters is relationship building, trust building, and ending stigma—this allows for support. Genuine support for people being oppressed by the state doesn't come through state violence. State violence pushes people further and further underground. These raids appear to be part of a gentrifying project."[22]

The complex stories and needs of migrant sex and massage workers, and those who provide genuine support independent of the state are ignored in favor of the simplistic framing of protecting women against sexual trafficking. Through this framing, the Seattle police were able to manufacture public consent for them to take money from migrant workers and shut down their workplaces in service of wealthy developers.

There may not be a right-wing figure or movement in the US and Canada that has *not* used claims about sex trafficking to promote the right's agenda. Fascist organizations like the Proud Boys claim that they are defending women and children against sex trafficking, and the far-right QAnon movement convinced millions in the US of the existence of an international sex-trafficking cabal made up of devil-worshipping Democrats conspiring against Donald Trump. Newly emerging right-wing formations like Moms for Liberty also lean on these tropes, claiming that library books that represent LGBTQ+ people are "grooming" kids for sex trafficking. Anti-abortion organizations like Focus on the Family use fears about sex trafficking to argue that the abortion pill should be outlawed, because sex traffickers use it to force their victims to have abortions.[23]

But the right are not the only ones using the modern slavery panic to advance a carceral agenda. Carceral feminists have played a part from the panic's inception and use it to promote very similar policies—more cops, more border security, more white saviors. As an example we can look to Seattle again, when in 2018, it came to light that Demand Abolition, an anti-trafficking and anti–sex work organization founded by the wealthy daughter of a Texas oil billionaire, had given millions to at least half a dozen police forces in the US in exchange for arrests and prosecutions of sex-work customers. The documentation shows that Seattle-area police worked hand-in-hand with Demand Abolition on planning the police tactics and on the media strategy to falsely reframe sex work arrests as sex-trafficking arrests.[24]

Sex work organizations and academic researchers have documented the inaccuracy and social harms of the modern slavery panic for decades, most recently in the books *White Supremacy, Racism and* the Coloniality of Anti-Trafficking, edited by Kamala Kempadoo and Elena Shih; Trafficking in Antiblackness: Modern-Day Slavery, White Indemnity, and Racial Justice by Lyndsey P. Beutin; Manufacturing Freedom: Sex Work, Anti-Trafficking Rehab, and the Racial Wages of Rescue by Elena Shih; Trafficking Harms: Critical Politics, Perspectives and Experiences, edited by Katrin Roots, Ann De Shalit, and Emily van der Meulen; and Sex at the Margins: Migration, Labour Markets and the Rescue Industry by Laura María Agustin. Sex work organizations on every continent have also reported harmful effects of anti-trafficking measures on sex workers' safety and dignity, including increases in criminalization and violence, poor working conditions, and the suppression of sex worker organizing.[25] Anti-trafficking measures have harmed sex workers across the globe who live in very different political and cultural contexts, largely owing to the overwhelming power of the US state to export and impose its agenda to punish sex workers on the rest of the world.

But historically, the right and the carceral left have discredited these attempts to question the validity of the sex-trafficking framing by accusing them of denying or minimizing violence against women and children who need rescue. Even when community organizers speak out on what is really happening, their voices are overshadowed by the police and anti-trafficking organizations. This tactic, to position any challenge as "pro–child sex trafficking" or "pro-slavery," is a cynical co-optation of actual social justice. It is a similar strategy that carceral feminists and the right used when they claimed that the US invasion of Afghanistan was necessary to rescue oppressed brown women from patriarchal brown men, and accused anyone who opposed the invasion as indifferent to the oppression of Afghan women—oppression that the US conditioned and worsened by waging war in the country.[26]

The near total absence of migrant sex workers and migrant sex worker organizing from leftist movements has meant that the left lacks the analysis and strength to challenge police, politicians, developers, or carceral feminists who use the modern slavery panic to claim that surveillance, policing, gentrification, and border restrictions will save

migrant women. Migrant sex workers and migrant sex worker organizers have a unique understanding about how the state uses modern
slavery as a way to extend its power, and they have the will to fight and
the power to shake up society. To fight the right and carceral feminists,
leftist movements need the leadership of migrant sex workers and migrant sex worker organizing.

HERE COME THE BUTTERFLIES

Migrant sex workers are the experts on their own lives, struggles, and
resistance. We have included their stories, interspersed throughout
the book as four "interludes," where they say who they are, demand
what they want, and share their dreams. Storytelling is an important part of the work of Butterfly: Asian and Migrant Sex Workers
Support Network, and over the years, we have built a community in
which the workers share their stories every day, talk about the issues
they face, and describe their joys and challenges. This is a key part
of our approach to supporting the workers' participation in organizing and policymaking processes. We collaborate with researchers on
reports and policy recommendations to lend academic legitimacy to
the oft-discredited stories and demands of the workers, and we use
this research, as well as community art projects, events, and meetings,
to inform policy advocacy and training materials. While names and
identifying details (such as country of origin) have been changed, all
the stories in *Not Your Rescue Project* have been shared with permis-
sion. Migrant sex workers shared them with us because they want people to listen and support them.

We think that the butterfly is an apt metaphor for migrant sex
workers who protect their freedom, despite the world's attempts to
trap, suppress, and control them. Like butterflies, migrant sex workers can fly high, clear above all the oppressions they face and the police, prisons, and borders that try to stop them. Together, they can
be powerful, happy, and strong. Butterflies are also synonymous with
transformation. Migrant sex workers are building a transformative
movement and solidarity across the sex work, migrant, racial justice,

gender justice, labor, anticolonial, and police and prison abolition movements. They are working with friends and allies, building community, and building power to fight for a world where everyone can live with freedom, safety, justice, and dignity, without oppression and beyond borders.

Not Your Rescue Project is a call to action. It is an invitation to defect from the victim/savior paradigm, by listening to migrant sex workers and backing them in their fight against the real enemies— state violence, labor exploitation, poverty, borders, police, prisons, and surveillance. This book comes from our vision of a world where migrant sex workers are valued and are recognized as strong, capable people struggling for a just world where people have what they need to thrive. We hope that you join us.

PART I

MIGRANT SEX WORKER REALITIES

CHAPTER 1

WHO ARE MIGRANT SEX WORKERS?

What do you know about racialized migrant sex workers? Where do they come from, why do they migrate, and why do they sell sex? What are their concerns, goals, and dreams? As organizers who have built friendship and solidarity with migrant sex workers, we have learned how powerful, valuable, and beautiful they are. Migrant sex workers in the US and Canada come from all over the world. Their experiences are extremely diverse and are strongly affected by their race, class, gender, language, sexuality, and immigration status. They have a million different dreams and goals for themselves. The stories that society has been told about migrant sex workers have rendered their lives (and their choices) incomprehensible to many. They are positioned as nothing more than their pariah status, as existing in some separate underworld. But migrant sex workers live in the same social, political, legal, and economic contexts that the rest of the world live in. In the next two chapters, we introduce migrant sex workers and what we have learned about their decisions to migrate and sell sex. We reposition them out of an imaginary underworld and refocus on how their social and economic oppression along the lines of immigration status, class, gender and sexuality, race, disability, and their labor as sex workers directly shapes their decisions and their experiences of exploitation, coercion, and violence.

THEY ARE MIGRANTS

There are roughly 281 million migrants in the world, and sex workers are among them.[1] Migrant sex workers have distinct experiences, but they are not unlike other migrants. Their reasons for migrating and the struggles they face are often similar. They move in search of work, to escape persecution, to search for better lives, to experience new things, to be close to family and friends who have already migrated. And they face the same set of social and economic conditions as other low-income, racialized migrant women and LGBTQ+ people. They lack the resources, information, or legal rights and freedoms that they need to migrate safely. Their movement is criminalized, and it is unsafe. Migrant sex workers' lives and safety are strongly shaped by migrant injustice.

Many people assume that sex workers' migration is not voluntary, but the result of human traffickers who have forced, tricked, or coerced them into moving across borders or from rural areas into cities. Yes, many migrant sex workers have been coerced into involuntary movement—but for the same reasons as other migrants. Like tens of millions of people, they are displaced people, pushed out of their homes by poverty, conflict, persecution, unlivable climates, and violence. Women and LGBTQ+ people are also pushed to leave in order to avoid their family's expectations of heteropatriarchal marriage. Some are Indigenous or ethnic minorities whose lands have been seized or sold by colonial governments over the course of generations, or who can no longer earn a living off their land due to unfair trade agreements or climate change. Much of the world's movement is unwanted, and this holds true for sex workers as well. They migrate because they are survivors of mass displacement, not the dupes of "bad guys."

Western governments and multinational corporations bear an outsized responsibility for creating the "push" factors behind mass displacement, including that of sex workers. Their environmental, imperialist, and corporate policies have destabilized democracies, fomented conflict and genocide, and economically exploited the Global South for centuries, most recently through neoliberal trade agreements that rob people of their land and impoverish working people. Western corporations and militaries are also responsible for most of the climate change that has devastated the Global South. For centuries, Western powers also imposed colonial legal and cultural frameworks that targeted non-European gender systems and reduced women's so-

cial status, making the world less safe for women and LGBTQ+ people. Essentially, ruling-class governments and corporations of the US
and Europe have created millions of economic and political refugees.
These are the real human traffickers, forcing tens of millions of people
to leave home and into unsafe migration.

For low-income women and LGBTQ+ people in the Global South,
leaving home can be very difficult, if not impossible. Poor and working-class people of color have nearly no pathways to safe, legal migration and legal status, especially not to the wealthier countries where
they hope to find work. They cannot apply for special work or student
visas because Western governments view them as "low skilled" or having too little formal educational achievement. Women and LGBTQ+
people face additional barriers. The large majority don't have the same
social networks that many heterosexual men use to help them find work
abroad, they face more discrimination and harassment in finding work
abroad, they are more likely to be responsible for supporting children
and other family members, and they are more likely to work in feminized sectors that are underpaid and undervalued as "unskilled labor."

Sex work is a solution to these problems. It is low-barrier work
that allows migrant women and LGBTQ+ people to earn a living
wherever they go, irrespective of their immigration status. It does not
require any capital investment, professional certification, educational
credentials, or language fluency. Sex work can provide migrants with
the means and the money they need to leave home, for any reason. It
can be a crucial source of survival for poor, undocumented people
on the move who do not yet have a home or immigration status. And
it can provide a source of stability for migrants who are establishing
themselves in their adopted new homes.

The mass media portrays migrant sex workers in a biased, one-
dimensional way: as ignorant and uneducated victims being moved under the cover of the night by gangsters and living without legal status
in the back rooms of massage parlors. But the reality of their circumstances are more like that of other migrants. They move about, dealing
with the same immigration laws and regulations as other migrants—
only with heavier restrictions and stigma. And as with other migrants,

immigration status among migrant sex workers can vary widely. Some migrant sex workers have citizenship, or they have permanent residence or temporary residence (with or without a work permit). Some migrant sex workers have precarious immigration status, and some eventually lose their status and become undocumented—for example, those who lose their student visa after their schooling ends or asylum seekers whose applications have been denied.

The movement of migrant sex workers is fluid and can take many forms. For some, it is seasonal or temporary. They want to come and go between their home base and the US or Canada, depending on the availability of work. Other migrant sex workers see the US or Canada as their permanent new home but may never get permanent status or only have temporary or precarious status. Some have permanent residency or citizenship and stay for twenty years, but never view Canada or the US as their "real" home. They may stay long enough to earn money, raise a family, and then return to their real home after their children grow up. Some see themselves as temporary residents but cannot go back home owing to dangerous conditions there. Some make a refugee claim or are being sponsored by a family member, and thus cannot leave the country while their claim is being assessed—a process that can take years.

Migrant sex workers are deeply impacted by immigration policy and enforcement. Their immigration status can change overnight because of new policies, and their safety is highly affected by immigration police. Rules that limit migrant sex workers' independence and control over their own mobility open up the potential for abuse. When migrants can't go where they want, they are forced into unsafe migration—they migrate without rights. Unsafe migration increases the chances of the migrants suffering exploitation and abuse by unscrupulous immigration agents, smugglers, or husbands who know that they don't have many choices. For example, when migrant sex workers are subject to formal travel bans, they must cross borders secretly to hide from immigration control. This puts power into the hands of third parties such as smugglers who can help them get across borders undetected. Some smugglers serve a positive function for migrant sex workers because they help them get where they want to go. But without immigration rights, migrant sex workers can be at the mercy of smugglers who extort bribes, abuse, or rob them. Or migrants who want to obtain immigration status or avoid being deported may seek a way to stay in the US or Canada more permanently, such as getting into a marital arrangement. Being vulnerable to deportation puts power into the hands of migrant sex workers' partners, who can use it as a tool of control over their partners. Immigration prohibitions increase the risks of intimate partner violence.

Not all migration is unwanted, and the same is also true for sex workers. Like other poor and working-class people, some sex workers want to move where they can find better wages or to reduce their living expenses. For example, some travel to another city or region to take a job at a workplace where they can also live, which lowers their housing costs. Also because of the likelihood of stigma, some sex workers leave home because they do not want to live and work in the city or region where they might run into their family members. Some sex workers migrate because they are ambitious and adventurous and want to explore the world beyond their home and earn more money. Some are adept travelers, independent adventurers, and small business entrepreneurs. They have the courage to take risks, to use sex work to set out on their own and explore the world, and to earn money through their own ingenuity. For many different reasons, sex work is a distinctly migrant job.

White people with money can decide to temporarily or permanently move to countries in the Global South and become "expats" or "digital nomads," but when low-income women of color move to the Global North, especially when they are traveling without a husband, they are much more likely to be seen as "out of place" and surveilled, interrogated, and denied entry by immigration control agents who profile such women as suspected sex-trafficking victims.

THEY ARE WORKING CLASS

Migrant sex workers are part of the working class, and, like millions of workers under capitalism, they are strongly affected by labor oppression and exploitation. They are denied fair or livable wages; fair hours of work; access to paid time off, sick pay, disability benefits, and parental leave; protection against discrimination (such as when employers pay migrant workers less than others); wage theft; quotas (such as a required minimum number of drink or service sales); and retaliation, such as being fired for organizing a union.

Sex work violates the terms of immigration status in the US and Canada, which means that even if, technically, migrant sex workers have legal residency, they are made illegal by the travel ban on migrant sex work. This has consequences that are akin to being undocumented, such as surveillance, detention, law enforcement abuse, and deportation. Working for illegal businesses and/or working without legal status means that they lack any formal recourse for unfair working conditions or unsafe work sites. Their precarious immigration status makes them vulnerable to labor exploitation, abuse, violence, and workplace injuries (such as when massage workers regularly sustain injuries that result from a lack of education on safe bodywork practice).

Sex work is economically exploited labor. Some people believe that being paid a wage for sex is itself sexual exploitation but that overlooks the labor component of the work. Sex workers, *as workers*, are economically exploited when they are not paid wages high enough to reflect the actual value of their labor, or when they are paid less than white, English-speaking sex workers. The services offered by migrant sex workers (which may include sex, massage, companionship, and more) are very valuable to some customers, yet many migrant sex workers cannot earn high wages. Some can earn good money and can afford to send their children to private school or invest in buying their own business, but most cannot.

Like other working-class people, migrant sex workers suffer poor working conditions under capitalism. When migrant sex workers face exploitation at work, this is *labor exploitation*. When they face abuse at work, this is *labor abuse* or violence against workers. When they are forced to sell sex (or to sell sex in ways that they do not want to), this is *forced labor*. Their problems are worker problems.

Migrant sex workers have diverse economic, social, and educational backgrounds. Most migrant sex workers come from poor and working-class families, but not all do. Some migrant sex workers have extensive education and professional qualifications from their home country, but their credentials are not recognized, or they are not able to find decent work. Butterfly has worked with migrant sex workers who were accountants, lawyers, and government officials in their home country. Some migrant sex workers are international students with degrees from their home country, but they work in the sex industry because it provides higher wages and more flexibility that allows them time to pursue their studies. Some international students also value sex work for the support and connections they get from coworkers and clients to further themselves academically, financially, and personally.

THEY ARE WOMEN, LGBTQ+ PEOPLE, AND MOTHERS

Racialized migrant sex workers are mostly women and LGBTQ+ people who are affected by systems of gender injustice, such as patriarchy, homophobia, and transphobia.[2] Many women sex workers are single mothers with significant caretaking responsibilities.[3] LGBTQ+ people are overrepresented in the sex industry for several reasons, including that sex work gives them access to higher wages and because they are discriminated against in other employment sectors. Sex work is an especially critical source of income to transgender migrant women who are pushed out of schools and locked out of nearly all other forms of work because of social and economic discrimination. The higher wages of sex work also help to cover the costs of health care for LGBTQ+ people who do not have health insurance, or whose care is not included in insurance plans (for example, HIV/AIDS care and certain types of gender-affirming surgeries). Gender justice is a migrant sex worker issue.

THEY ARE OLDER, SICK, AND DISABLED PEOPLE

Illness and disability are among the chief reasons people choose sex work, including migrants. About half of the Asian migrant workers in Toronto massage businesses are over forty-five years old, and, to our knowledge, many of them are disabled or are caring for elderly, sick, and disabled family members.[4] Sick and disabled migrants choose sex work because the conditions in many other workplaces are physically damaging or impossible to bear. Many of the jobs available to low-income racialized migrants are extremely physically demanding with inflexible schedules and without accommodation for disability. Workers have limited ability to rest, eat, drink, or take time off. Because the sex industry offers more flexibility, sick and disabled people can more easily find a way of making money that works for their bodies and minds. For some, that might be working for themselves; they can set their schedule, cancel work, work online, or work over the phone. Some sex workers piece together an income from a few sources outside sex work, and conduct sex work only a couple of times a month when they are running short on cash. Because migrant sex workers' needs and struggles are frequently related to issues of disability and aging, disability justice is an important migrant sex worker issue. Sex work can be a way that sick and disabled people cope with and resist the ableism of other workplaces, but it is overlooked as an important site of survival for this group of people.

THEY ARE PEOPLE OF COLOR AND INDIGENOUS PEOPLE

Not Your Rescue Project focuses on racialized migrant sex workers whose migration and sex work are heavily constructed as being inherently forced and coerced. But they are like other racialized migrants—fleeing poverty, dispossession, destruction of their lands, and persecution resulting from the imposition of Eurocentric conceptions of gender and sexuality. They face racist immigration restrictions and hostility from white supremacist countries that view them as permanent outsiders and expect them to be servile and impoverished, performing the backbreaking jobs that white people don't want, without a right to citizenship, labor protections, or full participation in democratic governance. White supremacy frames migrant sex workers as a social problem and as a dangerous threat to Western values, families, and border security. Racism heavily shapes what *kind* of danger migrant sex workers are assumed to pose. For the previous few decades, police and immigration agents in the US and Canada have frequently high-lighted race in their raids on Asian business by referring to Asian-run sex work businesses as "Chinese organized crime" and characterizing Asian women as passive slaves. They frame Asian people as outsiders, who band together into "crime rings" to become more powerful and dangerous. On the other hand, police have been more likely to frame Black sex workers as animalistic, aggressors with inhuman strength, and to view Black-run sex work businesses as pimping and enslaving.[5] Like other racialized people, racialized migrant sex workers are targets of different forms of racism.

THEY ARE SEX WORKERS

Sex workers are the targets of a distinct form of oppression—*systemic whorephobia*. This term refers to interlocking systems of institutional power that structurally oppress sex workers and people who are asso-ciated with sex work. Systemic whorephobia affects everyone in the sex industry, but it does not affect them equally. Systemic whorepho-bia occurs at the intersection of race, class, gender, labor, and sexual-ity. As an inherently intersectional system of oppression, it lands the hardest on poor and racialized women, both cisgender and transgen-der, who are sex workers or associated with sex work. It is justified through attitudes of contempt and dehumanization, such as the ideas that sex workers are immoral; lack intelligence, skills, and the capacity to self-govern or parent; don't have self-esteem, family or community; pose a danger to children; and are too "damaged" to understand their own experience. But systemic whorephobia it is more than a form of prejudice—it is structural and includes severe discrimination, exclu-sions, exploitation, and violence that is both enacted and facilitated by the state.

Migrants work in every sector of the sex industry. We understand sex work as the exchange of sexual services for some sort of compen-sation, including money, shelter, and immigration status. Sex work-ers do not sell their bodies, they sell sexual services. These services can include sensual touch, massage, blow jobs, hand jobs, and what is called "full service," which includes intercourse. It can include online performances and chat, dancing, lap dances, or BDSM. Sex work also includes the emotional labor of companionship, kindness, and intimacy. Most sex work takes place indoors in sites such as massage parlors and strip clubs, in apartments where clients come to the sex workers (this is called an "in-call" location), at clients' homes (an "outcall" location), or at a webcam or adult film set. Some sex-work sites are stable, and others are temporary, as some sex workers find clients in nearly any location, including in motels, shelters, truck stops, bus and train stations, restaurants, casinos, bars, prisons, detention centers, refugee camps, and the back rooms of their other workplaces.

We use the term *sex work* to recognize sex workers' labor, even though not everyone involved in the sex industry identifies as a sex worker. We may also use the term *people in the sex industry* to describe people who trade sex in exchange for things they need and do not see this informal labor as a job. And we include those who see themselves as workers, but not *sex* workers, because they do not consider their services to be sexual. Sexuality is a social construct, and many Asian massage workers, for example, do not consider touching a client's genitals with their hands to be a sexual act, but rather as part of a massage. We have also included massage workers in some of our discussion and profiled their stories because, as low-income, racialized women who are associated with sex work, they are also affected by systemic whorephobia, whether or not they sell sexual services.

Migrant sex workers are powerful survivors and dreamers. They imagine a better life—and dare to pursue it, wherever that takes them. They break immigration rules. They refuse to stay put. They go where they want, not where the state tells them to. They refuse the jobs that corporations have in mind for them in factories, farms, and care facilities, instead working for themselves or in small sex work businesses. They refuse to be "good girls" and provide sex to just one man—a husband. They challenge control over women's work, their movement across borders, and their sexuality. Here is how our sisters from Empower Foundation–Thailand describe the skewed perception of resourceful and strong migrant sex workers:

If this was a story of a man setting out on an adventure to find a treasure and slay a dragon to make his family rich and safe, he would be the hero. But I am not a man. I am a woman and so the story changes. I cannot be the family provider. I cannot be setting out on an adventure. I am not brave and daring. I am not resourceful and strong. Instead I am called illegal, disease spreader, prostitute, criminal, or trafficking victim. Just like the women fighting to be educated, fighting to vote, fighting to participate in politics, fighting to be independent, fighting to work, to love, to live safely . . . we will not stay in the cage society has made for us, we will dare to keep crossing the lines.[6]

INTERLUDES I

In these interludes we share stories by migrant sex workers, collected by Elene and other Butterfly members while working with communities of Asian and migrant sex workers, in Canada, the US, and internationally. Some of these stories have been published, and some are shared here for the first time. You'll notice shifts in point of view between the stories. Some of these stories are told in the first person, from the worker's point of view, others were written in the third person by the Butterfly member who collected them. We've preserved these points of view, only editing the stories for clarity. In these stories, which were collected between 2018 and 2023, we see the themes and struggles shared by migrant sex workers living and working across the US and Canada.

SU'S STORY[7]

Su was from a small Asian city where she took care of her father for many years. After his death, she realized that she had sacrificed herself for her family for almost her whole life. She was also facing increased pressure to marry, as it is the only way out for women in her community. Su wanted to be free, go to new places, and to find her own way. She decided to leave home. She'd heard about people traveling to Europe and North America to work in the sex industry, and at that time there were still a lot of ads in the papers looking to recruit people to work in the sex industry. Su called up a few different agents to get more information, and after speaking to one, she decided to go to Toronto. Everyone told her that it would be too cold for her, but she wanted to see snow.

Through her conversations with agents, Su realized that she didn't actually need to rely on them to go to Canada; she could do it herself. She bought the airline ticket, booked a hotel, and started her journey. After she arrived, she bought a few newspapers, because she'd heard from the agents that massage businesses advertised in the Canadian newspaper there, too. Su called a few different ads and decided to work with a woman named Ching who seemed nice and spoke her language.

When Su began working with Ching, she did not know what to do. She'd never worked in the sex industry and had only had a few boyfriends and not that much sexual experience. Ching told her that she could let her know if she had any problems, and found Su an old client who was more experienced and caring. Even though Su felt that she did not know much, she was happy and satisfied. After her first short session, when she held the money in her hand and watched the man walk out from the room, she felt that this was the "new her" in her new life. But there were too few customers, so after a few days, Su didn't want to work with Ching anymore. She was seeing only one or two clients a shift, which meant only a few minutes of work each day because men "do not last very long!" She felt bored just waiting around for customers. She met another worker who said that there was a place in a busier part of town that had more clients. Su told Ching that she was quitting, and Ching told her that she was welcome to come back anytime.

Su started working in another place that had eight to ten workers; some of them were part-time, and some of them were full-time. They had a lot of clients—so many that the clients sometimes needed to wait. One of the other workers invited her to do a "duo." This is a session with two sex workers and one customer. Su agreed to the duo, and it was a positive experience for her because she had never had sex with another woman. She did not feel sexually aroused, but she enjoyed touching and feeling another woman's very soft body. She also found that working with another woman was less work, saved a lot of effort, brought in more money, and taught her a lot of skills, such as how to handle clients with big penises and how to get the clients to do what she wanted. She found the work to be interesting. Her days were a mix of good and bad clients, particularly at the beginning when she did not know how to stop clients from hurting her (for example, by putting their dry fingers inside her). But after working with a few other women, she learned how to set boundaries

and felt more confident. She particularly liked to work with customers who were not born in Canada. She knew they were alone in Canada, and she would sometimes meet up with them on holidays like
Christmas and New Year's Day. She felt more connected with them
than her white Canadian clients and felt that she could comfort their
lonely souls by making them feel her warmth. Her English was limited, but she felt proud when her customers would smile from their
heart after the session. Of course, not everyone was like that. Some
of them were very shy, some of them were rude, and some of them
did not even want to look at her.

Three months later, the owner sold the parlor to some of the other
workers. This was his business strategy—to open a place and run the
business, and then once the place got busy, he would ask the workers
if they were interested in taking over and buying it from him. Su did
not want the responsibility of managing a business, paying rent, or
managing other workers. She preferred the flexibility of just being a
staff member who could come and go. After it was sold, a new boss
came in who was too pushy, so Su left. She found a new parlor where
the clients mainly spoke her language. One of her clients helped her to
rent a place and get settled in Toronto.

Five years later, the Toronto police raided the massage parlor Su
was working at as part of an anti-trafficking investigation. A neighbor had complained to the police about suspected sex trafficking. The
police found no trafficking victims, but sex work is prohibited by Su's
immigration visa. So the police arrested Su and detained her in a cell.
She knew about Butterfly through their outreach in the massage parlors where she worked, and she was able to contact them. But Su was
still deported. The Canadian government also issued a ban that prohibited her from returning to Canada.

This did not stop Su from traveling. She did not want to be kept
in a cage. She went to Dubai, New Zealand, England, and Australia.
However, she found that no place was like Toronto, where she felt at
home, where she had friends, felt safe, and had established clients. It
hasn't been easy for Su in other countries. She was robbed, sexually
assaulted, and injured at work. She still dreams of coming back to

Canada, but it may be very hard for her due to the immigration ban. She still has the picture of the snow that she took on the first day she arrived in Toronto, set as her phone's wallpaper.

SEAN'S STORY[8]

Sean was a graduate student in a Canadian city who had moved from his home in Europe to pursue postsecondary studies. Because of the high unemployment rate in his home country, he was hoping to stay in Canada after graduation and find a new job. Sean's tuition fees were about triple what they were for Canadian students, so he needed to find work. He was fluent in English, but, lacking any Canadian experience, it was still difficult for him to find a good job. His immigration visa prohibited him from working more than twenty hours per week, and he also really wanted to focus on his studies rather than working long hours in a low-paid restaurant job. To build his professional experience, he also needed to be available to take unpaid internships, and he wanted to contribute to local community work and meet more people. Sean had done sex work occasionally back home in Europe as a way to connect with sexual partners while also getting some income. He decided to start escorting to bring in good money without long hours. In the beginning it was good—he met clients and made money while being able to concentrate on his studies. In the news, he'd heard about migrant sex workers being targeted by the police in anti-trafficking raids, but he'd never experienced any problems with the police himself.

Sean met a man who paid him very well and became a stable, regular client. Sean was happy because this allowed him to spend less time finding new clients. Sean and his client spent more and more time together, sometimes taking photos and videos together. Over time, the client started to become controlling and jealous. Sean was not comfortable with it and wanted to stop seeing him, but the client got angry. He was linked to Sean's Facebook account and threatened to tell Sean's family and friends by sending them explicit photos and videos he'd taken. He also threatened to report Sean to immigration authorities. Sean couldn't tolerate the client's abuse and control, so he decided to leave anyway. He tried seeking support from anti-violence organizations, but most of them only supported women and didn't understand his situation.

Sean's abuser carried through on his threats and sent the photos and videos to Sean's friends and family. He also reported Sean to immigration authorities, providing them with copies of Sean's sex-work ads and his phone number to show that he was a sex worker. Sean received a letter from immigration authorities that said they had received information that he was working in the sex industry and demanded that he submit to questioning. He tried getting information about his legal situation and hired a lawyer, who told him not to worry because the Canadian laws don't criminalize independent sex work. Initially, Sean was reassured, but then he did his own research and found out that his work permit prohibited him from working in any part of the sex industry.

His abuser continued stalking him, but Sean was afraid that if he reported his abuser, he would lose everything, including the fortune he'd spent on travel and tuition fees and his student visa, because he'd violated its terms. And what if he was barred from applying for immigration status as a permanent resident in the future? Instead of reporting his abuser, Sean reached out to the student center at his school, and, luckily, he finally found someone supportive. The student center staff helped Sean to withdraw for a semester without having to pay tuition fees so he could take care of the legal and emotional issues of the abuse without having to drop out.

Sean had to go into hiding. He changed his phone number, closed all his social media accounts, and moved to another city. Another client helped him with the move, giving him some money and driving him to his new home. That client had heard about Butterfly in the news and introduced Sean to the group. Butterfly connected Sean to a lawyer who understood the immigration restrictions and Sean's options. Sean was also able to connect with other sex workers, who gave him support and advice on how to talk to his family and explain the videos and photos. Sean has managed to escape his abuser, but he remains afraid to engage in community work for fear of being traced and identified and stalked again.

LISA'S STORY[9]

My name is Lisa. I came to Canada in 2015, and I am sixty-one years old. I like Canada's nature, blue sky, and the fresh air. When I first came to Canada, I worked as a dishwasher and a factory worker, including in a wedding dress factory. These jobs were very tiring, the salary was low, and the working hours were long. I washed the dishes for ten hours a day without much time to rest. My body couldn't take it. Later, others introduced me to work at the fruit factory. It was easier than washing dishes, but the fruit factory was very cold, the wages were even lower. The agents would also charge transportation fees, so the money I actually got was very little. After working for more than a year, I fell ill and needed an operation, so I left. I still needed money for rent and food. After taking a break after the operation, I went out to look for a job near my place and saw a few massage parlors with Chinese recruitment notices, so I decided to give it a try. The temperature inside the massage parlor is very comfortable, not as cold as the fruit factory. I only need to work when there are customers. I have flexible hours and more rest time. After trying it for a bit, I felt that it was suitable for me, so I have been doing it till now, and it has already been four years.

We often face inspections by law enforcement when we work in massage parlors. The boss told us not to irritate them and not to cause trouble for ourselves. If they cannot find any violation among our workers, they will pick on the shop. In many cases, a ticket was issued for some inexplicable reason, such as not covering the drain in the bathroom. Our English is not fluent, and we didn't understand the government's procedures, and we didn't know anything about the discriminatory policies. Many people did not understand us at first and discriminated against us. Later, through communication and public education, they understood our story and understood that this job is what we choose to do, to support our family and ourselves, and it is much better than other jobs. I rely on myself and make money with my hands; I can pay the rent. The customers can relax through my service. I remember a parent bringing their child to the store to experience a massage. At the end, we even took a group photo. Everyone was very happy.

I think this job is respected. Now I am proud of my job. But it is impossible for me to go back to school and get a certificate. I have to pay tuition and study. I am sixty-one years old. I only know how to work. Even if I have time and money to attend classes, I can't speak English and I will never get a certificate. If I can't work, I can't pay for the rent or food. I find new regulations about the massage spas very ridiculous. The regulations on training are to make it difficult for people like us. If the massage parlor is forced to close, we cannot survive. Police are causing us a lot of trouble. They will always ask us if we were trafficked, if there were any trafficker, how much money we give to the trafficker, et cetera, but we only go to work normally, and we are not forced. Here, I don't need fluent English to serve the customers well. With the experience, I can tell where my customer hurts just by touch. I already have a lot of experience and don't need the English exam and certificate. This is discrimination, bullying, prejudice against the massage industry, and ignorance. It is to oppress us. I understand that it is not something that can be done in a day or two to fight against the government and society's discrimination against our industry. But we must still unite and fight for our own interests.

CHAPTER 2

WHY MIGRANTS SELL SEX

For many women of color, prostitution is not what you do when you hit rock bottom. Prostitution is what you do to stay afloat, to swim rather than sink, to defy rather than disappear.

—Pluma Sumaq[1]

MIGRANT SEX WORK AS SURVIVAL

We have just described who migrant sex workers are and shared some of their stories in a way that we hope restores their humanity and the social, legal, and economic context of their oppression. Now we want to explain why the sex industry is preferable for some migrant workers. Low-income women and LGBTQ+ people from the Global South choose sex work because it can be an effective strategy for survival, a way to resist unfair conditions in their work and home life and create new possibilities for themselves.

We want to first address a problematic question we are often asked: "Do migrants actually *choose* sex work?" Many people believe that migrants are too oppressed by the forces of domination, poverty, and social inequality to meaningfully consent to sex work. When questions about consent are raised—whether stated or implied—it is usually in reference to cisgender Asian and other racialized women from the Global South who migrate to the US and Europe. Perhaps, goes the thinking, they are just too traumatized to speak for themselves? Too naive to know they have been trafficked?

These questions reveal the problem, which is the prevalence of colonial, racist, and sexist assumptions that sex work is violence (not labor) and that certain racialized women are helpless, rather than strong, smart, and savvy. White supremacy, sexism, and whorephobia strongly affect how people understand migrant sex work, especially that of Asian women. Under conditions of poverty, limited opportunities, and social inequality, workers make choices about their best options. This includes migrant sex workers. Other labor activists do not need to prove that workers are capable of consenting to their labor, even though capitalism forces everyone to work to survive. For the most part, working-class people don't get to decide *if* they will work. They must work or they would not be able to survive, afford food, housing, health care, or education, or have the means to raise their children. In other words, everyone, except a tiny wealthy elite, is coerced into working so that they and their families can live. If we can't say no to waged work without suffering or dying, then we aren't really consenting to it. As anti-capitalists ourselves, we understand the concerns about economic coercion. But viewing work in the sex industry (and migration for sex work) as uniquely coerced and exploitative conceals, minimizes, and justifies the everyday exploitation and coercion of labor under capitalism. And viewing Asian women as prone to enslavement legitimizes sexist, white supremacist narratives about Asian women.

WAGES AND WORKING CONDITIONS

Migrants who choose sex work do so because it is the best job available to them, within a set of constrained job options. When compared with other migrant labor sectors in the US and Canada, the sex industry can offer substantially better wages and financial opportunity, more mobility and flexibility, and less disabling work conditions.

Some believe that because the sex industry offers little protection against discrimination, exploitation, abuse, and violence, migrants would not willingly choose to work in it. It is true that when a client cheats a sex worker out of their wages, there is little they can do. However, there is no labor sector that provides protections to low-income racialized migrant women and LGBTQ+ workers. While it may be technically against the law to cheat migrants out of their wages, or force them to work in unsafe work sites, or sexually abuse them, in practice these laws are not enforced, or they *are* enforced but in a way that puts the workers at risk. In effect, all low-income racialized migrant workers do not have meaningful protection against unsafe or unfair working conditions.

To understand the choice to sell sex, we must understand it within the context of other available work options. It's not that sex work is necessarily good, it's that it can often be *better* than other work. The jobs available to low-income racialized migrants in other sectors are some of the worst jobs in the world. Work in agricultural, manufacturing, construction, warehouse, and domestic labor sectors is notoriously poorly paid, punitive, relentless, exploitative, and dangerous. Harassment, wage theft, and abuse are common, as are injuries, illness, and long-term disability. Workers have no control over their wages, working hours, or working conditions. They are closely monitored and made to work at a breakneck pace while being paid as little as legally possible (sometimes even less than the minimum wage). Employers provide little to no job security, health insurance, or even basic health and safety protection. Migrant workers in sweatshops work eleven to thirteen hours in windowless buildings with no emergency exits and little ventilation, where they are not paid overtime. They live in company housing that is crowded, vermin infested, and cold, and offers them no privacy or safety. Also, migrant workers' mobility is strictly restricted. Most temporary migrant workers in the US and Canada are trapped in their jobs and in a single location because their immigration status is tied to their job and to a specific employer. Western governments make it nearly impossible for poor and working-class migrants to enter the country, except through temporary work permits that shunt them into these grimly exploitative, dangerous, and precarious jobs. But migrants take them because they badly need the money and it offers a way to stay in the country.[2]

Temporary work permits provide all the advantages to the employer and very little to the worker. They essentially treat migrant workers as bodies to be used up for profit and then disposed. Governments and corporations lie about the jobs, the conditions for workers, and the wages. The government of Canada claims that "if you are a temporary foreign worker, you have the same rights and protections as Canadians and permanent residents. . . . Your employer can't force you to do work that you think is dangerous."[3] This hides the reality that migrant workers are paid less, cheated out of wages and benefits, and made to work in unsafe conditions all the time.

The US and Canada offer migrant workers a very limited pathway to citizenship and no legal protections that ensure a legal right to stay. The constant danger of being deported keeps workers in line. This is why migrant workers in warehouses, processing facilities, and eldercare homes were among the communities most devastated by the COVID-19 pandemic. The workers were unprotected but also unable to refuse their dangerous working conditions. Undocumented workers have even less control over their wages and working conditions and are subjected to routine exploitation, danger, and abuse. When the alternative is deportation, arrest, and poverty, millions of migrants are coerced into brutally exploitative labor contracts. Migrant worker activists including, Harsha Walia, have described these conditions as modern indentureship, and in some cases, "systemic slavery."[4] The conditions of these work permits are deceptive, coercive, and unfree. In the following pages, we explain how sex work provides migrants with a significant improvement over these conditions.

BETTER WAGES AND WORKING CONDITIONS

Perhaps the top reason that some racialized migrant women and LGBTQ+ people choose sex work is because it offers higher wages than elsewhere. The sex industry is one of the only labor sectors in which, on average, women earn more than men. It is not uncommon for sex workers to earn double or triple (or more) what they would earn in other labor sectors. It cannot be overstated what an enormous difference it makes to the lives of low-income, racialized migrant people (most of whom are parents and/or disabled) to be able to earn higher wages through sex work.[5] For poor people, this increase in wages can be life-changing.

Sex workers' wages are higher because they keep a higher share of the value of their labor than labor in other sectors. Sex workers who work independently keep all the money they earn, outside of their overhead expenses such as rent. But even those who work for others retain more of the value of their labor. A migrant massage worker might charge a hundred dollars for a massage and a sexual service such as a hand job. In some establishments, sex workers split half their earnings with the owners, so the worker would keep fifty dollars for their hour of work, a wage that is much higher than they could earn in other jobs.[6] In some massage businesses, the sex worker might receive a low base fee (say, twenty dollars for a massage), but they keep all the money they charge as "tips" for sexual services. In the sex industry, "tips" can be significantly more than a base wage.

This speaks to one of the other unusual advantages of the sex industry—sex workers can often independently negotiate their wages. This has its advantages and disadvantages. On the one hand, being in the informal labor sector means that sex workers have no guarantee of a minimum base wage. But on the other hand, working in the informal sector offers financial opportunity for workers who develop some entrepreneurial skills and learn how to negotiate for more money. In most jobs, the employer has total control over the workers' wage and relinquishes only a tiny fraction of the value of their labor to the worker, perhaps minimum-wage compensation or even lower. Such low wages are especially hard on women who support multiple family members, including their own children. For most migrant women, it is nearly impossible to earn enough money to support their family, pay for their education (or their children's education), and build financial stability through nonsexual labor. For example, nearly eight out of ten domestic workers in the US don't even have food security.

These workers have little power to negotiate their wages, especially if they are undocumented. By contrast, the sex industry offers workers some opportunity to influence their wages. Many migrant sex workers learn how to encourage their customers to tip them well, see them regularly, spend more money on them, bring gifts, and help them out financially when needed, such as with money for their child's education. This is one of the many reasons that the sex-worker community is so crucial. Sex workers develop practical, effective negotiation skills that will work in their specific circumstances by being in conversation with other sex workers who share their experience.

This does not necessarily mean that sex workers' wages are *high*—just that they are relatively *better*—and nor does it mean that making money in the industry is guaranteed. Income in the sex industry can be very unreliable, and many migrant sex workers are just getting by. For some migrants, especially those who are LGBTQ+, sex work is their only economic option, and the alternative is homelessness and hunger. But some sex workers can earn enough to save, open their own small business, build financial security, and support other family members. The International Labor Organization estimates that globally, the average sex worker is financially supporting five to seven family members.[7] Sex work allows migrants to provide for their families in ways that the government and other employers refuse to do.

GREATER INDEPENDENCE AND MOBILITY

Migrant sex workers usually have more independence and mobility than those in other migrant labor sectors because they are typically working secretly, so their immigration status is not formally tied to one employer. Free from the restrictions of a temporary work visa, they can quit their jobs, change employers, or move to another town without risking their immigration status (as long as their work remains hidden). This provides migrant sex workers with much more control over where they want to live, go to school, raise their kids, and who they want to work for. If business is better in another city, or if they want to move closer to their school, friends, and family, they can. These are basic freedoms that white citizens take for granted, but they are out of reach for many low-income migrant workers on temporary foreign worker visas. Working under the radar of the state allows sex workers to be mobile in ways that would otherwise be closed to them.

GREATER FLEXIBILITY

Sex workers often have more flexibility and control over their time than migrants in other labor sectors. Work shifts in the sex industry can be much less regimented than other kinds of work. Those who work in establishments such as massage businesses or strip clubs can sometimes schedule their shifts around their parenting or their school schedule. Sex work is not based on models of mass industrial production where employers closely monitor workers' movements and keep them in constant unceasing motion to maximize profit at every moment. It is also not based on the model of "women's work" in the home, either, where domestic workers can be expected to be on call and available to work, around the clock, seven days a week, 365 days a year.

Independent sex workers (those who work for themselves) can set their own hours. Most sex work is conducted on a fee-for-service basis, where there are often long periods (hours or days) with no clients and therefore no work. Sex workers can rest, take breaks, study, or go home early during slow periods when there are not many clients. If anything, sex workers often long to find more work and more clients so they can earn a steadier income.

LESS DISABLING

Sex work can be very physically demanding and sex workers experience injuries at work, as well as exhaustion, violence, and abuse. However, for many older and disabled women and LGBTQ+ people, sex work is more accessible and less dangerous and disabling than the physically punishing manual work that migrants are otherwise relegated to in other labor sectors such as food processing and home health care. Sex work can offer more time for workers to put into caring for themselves and their loved ones.

Working conditions are extremely important for migrant women who are older, sick, or disabled, or are single parents or sole caregivers for their own parents. The regimented schedules, long hours, and backbreaking physical labor of most migrant work sectors are difficult or impossible for those who cannot pick food, lift people, or walk for miles in a day. Many migrant labor jobs are disabling. Workers in Amazon warehouses walk on average ten to thirty miles *per day*. Agricultural workers are required to work in the rain, snow, freezing cold, and during heat waves, near wildfires without protective gear, and sometimes even while toxic chemicals are being sprayed on their worksite. These workers are sometimes accompanied by their children, who endure the same conditions and develop illnesses. Non–sex industry migrant workplaces exert extreme control over workers' bodies. In factories, warehouses, sweatshops, and farms, migrants are often under the surveillance of bosses who monitor their every movement and restrict their ability to slow down, sit, eat, drink water, take breaks, use the bathroom, tend to any injuries, or deal with unsafe conditions (such as protecting themselves from toxic substances). Management pushes workers into a relentless pace to meet grueling production quotas. Migrants who work in private homes are also not exempt from such invasive control and often must be available outside of their paid work time, for free. For example, 25 percent of domestic workers report that they don't regularly achieve even five hours of sleep a night, owing to the around-the-clock demands of their employers.[8]

Sex work can offer workers more control over their bodies, including the ability to work fewer hours, take unexpected days off to care for themselves or a family member, and sit down and rest when they need to. It is rare for sex workers to have to stand for an entire shift (exotic dancers who stand, dance, and circulate through a club talking to customers can still take breaks). In our capitalist societies, being disabled or being a caregiver is expensive, but poor and undocumented migrants are mostly excluded from social and economic support systems like health insurance and unemployment insurance. The higher wages of sex work can help to make up for their exclusion from these kinds of supports in the US and Canada.

REDUCED INSTITUTIONAL RACISM

For migrant women, there is no escape from structural and systemic racism, and this is true in every labor sector, including the sex industry, where migrant sex workers often deal with racist clients and are not able to charge rates as high as those of white sex workers. And yet, the sex industry can still be a *less* institutionally racist option than other labor sectors. For example, migrant sex work businesses are often owned and managed by racialized migrants, not wealthy white corporations. The owners or managers of migrant sex work businesses have their own tools of control, but these tools do not usually include access to state power. Migrants running sex work businesses cannot keep workers in line by threatening to call immigration enforcement, because this would expose the owners to the risk of state violence as well. Working for a racialized boss does not by any means ensure sex workers decent working conditions. However, it bears repeating that migrant women have no enforceable protections or recourse in *any* labor sector. Sex work businesses run by migrants (who are sometimes women and former sex workers themselves) can be less institutionally racist and more culturally respectful. When sex work businesses are in immigrant neighborhoods, their customers are also often other working-class migrants from their own home country or region of the world. As racialized people living in a hostile country, some sex workers find these clients to be a welcome source of companionship.

By comparison, most non–sex industry jobs available to low-income migrant women and LGBTQ+ people of color are jobs working for multinational corporations, owned by rich white people who have the power to use state violence such as the police and immigration control. They can call the police on workers, they can bust any attempts to resist unsafe working conditions, and they can threaten workers with arrest and deportation for leaving their jobs.

NAVIGATING RACISM, CAPITALIZING ON RACIST IGNORANCE

Some racialized migrant workers choose the sex industry because they feel they have more power to navigate racism in their workplace. Racialized workers are affected by racism in whatever industry they work within. But work in the sex industry, in particular, Asian women's sex work, raises concerns about the ways that Western culture has for centuries fetishized Asian women, representing them as sexually immoral and hypersexual objects of desire. After the 2021 shootings in Atlanta, in which a gunman killed eight people—six of them Asian women—in three massage businesses, many in the Asian community pointed to racist mythologies about Asian women's sexuality as one of the key cultural factors that led to the violence. It is important to challenge these stereotypes, which are used to justify vigilante violence of the kind we saw in Atlanta and other attacks on Asian women. However, it is also important to recognize that Asian sex-working women are not objects who passively allow themselves to be sexualized and fetishized by racist Westerners, and they are not responsible for violence. Instead, through the sex industry Asian women resist more controlling and exploitative work and are sometimes able to use Westerner's racist ignorance and fetishization to get what they want, to access safety and resources, and attain economic, social, and immigration status.

Asian migrant sex workers deal with oppressive Western stereotypes about them in many ways, including by leveraging those myths to earn more money. For example, recognizing that Westerners view Asian women as younger than their years, middle-aged and older Asian women—well into their forties, fifties, and sixties—can strategically take advantage of their "youthful" image to make more money from white male clients. In doing so, they can transition their aging bodies out of dangerous and disabling work in factories, food-processing plants, and care-giving jobs into more accessible and better paying sex work. They are savvy and resourceful, not simply passive objects of sexual racism. As Asian sex worker Lienne Dagger writes: "Harnessing the power of female sexuality in a violent patriarchal world is a double-edged sword. Doing so puts me in even greater danger and exposes me to people and institutions who fetishize and marginalize me. But at the same time, sex work is one of very few avenues that allow me to earn a livable income as a neurodivergent, queer Asian immigrant."[9]

It can be complicated, but intentionally playing into oppressive stereotypes to gain control and to access power and economic resources is not unique to migrant Asian sex workers. The problem is not that the sex industry inaccurately portrays Asian women as "too sexual." It is that Asian women do not have the social and political power to define their own sexuality, on their own terms. We still need to change racist ideas about Asian women—and not only them, as many women of color are objectified and sexualized. But instead of taking away the power of sex work, the question is: How can we offer Asian migrant sex workers more support?

CONNECTION TO COMMUNITY OUTSIDE OF WORK

Many sex workers have more contact with people outside of their own workplace compared with low-income migrant workers in other labor sectors. For instance, sex workers often work in urban areas where they have access to immigrant communities, local shopping, friends, and other networks. There are both good and bad clients, but it is common for sex workers to create relationships with a handful of good clients who become part of their support system. Good clients provide help to sex workers during financially stressful times, introduce them to opportunities to learn the culture and language of their new country, and can provide access to resources and information. Some sex workers who are facing abuse, either at work or at home, rely on connections with trusted customers to help them escape. Domestic violence survivors in the sex industry are sometimes able to rely on a good client who helps them escape abuse by providing use of a phone, a place to stay, extra money, or a ride to a new home or city.

Many other migrant worksites, such as farms and food processing facilities, are isolated in remote and rural areas where workers are surrounded by racist white locals, lack access to transportation and other services, and are far from community members and friends who speak their language. Even migrants in urban areas can be quite isolated if they work in private homes as live-in caregivers, where their entire life is spent behind closed doors, with no other colleagues who speak their language.

CHEAP HOUSING, BETTER BUSINESS

Many migrants live at their workplaces, including agricultural workers and live-in caregivers. Sex workers often choose to live at work, too, and will rent the room they work out of because it makes financial sense. Many people think that sex workers are part of an organized crime ring when they live at work or move to different locations with the help of their friends, boss, or an agent. In the sex industry, moving to new locations or new cities is common and referred to as "touring." Some workers, including massage and sex workers, prefer touring as their work arrangement. They earn more money by seeing new clients, and save money by renting space in their workplace rather than paying for separate housing. Some also prefer to live at their workplace because it makes it easier for them to avoid being targeted by law enforcement—they can easily move to new locations or cities if the police become active in their area.

Some migrant sex workers work from their home in an apartment or hotel room to save time and money. Working from home saves travel time getting to work, which allows them to see more clients and, as a result, make more money. For migrants with precarious immigration status, traveling back and forth to work can be stressful, risky, and expensive. Many migrant sex workers do not have driver's licenses. If they do have licenses, driving opens them up to the risk of being pulled over by the police and reported to immigration. Leaving the house at all increases the risk that neighbors will report them. Navigating transportation systems (that may be inferior to those in their home country) in another language can be stressful and frustrating.

Working from home also allows migrant sex workers to save a lot of money by not having to pay for transportation or rent on a hotel room or second apartment for work. This way, they don't have to pay for two spaces when they travel for work and tour, or when they leave town to visit family and friends. The issues that migrant sex workers deal with related to housing are pragmatic—like buying a bed that is soft enough to sleep on but firm enough for work, finding a good rice cooker, getting groceries nearby, and so on.

Sometimes migrant sex workers don't leave their home/workplace for long periods, which people may interpret as a sign of their captivity by human traffickers. But the actual reason is usually that migrant sex workers are at risk of being reported every time they are seen in public. Thanks to decades of public discourse that links Asian women and other women from the Global South in the sex industry to sex trafficking, their neighbors and landlords are encouraged to surveil them and to report them to the police. Being seen in public is dangerous, and some sex workers will try to minimize that risk by staying home or at work as much as possible.

In some cases, migrant sex workers don't leave home much because they are experiencing intimate partner violence and their partner keeps them restricted to the house. Much of the abuse that people think of as human trafficking is actually intimate partner violence (IPV), involving the sex industry. Framing survivors of IPV as human trafficking victims (and criminalizing them as such) means that they may become the targets of a criminal investigation and are forced to hide from supportive neighbors, friends, and medical and social service providers who might help them to escape their abuser.

A WAY OUT OF HETEROSEXUAL MARRIAGE

Around the world, low-income women have limited economic and social opportunities, and for many, marriage is their only way to gain economic security, social status, and some degree of physical security from the threat of violence by other men. Similarly, LGBTQ+ people can face strong expectations from their family to marry, have a normative sexuality and gender, and have children. In addition to social pressure, it can be very difficult for low-income women and LGBTQ+ people to survive without the income of a husband. Migrant women and LGBTQ+ face these issues as well. Being in a different country where they may be isolated and have few economic options can put even more social and economic pressure on migrant women and LGBTQ+ people to marry. For them, the higher wages of sex work provide a way to be unmarried, queer, widowed, or divorced and still survive. And working with other sex workers can be a way to stay safe from the violence of men who may deliberately target women and LGBTQ+ people perceived not to "belong" to a man, such as a husband or father. For some, sex work is a way to resist (or delay) heterosexual marriage and other gender-role expectations.

SEXUAL EXPLORATION

Sex can be a source of power even for sex workers who face a lot of racism or other difficult conditions. Certainly, the space for personal enjoyment in sex work is limited by many factors. Not all migrant sex workers experience enjoyment at their jobs. For some it is just work, for others it is shitty work that they just need to do. Some hate it. But some find sex work itself is complicated, interesting, and fun. Through the work, they explore feeling desired, taking on different roles, becoming sexually confident and knowledgeable about human sexuality. Every culture has its own historical relationship to sexuality, and some workers who have had less exposure to the Eurocentric Christian value system do not always have the same burden of shame around sex. For example, some women do not have a romantic view of marriage. For them, marriage is more important as a means of economic exchange offering financial stability. Within this view, the body is the woman's asset for securing her safety and income. Those who do not have a strong connection to moralistic Christian views of gender and sexuality are less influenced by sexist ideas about women's sexual purity. We rarely hear these stories, but that doesn't diminish their legitimacy. College-educated white people aren't the only ones who have nuanced, complex, and powerful relationships to sexuality.

IMPROVED SAFETY FOR RACIALIZED MIGRANT WORKERS

Some racialized migrant women and LGBTQ+ people choose sex work because it is safer and less physically demanding and damaging than their alternatives. Most people assume that non–sex industry jobs will be safer than sex work, owing to the risk of abuse and violence in the sex industry. These dangers are real—some sex workers experience abuse and violence on the job. However, when people imagine that the sex industry is uniquely dangerous, it is because they believe not only that work related to sex is inherently dangerous, but also that other kinds of work—unrelated to sex—are naturally and normally *not* dangerous to racialized migrant women. This minimizes the harms that migrant women face outside of the sex industry, including exploitation, coercion, and abuse. Or these harms are viewed as acceptable, so long as the woman does not work in the sex industry. Harm and exploitation are not acceptable in any form of labor and migrants smartly choose the work that best protects their safety. Sometimes that is sex work.

Sex workers' ability to change employers also protects them from abuse. They are more likely to be able to leave an unfair, dangerous, or abusive job than other migrant workers because their job is not tied to their immigration permit. Quitting their job does not risk their immigration status and deportation.

Additionally, the higher wages in the sex industry serve as their own form of protection against abuse and violence in the home. One way that low-income, racialized migrant women and LGBTQ+ people avoid poverty is by getting into a romantic relationship with a man who can provide them with economic stability. Earning higher wages in the sex industry means that some are more able to avoid an unwanted relationship with a man or to leave if the relationship becomes abusive because they can more easily afford to pay for new housing, phone costs, transportation, medical care, legal advice, time off work, and so on. As we mentioned, in some cases, good sex work customers can also be a source of safety, helping migrant sex workers to leave a home or a job and settle in a new location.

THE UNIQUE BENEFITS OF MASSAGE BUSINESSES

The massage sector in US and Canadian cities is largely composed of Asian migrants. People sometimes ask us why migrants are so highly represented in the massage businesses, like spas and parlors.[10] They have heard anti–sex work organizations claim this is because secretive cartels are "importing" Asian women and forcing them into "modern slavery" in the massage parlors. But this is a myth rooted in assumptions that Asian sex workers cannot make their own decisions. Asian migrant women choose the massage sector for three main reasons: the economic and personal safety benefits and increased bodily autonomy.

Massage businesses are typically more economically beneficial to new migrants than other parts of the sex industry because they require much lower overhead costs than working independently and can offer low-cost housing. People who work for themselves need to have enough money upfront to pay for overhead costs like advertising or rent on a worksite. Massage workers do not. The business owner or manager is responsible for these costs. Massage businesses offer a financial advantage that is unlike other parts of the sex industry—the ability to live at work for very little money. Most other sex work businesses do not provide any form of accommodation to workers. Even if the accommodation is basic, this is attractive to migrants who are new to the country, do not have much money, and are trying to get an apartment in an expensive urban market. It can be very hard for migrant sex workers to rent an apartment. They may not have an established credit score, references from previous landlords, or official proof of income. Living at work also reduces their transportation costs.

Second, migrant women can also find working conditions in massage businesses to be safer and more enjoyable than in other parts of the sex industry. Working in a massage business can reduce the risk of arrest and other forms of state violence. Although massage businesses are *associated* with sex work, they are still less criminalized than other types of sex work. Not all massage businesses offer sexual services, and many (if not most) do not. To some extent, this allows migrant women to hide their participation in sex work from neighbors, the community, and the police. Also, when advertising their businesses, independent workers have to navigate language barriers and the danger of being arrested for running a sex work business. In a massage business, it is the owner or manager, not the worker, who bears the responsibility for renting a worksite, obtaining and renewing licenses, advertising the business, and so on. They take greater financial and legal risks than the workers. Also massage businesses usually have multiple workers on shift at the same time who speak a shared language, and are often located in an urban or suburban setting, which is less isolated than working alone in an apartment.

Massage businesses can also provide sex workers with more bodily autonomy than working independently in an apartment. Workers in a massage business are more likely to have the choice—to sell sexual services or not sell them—depending on their financial needs and their sense of safety or comfort with a client. Because not all massage businesses offer sexual services, their clients do not have reason to assume that they are able to receive sexual services. Because the expectation isn't there, massage workers have more flexibility to choose whether to offer sexual services, when, to whom, and for how much. This increases their comfort, their safety, and their control over their sexual services, boundaries, and earnings. The common understanding is that apartment businesses always offer sexual services (though they may *also* offer additional services, including massage), meaning that clients come to them expecting sex. These workers have less flexibility over whether they offer sexual services—though for some it is worth it because their rates are typically higher than those of massage workers.

There is a cultural and legal assumption that racialized and non-English-speaking women in the sex industry are forced to provide sexual services. But this is based on presumptions of their helplessness. In reality, non-English-speaking sex workers find ways to negotiate their sexual and labor boundaries despite language barriers. The following quotes from sex workers help illustrate how they negotiate getting paid and making decisions about sexual services:

> We aren't stupid. If they don't have money, then we don't do [the sexual service]. Usually they give $20 tips for extra service. If you don't have money, we don't do extra.
>
> I feel I am happy, and enjoy the job. . . . I don't let them feel I really enjoy the sex, though. . . . Sometimes if I don't have the mood, I won't provide a good service. I will watch TV and have sex with the customer. . . . I kicked him out in less than ten minutes."
>
> I won't allow a client to touch me if I don't like him. I'll strictly say it. . . . I usually ask my client to give me the tips when I [have done] half of the job.

MIGRANT SEX WORK IS A GLOBAL JUSTICE ISSUE

Migrants sell sex because migration, paid work, and sexuality (not just sex work) are all strategies of survival.[11] Some migrants use sex work because it grants them more control over their work, their wages, their mobility, their bodies, and their sexualities. When many people look at migrant sex workers, they often do not see someone who has made a daring escape—someone who may have defied poverty, fled from war or conflict, indentured labor, an unwanted marriage, or dictatorial control by bosses and racist immigration restrictions on where they choose to live or work. A migrant sex worker is someone who dares to cross the line.

Sex work increases everywhere there is a social or economic crisis. For example, online sex work skyrocketed in the first few years of the COVID-19 pandemic as people lost their jobs in other sectors and entered the sex industry to economically survive, while doing work that did not expose them to the risk of COVID transmission.[12] People from oppressed groups everywhere in the world use sex work as an economic survival strategy, especially those who are poor, racialized, and migrant. People who need money for food, shelter, safety, and transportation but no access to capital have one form of capital available to them—their bodies. An estimated 60 percent of the total sum of the world's paid work is informal, and sex work is an important part of that economy, allowing people to make money by selling their own labor informally but without being detected by government, law enforcement, and other authorities. Poor people, undocumented people, people in jails and prison, unhoused people, women fleeing domestic violence, stateless people, people displaced by climate, war, and persecution—people from all of these groups trade and sell sex to get by. And this isn't exclusive to women and LGBTQ+ people—straight men survive through sex work, too.[13]

Migrants also sell sex because their families depend on them. Given that on average, each individual sex worker supports five to seven people other than themselves, the economic effects of sex work are manifold. An uncounted number of poor and marginalized families and communities quietly depend on sex workers for their economic survival, though it is often hidden and stigmatized. Sex work should not be considered something that only affects a small part of the population, but as a global social and economic justice issue. Most oppressed communities are in some way affected by sex work stigma, discrimination, and criminalization. The oppression of sex workers and people in the sex industry—especially those who are poor, racialized, and migrant—should be understood as a threat to the economic survival of all oppressed people.

When we say that migrant sex work is resistance, it is not to glamorize migration or sex work. Many people do not want to leave home, and selling sex can be hard, unsafe, and miserable. Yet we respect that racialized migrant sex workers are strong people, intelligently wresting control over their lives against economic and political systems that are set on controlling and exploiting them. In the next chapter, we explore their lived reality of one of these systems—state violence.

INTERLUDES II

DAISY'S STORY[14]

Daisy was an escort in her mid-thirties who had permanent residency, which meant that she could still be deported for a criminal conviction. She had worked in the sex industry for years, but she did not have enough yet to buy her own home, so she rented an apartment, where she also saw clients. The work was not easy, but it helped Daisy on days when she was very lonely. Sometimes good clients would take her out for dinner, show her around the city, and take her out of the city on hot summer days to their vacation homes—a rare privilege for working-class women in the city. It made her feel less lonely, and supported and cared for. Daisy moved into a new building, where she worked with her friend Candy, who was in Canada on a tourist visa. After three months in the new place, the police knocked on her door to interrogate her about whether she was a sex-trafficking victim. The police were using what they claim was a "victim-support" model of investigation, where instead of raiding a suspected sex-trafficking business and arresting everyone, they "talk" to the suspected victims. But even though it was not a raid, Daisy was scared—and with reason. Candy did not have residency, so the police could arrest her. The police stole Candy's money and jewelry, and she was indeed deported.

The police also told Daisy's building management that they suspected Daisy was a "sex-trafficking victim." The management responded by accusing her of "criminal activity" and terminating her year-long lease. They demanded that Daisy pay the remaining nine months' rent for violating the lease and sent her a letter from their lawyer threatening to sue if she didn't pay. The building management also sent a letter to all the residents of the building to "watch out," and encouraged other residents to report to management if they saw any evidence of suspicious activity, such as "strange men coming in." They warned Daisy that she should stop engaging in illegal activity and offering sexual services, or they would call the police. Shortly after, the building manager locked Daisy out of her own apartment by changing the front door passcode and the intercom code. Panicked, Daisy called Butterfly, worried that she wouldn't be able to retrieve any of her belongings, identification, or money. Butterfly contacted the building management on her behalf, and Daisy was able to get her things. She didn't want any more trouble and moved out very quickly. Daisy didn't have the money to pay the remaining nine months on her lease, so she left without paying, but this claim remains on her credit report.

Daisy moved to a new place where she hoped to have less trouble, but the building management again suspected her. This time, they installed a closed-circuit security camera on her floor to monitor her. She didn't know if this was legal, but there was nothing she could do. When a client raped and robbed her, Daisy suppressed her instinct to scream to avoid having the police called.

The police came to her door again anyway, under the pretext of a "human trafficking" investigation. They said they wanted to protect Daisy and asked her to collaborate with them in their investigation into human trafficking. They promised that they would help if she collaborated. Daisy refused. The police returned with a search warrant and said that they were there to "protect her," to make sure she was safe. Instead, they searched her place and interrogated her, demanding that she answer personal questions, including if she was working with anyone and whether anyone answered her phone when potential clients called or advertised for her. These would all be trafficking offenses. The police asked if she had any family members or a boyfriend. Daisy refused to talk, as that would incriminate her friends and family. During the search, the police took photos of Daisy's identification cards and forced her to show them her text messages and her contacts list. Police took screenshots of her call history to record the numbers of everyone she had been in contact with. Her friends, family, and clients were all on her call history. Daisy felt so afraid even after the police left because she didn't know if she or those around her would get into trouble. The police still have Daisy's call log, which means that any of her friends or family, like Candy, could be investigated for human trafficking, criminally charged, or deported. After the investigation, the management of the building told Daisy that she was not allowed to stay and work there anymore, and she got evicted again.

After the second eviction, Daisy moved to a third building. Again, the building management suspected what Daisy was doing, but this time they requested bribes. The management subtly made it clear that they would not report Daisy to the police as long as she paid them an additional $1,000 per month on top of her rent. She knew there was another worker in the building who was only paying $500 in monthly bribes, and she was angry that she was being forced to pay $1,000, but she felt it was her only option.

Daisy's bank also told her that they were terminating business with her and closing down her account based on transactions that they described as "abnormal activity." She never knew if this was because the bank flagged something from her cash deposits as suspected "human trafficking," or because the police had notified them of their investigations into her as a suspected sex-trafficking victim. Without a bank account, Daisy had to keep all of her money in cash, in her house, putting her at great risk that everything she earned could be seized as "proceeds of human trafficking" or stolen by the police, or stolen by thieves. To protect her earnings, Daisy began to rely on a friend to deposit the money for her into her friend's bank account every month. This hurt her chances of ever owning her own home where she can live and work free from police "rescue," but it was a better option than the risk of losing it all in a police or client robbery.

BLUE'S STORY[15]

In 2009, my family was facing some political issues and they thought that it would be much safer for me to leave my home country. Instead of applying as a refugee, where there is a lot of uncertainty in the immigration process and stigma, my family decided that it was better for me to come to Canada with a student visa because my score was quite high and I had graduated from the university in my hometown. I came to Canada and began studying in a degree program at a university.

We knew that it would be expensive. I had to pay over $45,000 a year in international student tuition and living costs, but it was also important for me to leave the country. For the first year, my family was still able to send me money. I could manage my school fees in the first semester. But after that, they were having some difficulties and were not able to send me so much money. I had a very heavy course load, and it was very challenging for me to find a paid job. Most of the jobs available were cash jobs in restaurants or factories. I had studied engineering, and I really wanted to spend the time on my schooling and getting relevant experiences. As an international student and a girl, I was not able to find internships or part-time jobs in the engineering field so easily. Then, because of the financial crisis in Asia, my family could no longer help support me. I needed to earn more money to pay for my school fees, right away. I looked at the job ads, but most of the jobs were for long hours doing low-paid labor. I saw that a massage parlor was hiring. I contacted a boss, and she told me that I could work flexible hours so that I could continue to study and accommodate my school schedule. I would mainly take the night shift so that I could earn more money without it affecting my school, volunteering, or needing to deal with family issues. I earned between $100 to $150 per hour instead of $10 per hour. When I worked in massage parlors, I mainly offered massage, and sometimes "body slide" and hand jobs. I did not do full service, but it was okay. Some girls did it, and some didn't. This was my bottom-line boundary, and I had enough clients to survive. I did not offer full service, but I also didn't discriminate against the other girls in the spa who did. I offered the services that I was comfortable with, and I deserved the money I earned from that.

I have to tell you—it may sound a little bit crazy—but I really enjoyed seeing the men "come." It gave me a lot of satisfaction. It was like a little miracle. It's hard to explain. I do not know why I feel this way, but this is how I feel.

In 2015, law enforcement came to the massage parlor where I worked, and things took a major turn for the worse. It was a nightmare. I thought Canada was a place that respects human rights, but I found that it is not true when you are not a citizen and speak

English with an accent. They saw us as illegal and bad people. My massage parlor was legal and registered. But on that awful day, the police abruptly opened the door of my service room. I was cleaning up. They told me that the police were coming to do an investigation. They asked me who brought me here to Canada and who was my boss. I told them I found this job myself and the boss was not here. Then they looked at me very rudely and ordered me to tell them the truth. They asked me if I was being controlled and who was the person behind me. They told me that they were investigating human trafficking. I told them I was not trafficked and I was voluntary.

Then, the police ordered me to stand inside the room while they searched the entire room, my bags, and other personal belongings. I was so scared, but they were still very rude. My boss asked to see a search warrant. He asked them to show a warrant or stop the search. The police kept searching and brought me to the other room.

Four big guys stood around me. They did not allow me to leave that little room for almost two hours. They asked me for my immigration documents. I showed the police my work permit and told them I had legal status and I was allowed to work. They did not even allow me to sit and kept me standing for that whole two hours. Then, I heard the police calling the immigration authorities as the other three police officers continued to interrogate me. I was so frightened and so frustrated that I did not know what to do. I did not know why I was being asked many questions over and over—like why I came to Canada and why I worked in a massage parlor. Overwhelmed and insulted, I eventually started to cry. I repeated to the officers that I wasn't doing anything illegal. When the border agency officials arrived, they saw my student ID and work permit. They continued to interrogate me and would not allow me to leave or make a telephone call.

I don't remember how long that lasted, but it was quite long. The immigration officers left the room and the police officers asked me to leave immediately and never come back. I was warned that if I returned to work there, I would be arrested and deported. I was not sure what kind of laws I breached, but I tried to leave as soon as possible. I heard that the boss had received a ticket after I left.

I was so terrified, I could not sleep for almost a month. I kept thinking, *Why did it happen to me?* I was so traumatized that I could not forget that scene even until now. I was so afraid, as I had never been treated this way. I was really worried that they would arrest me, and I decided to move and live in another place. I really did not want to see them again. However, I really needed to work and make money, and the boss begged me. He told me that some regular clients really want to see me. I really needed money. I had tried to work in a massage parlor again; however, I left after staying less than an hour because my heart could not stop beating and I was really afraid that the law enforcement would come again.

I wanted to continue working at the massage parlor, where I felt like I had more control, more support, more power to choose who I provided services to, and more ability to negotiate with clients. However, I did not want to take the risk and I did not want my family to be disappointed, as they had spent all their money to send me to Canada. I knew that some women were working in apartments and they had less chance of being investigated by the police. But I also knew that this job involved providing "full service" as opposed to the hand jobs. But I had no choice. Now, I needed to pay for the rent on a work apartment, place advertisements, and do everything. It was not easy, but it was the only way I could earn money. It was very stressful as I had to manage everything myself. I also needed to work much longer hours, and I had to pay different costs every day. I was also afraid, as I had to work by myself instead of having other people around in case I needed someone to help me. It was so stressful—I was afraid of police, immigration, and robbers at the same time.

My working permit restricts me from doing any sex work–related job. One of my friends was arrested after the border agency caught her working in a massage parlor, and I had heard ten other women were deported. I had to be careful. The raid and police attention has put my immigration status at risk, so I no longer feel like I can ever call the police even if I'm in danger. I would risk losing my study permit and risk deportation. I would never make the call. But working in an apartment is much more dangerous. Many people target us because they know that we are like a money machine. I had never been robbed in massage parlors, but I've been robbed three times in my apartment. I didn't even scream when it happened because I was afraid someone would call the police. I can't believe this is happening to me in Canada. When I saw the news, they kept saying the anti-trafficking investigations were rescuing women. I don't know who they rescued. It is a lie. I don't believe it, and I hope others don't believe it. For me, they are just a horrible evil that keeps chasing you. Of course, I believe that the laws should be changed. Law enforcement is using the laws to target us. They are not protecting us. The laws should not be used against the people.

MI'S STORY[16]

Mi came to Canada from Asia in 2015. She was working as an escort in a city where escorts were in a legal gray area. The city required escorts to pay for a special license, but the license regulations prohibited sexual services. Mi was in Canada on a tourist visa and was not eligible for the license. The local city inspectors would racially profile all the online ads of Asian workers and conduct investigations. The officers found Mi and fined her for working without a license. She did not pay the fine because she was afraid that if she did, she'd risk being arrested. Shortly after, her visitor's immigration visa expired, and she became undocumented. Based on the combination of having an outstanding ticket and having no immigration status, immigration control issued a warrant for her arrest. The next time she was back in that same small city, the police found her advertisement and arrested her. She was detained and locked with chains on her wrists, waist, and legs. The police seized $10,000 from Mi, including all of her personal belongings and communication devices. The police interrogated Mi about whether she was a victim and whether there were others working with her. Despite the fact that Mi did not identify as a victim, she was held in detention while police "investigated."

"The officer asked me if I was being controlled, being forced or if anyone had assisted me to come and work in Canada," Mi said. "I told the officer that I did it voluntarily. No one received any money from me. I am over forty years old, and I know what I am doing. No one forced me. They also kept asking me if I was working with others, and they asked me again and again who helped to advertise. They found a money transfer record, and I explained that there was a person who helped me do money exchange. However, they insisted this person was not helping me, and they kept saying this person is a trafficker."

The police and immigration continued to demand that Mi provide a statement, but she refused. After seven days of Mi in the detention center, two individuals approached her identifying themselves as a "victim-support team" and invited her to talk with them. Mi confided in these individuals about her experiences of being robbed, raped, and almost killed at work. But she did not know that the "victim-support team" was a police officer and an immigration authority. Her statement was used against her to charge her for working illegally in Canada.

The immigration authorities decided to detain Mi even longer because they believed that everyone who was offering to assist her was her trafficker, and they justified her detention as a protective measure. In prison, she had no money, no interpretation services, and could not understand what was happening or how to navigate the complex prison system even to make a phone call. Because her phone was confiscated, she did not have the phone numbers of her friends. To be able to call Butterfly for help, she offered candy to others in exchange for instructions on how to make a collect call. Being in detention was the worst thing Mi had ever experienced.

"I was locked up in a prison. I was locked up almost two months. I might still be in prison if I was not helped by Butterfly," she said. "They took away my phone and didn't allow me to contact my friends and family. No one knew what had happened to me, as they did not allow me to access the phonebook. The judge [of detention review] did not allow me to leave, as they said they had to protect me. They thought my friends and clients were bad people and dangerous for me. They did not allow my friends to be a bondsperson to get me out of those chains.[17] They also would not release me to my friends.

"They said I was not allowed to get out because I did not have place to stay. But I told them that I would have a place to stay. All of my friends took care of me very well. They did not take my money. Some of them even gave me money sometimes."

Mi was released back to her hometown with the assistance of Butterfly. But she was still very angry and frustrated at the treatment she had received, particularly because the police refused to return her money and personal belongings. The police have since informed Butterfly that they are working on an application to be able to permanently seize the $10,000 they confiscated from Mi because she had worked illegally in Canada.

Mi explained, "I have asked them when can I get back my money, but they do not respond to me. During the interview, they said they will help me to get it back. However, they lied. They said that to make me talk to them. I did not know they were police because they said they were special officers who protect victims. They refuse to give the money and phone back to me, even after I have left Canada for three months now. Some of the money was what I brought to Canada. I still owe the lawyer fee and I cannot pay back the lawyer as I cannot get the money back." Mi continues to fight for the return of her money and phone with the help of Butterfly.

CHAPTER 3

MIGRANT SEX WORKERS AND STATE VIOLENCE

The state is the primary perpetrator of violence against racialized migrant sex workers, and it is responsible for creating the conditions for non-state violence as well. Migrant sex workers are more endangered by those who make the laws and those who enforce them (the police, immigration control, and city enforcement officers) than they are by organized crime. We use the term *state violence* to mean suffering and harm that is committed by state authorities. State violence includes both authorized and unauthorized forms of suffering and harm resulting from the actions of law enforcement, correctional institutions, border patrol, and other agents of the criminal legal system through surveillance, policing, immigration raids, seizure of wages and property, detention, prisons, expulsions, and travel bans. It includes the state's apprehension of sex workers' children and family separation, forced evictions, and denial of medical care, as well as the surveillance, arrest, detention, and deportations of migrant sex workers' family members and friends who are caught up in investigations. State violence includes legal and authorized processes such as criminalization. Criminalization is a social and political process in which society decides who and what behaviors or activities will be punished by the state. And state violence includes extralegal and unauthorized violence such as physical and sexual assault, sexual harassment, threats of violence, wage theft, and murder.

Most state violence against migrant sex workers is legal and viewed as legitimate, normal, and justified. We want to challenge the narrative that abusing, caging, and threatening migrant sex workers with death is considered human trafficking when it is committed by non-state actors, but that when the police do it, it is legitimate, helpful, and fair. In popular conceptions of migrant sex workers, they are very often imagined as victims of armed gangsters holding them hostage, withholding all their money, and forcing them to have sex under threats of violence. But it is the police who enter the workplaces of migrant sex workers with guns pointed at their heads. It is the police who are authorized to fatally shoot people for resisting an arrest or running from a raid. It is the police who are authorized to seize a sex worker's life savings. It is the police who are authorized to kidnap migrant sex workers and put them in cages—in a prison, jail, or detention center. And it is the police who sexually extort and assault them with impunity. The media's depiction of a human trafficker resembles a cop more than anyone else.

State violence touches every part of racialized migrant sex workers' lives and work, including their economic and housing security; their mobility, bodily autonomy, and freedom of movement; the quality of their relationships and their vulnerability to intimate partner violence; their wages, working conditions, and access to safe workplaces and safer sex; the level of openness and transparency they can have with their families; their participation in democratic processes like voting and policy decisions; their access to social services, medical care, and legal support; their ability to parent and keep their kids; and their ability to save money and build economic security.

CRIMINALIZATION OF MIGRANT SEX WORKERS

Migrant sex workers are caught within a web of carceral power. The strands of this web are made up of laws and policies—sex work laws, human trafficking laws, organized crime laws, immigration prohibitions, municipal regulations, and anti-trafficking policies for professional bodies like health care providers and social work agencies. The carceral web envelops migrant sex workers so that no matter their immigration status or type of sex work they do, no matter where they go or how they travel, the state can always use some form of law or policy to catch, control, and punish them.

CRIMINALIZATION OF SEX WORKERS

Migrant sex workers are criminalized for their work through laws related to sex work and organized crime, and also increasingly through laws related to human trafficking, at the federal, state/provincial, and municipal levels.

Sex work is criminalized through laws that prohibit sex work or activities related to sex work. The criminalization of sex work includes activities that could help sex workers be safer, such as using websites through which workers can find and screen clients and share information about problematic clients. It includes all forms of communicating and negotiating services with clients (in person, over the phone, or electronically). Working with other sex workers; renting a work space; hiring assistants for security, answering phones, or cleaning; or introducing clients to other sex workers are all prohibited by anti–sex work laws in the US and Canada. Some jurisdictions also criminalize the possession of condoms by using them as evidence of sex work.

The criminalization of sex work includes laws that claim to only criminalize clients and third parties. However, that claim does not hold up, because when any part of the sex industry is prohibited, sex workers are also criminally charged. This owes to the diverse roles that sex workers play in the sex industry. So, for example, when jurisdictions make profiting from sex work illegal on the basis that it is "sexual exploitation," even sex workers who answer the phones or rent space to other sex workers can be arrested and charged with an offense.

Sex workers work with each other in many important ways but these relationships are criminalized through third-party laws. In both Canada and the US, a sex work business staffed by more than one person can be considered an organized crime ring. People who work for the same massage business are considered part of what the police often mislabel a "sex trafficking organized crime ring."

Relationships between independent sex workers (those who work for themselves) are often organic, cooperative, and flexible—but no less criminalized. Independent sex workers sometimes work together by sharing the cost of a workspace, like a rented apartment that two or more sex workers use to see clients. Some may also rent out a room in their own home to other sex workers. Sex workers also work together by "touring" together—traveling to new places for work and sharing the cost of transportation, advertisements, and hotels—relying on each other for companionship and safety. Sometimes sex workers who see a similar clientele become business partners. Some sex workers want to work with a manager who will take care of the business side of their job. Sometimes good friends, spouses or lovers work together as part of their relationship. Sex workers also work together informally, by helping each other with any part of the job. This might be sharing information about which businesses are doing well so they can make more money, neighborhoods to avoid because the police or immigration control have been more active, how to get clients to spend more on them, information about a troublesome or abusive client, help with sending money home or figuring out how to use a new sex work advertising site.

All of the above activities are illegal under anti–sex work laws. In addition to the outright prohibition on sex work, sex workers are increasingly criminalized through human trafficking laws and zoning and licensing regulations that prohibit all working relationships between sex workers. In the US and Canada, working together in the sex industry is so heavily penalized that it can constitute an organized crime offense, a prostitution offense, a sex trafficking offense, an immigration offense, a banking regulation offense, and a municipal licensing offense.

MUNICIPAL CRIMINALIZATION

City licensing and zoning regulations are an important and underrecognized form of carceral control and criminalization. City regulations typically prohibit sexual services in massage businesses and other aspects of sex work, such as communicating for the purposes of sex work, renting space, and answering phones, and may also inhibit the presence of sexual health materials like condoms by classifying them as evidence of a license infraction. To carry out these regulations, municipal officers engage in surveillance, investigations, and raids of migrants who are sex workers (or Asian massage workers who are racially profiled as sex workers).

Migrant massage workers are subjected to specific criminalization in many places in the US and Canada through the heavy regulation of the industry, as detailed in the report *Un-licensed: Asian Migrant Massage Licensure and the Racialized Policing of Poverty*.[1] In some jurisdictions, only registered massage therapists can legally practice massage. Low-income, non-English-speaking migrant workers who do not have access to professional massage training because of the costs, language requirements, and prohibitive length of the courses are excluded from accessing professional certifications. Most migrant massage workers don't actually need the training because they already have the necessary skills and experience. But without legal certification, they are subject to intense surveillance and enforcement.

Other jurisdictions allow for massage services by non-registered massage therapists, but subject the therapists to extreme regulation because they are associated with sex work and racialized migrants. In New York State, for example, the penalties for offering non-licensed massage are so severe that they are higher than the penalties for a prostitution charge. In Toronto, massage workers must get special "body rub" licenses, may be required to complete criminal background checks, and may face very narrow restrictions over zoning that segregate non-registered massage spas from registered ones, forcing them into more isolated parts of the city. This isolation makes them more exposed to harassment and abuse by the police and predators. Obtaining a body rub license requires proof of immigration status (such as a work permit), despite Toronto being a "sanctuary city" where residents are guaranteed access to city services regardless of their immigration status. It also requires a medical exam, which is a violation of workers' bodily autonomy that is based in stigma, and discrimination as there is no evidence that mandatory medical inspections promote the health of sex workers, their clients or the public.[2]

IMMIGRATION EXCLUSIONS, INCLUDING TRAVEL BANS

Migrant sex workers experience discriminatory immigration policies that authorize the state to employ surveillance, racial profiling, arrest, detention, deportation, and other forms of restriction on people's move-ment. Migrant sex workers are subject to formal exclusion by both the US and Canada, as both countries' immigration regulations prohibit the movement of migrant sex workers across borders.

The US government maintains a travel ban on those who have been engaged in prostitution anytime in the previous ten years—and anyone who has been economically linked to the sex worker, including those in a shared household. In Canada, migrants with temporary work visas are banned from taking any job in any part of the sex industry, and working in the sex industry is a deportable offense. Permanent residents in the US and Canada may work in the sex industry, but can be subject to criminal offenses. Sex workers who are convicted through human trafficking laws and organized crime laws can also be deported.

BORDER SURVEILLANCE

The US and Canadian states use surveillance before, during, and after migrant sex workers cross borders to control their mobility. Immigra-tion officials require that certain migrants—especially those who are not from rich, predominantly white countries—disclose their occupa-tion, income, assets, passport (which includes evidence of where they have traveled), travel plan, and contacts in the country they are apply-ing to migrate to, and that they undergo questioning by an embassy official before they are allowed to legally enter a country. Disclosure of personal information functions as sex work surveillance. Migrants have to carefully disguise their sex work history, connections, and plans to avoid being denied entry through formal or informal discrimination.

Border guards function as the next level of control over mobility. At the border itself, immigration control agents racially profile women from the Global South and demand the same information that immigra-tion officials require, along with additional personal information. For example, if border guards have suspicions about a woman's involvement in sex work (which are usually based on sexist racial profiling), they will search her clothing for evidence of "sexy" underwear and go through her phone to see her texts and photos, asking about any sexting or "sexy selfies" they find. They will demand to speak to the person picking her up at the airport about their relationship, and, if it appears to involve the sex industry, the border agents can deny entry and issue a ban, based on merely the suspicion of sex work, without evidence or recourse.

Beyond the border, police and border agents racially profile migrant sex work businesses (and suspected sex work businesses) in an attempt to catch racialized migrants and punish them by stealing or seizing their money, issuing fines, or being abusive. And they may also arrest, detain, and deport them.

POLICE SURVEILLANCE

When the police single out Asian migrant women for surveillance, they typically claim to be conducting investigations into human trafficking or organized crime. What they actually do is monitor the "Asian" advertisements on massage and sex work websites and investigate the massage businesses in immigrant neighborhoods. This is racial profiling through surveillance, not legitimate protection against human trafficking. The police can subpoena sex workers' emails, text messages, and call logs between workers and their friends, family members, and customers. They can also demand that migrant sex workers provide them with information about any mutual aid funds (which investigations can deem human trafficking funds); information about their workplaces (which can be deemed organized crime rings); and community organizations that work with migrant sex workers (which can be deemed enablers of human trafficking or organized crime).

CIVILIAN SURVEILLANCE PRACTICES

Evading surveillance from multiple law enforcement bodies is increasingly difficult because surveillance has spread to nearly every corner of society. Private security firms, airport security, transit cops—and, increasingly, civilians such as health care workers, teachers, landlords, neighbors, and even truckers, bus drivers, and hairdressers—have been trained through their workplaces or through public education campaigns to identify and report their "suspicions of sex trafficking" to the police. But these trainings and public education campaigns only teach people how to identify sex workers—especially racialized sex workers on the move. The moral panic about "modern slavery" provokes a sense of urgency among civilians that they must react quickly and say something if they suspect someone is being enslaved. Many of the arrests of Asian migrant sex workers have been initiated by a neighbor calling the police because they found out (or suspected) that non-English-speaking Asian women were selling sex and concluded that they were being trafficked.

The moral panic about "modern slavery" also discourages people from having contact with migrant sex workers, because they do not want to risk becoming associated with people who might be under police surveillance. In some cases, this can work in the favor of migrant sex workers who want to work under the radar and be left alone. But this silence around them becomes a problem if they need help. For example, a neighbor of a migrant sex worker may not support discrimination and hate against migrant women in the sex industry, but will hesitate to reach out and support a worker who may be facing problems because it could bring trouble on the neighbor themselves. If the neighbor visits the migrant woman at work, for instance, the neighbor can be charged with an organized crime offense. So if a migrant woman is being abused by her partner, the neighbor may hesitate to offer help. What if the police become involved, and the neighbor comes under suspicion as well? What if immigration control agents are called and they ask about the neighbor's immigration status? The surveillance of migrant sex workers thus stops helpful bystanders from taking action to support them, leaving migrant sex workers isolated and more vulnerable to abuse.

TERROR, ABUSE, AND PUNISHMENT

The state authorizes law enforcement to punish migrant sex workers through legal and extralegal forms of terror and abuse. Police engage in surprise raids at dawn where they smash down doors and point guns at migrant sex workers. The workers are then forced to strip, are interrogated, detained, and caged, extorted for sexual services, must endure sexual and physical assault, and have all their belongings and money stolen or seized by the state as "proceeds of crime." Police can use the information they gather from surveillance and interrogation to criminalize the family of migrant sex workers, or anyone they have a relationship with (for example, their landlord or neighbor). They can criminalize sex workers who are survivors of violence, arresting them for reporting an incident that occurred while they were engaged in sex work. Law enforcement punishes migrant sex workers in many indirect ways as well. The police act as a pipeline to different types of state violence, such as, for instance, turning migrant sex worker survivors of violence over to immigration control to deport them, or reporting migrant sex workers to child welfare authorities so that their children will be apprehended. They can also "out" workers by disclosing their work to their landlords, families, or communities.

DEATH

State violence kills racialized migrant sex workers, as illustrated through the story of Yang Song, a thirty-eight-year-old woman who was killed on November 25, 2017, during a police raid at the New York City massage parlor where she worked. Yang grew up in a remote village in northeast China and immigrated to New York City with her husband in 2013. Her husband was disabled and could no longer work, so Yang tried to support them both by waitressing, and later, by training as a home care worker. As a Chinese-speaking woman without citizenship, her wages were not enough to support herself and her husband. To support them both, she began working in massage parlors. In 2017, she told her family back home in China that she'd been sexually assaulted at gunpoint by a police officer. She was also terrorized in multiple police raids on her parlor. These raids resulted in prostitution charges, meaning she was at risk of deportation. Yang was so traumatized by her interactions with the police that she told family members that she'd rather die than be arrested again.[3]

In the late fall of 2017, New York City police conducted yet another raid on Yang's parlor. To escape the police, the workers ran. One jumped out a window and was badly injured. Another hid all night on the wintry fire escape. Witnesses saw Yang flying out the fourth-story window. We don't know whether she jumped or was pushed. Some believe that she fell while running to escape another arrest or sexual assault by the police. Others believe that the police pushed her out the window to her death in an attempt to cover up the sexual assault. Either way, Yang Song was killed by the policing of her labor, her migration, and her survival. Her death catalyzed the organizing of massage workers in New York City to fight back against police power in their workplaces and lives. The grassroots collective, Red Canary Song (RCS), continues to lead in this effort, honoring Yang Song with an annual vigil.

Law enforcement agents also engage in unauthorized killings, as in the case of Juan David Ortiz, the US Border Patrol agent in the border town of Laredo, Texas, who attacked five sex workers, killing four. Ortiz described this as a service he was providing to this city by "cleaning up the streets" of sex workers, whom he claimed were "trash" and "so dirty."[4]

STATE-FACILITATED HARMS

The state's targeting of migrant sex workers has far-reaching impacts on every aspect of their safety and well-being at work, at home, with their associates, and even with strangers. Instead of protecting migrant sex workers, the state creates or worsens the conditions that make them vulnerable to exploitation, abuse, and violence. Violence against migrant sex workers is not inevitable, it is a choice by the state to expose them to harm.

EXPLOITATION AND ABUSE AT WORK

Migrant sex workers have spoken about the effects of criminalization in their own words, collected in "Stories of Migrant Sex Workers." One sex worker, Ding Ding, shared how criminalization affects her work:

Some of the sisters are scared to blame their bad bosses for their oppression because the boss would occasionally threaten them by saying they had no legal status. Some of the sisters did not dare to call the police when robbed because the police did not solve any problems. To add salt to injury, immigration bureau staff were brought in, and they detained or even deported those victims. I have a sister who called the police for being robbed. The police did not do the investigation. Instead, she was arrested and handed over to the immigration authority. She was finally released. To avoid being arrested again, she fled to other cities."[5]

Criminalization directly contributes to poor working conditions, such as wage theft, unsafe worksites, unfair labor practices, and abuse by bosses. On top of the precarious, unprotected conditions that racialized migrant workers in all labor sectors are often forced to work under, migrant sex workers face an additional layer of criminalization that further reduces their access to fair working conditions, unions, or even worker associations. Migrant sex workers deal with bosses who refuse to maintain safe conditions in the workplace, fail to follow through on agreements about wages and scheduling, discriminate in hiring and firing decisions, engage in sexual harassment, extort sexual services, and refuse to ban problematic clients from returning. But what can a criminalized migrant working in a criminalized business do if they have a bad boss? They cannot report these conditions, and they cannot organize a union. As a result, some workers are forced to accept poor working conditions, such as unsafe worksites and unfair labor practices. Criminalization fosters a welcoming environment for exploitative managers who know they are entering a sector where workers cannot protect themselves against state and interpersonal violence, and where the managers are unlikely to face any consequences for exploitation or abuse. Criminalization also creates unsafe working conditions that endanger sex workers' health and bodily autonomy. For example, criminalization is responsible for up to 46 percent of HIV infections among sex workers because it drastically reduces sex workers' control over their own health and safety. Criminalization increases violence against sex workers, including sexual assault, and it reduces access to health care, such as HIV prevention and treatment. Under criminalization, sex workers cannot openly communicate their services and boundaries (such as their safer sex practices) in advertisements and in negotiations with clients. And some jurisdictions use the presence of condoms to prosecute sex workers. As a result, their ability to negotiate and implement condom use is drastically limited.[6]

WORKPLACE VIOLENCE

In Butterfly's research on migrant sex workers, more than 60 percent reported experiencing violence.[7] By making safety measures illegal, the state increases vulnerability to abuse by clients and aggressors posing as clients. Dorothy, an Asian migrant sex worker who works out of an apartment, shared her experiences with Butterfly, reporting:

> They (the robbers) treated us like a money machine. We were robbed four times in one week. All the girls were afraid, and some girls were injured. They came with weapons, and they had a gun. We could not call the police; otherwise, we would have had more trouble. I told the police about this while I was detained, but they did not care. They just wanted to arrest us."[8]

Many migrant sex workers cannot use bank accounts or credit cards because of their undocumented immigration status. But also many cannot use banks because they risk losing all of their money. Banks surveil their customers to detect sex work businesses and can report migrant sex workers to the police, freeze their accounts, and seize their money if they suspect that an account is being used as part of sex work. Some workers are able to get around these rules but many cannot. As a result, workers are more likely to keep cash in their workplaces, which increases their chances of being robbed by thieves or having their money seized by the police. Some cities prohibit locks on the treatment rooms in massage businesses as part of their efforts to increase surveillance—even though workers in these establishments use locked rooms to find safety in the event of a robbery or other violence. And many cities zone migrant sex work businesses in industrial areas with poor lighting and transportation options and where there are few people around, leaving workers isolated and at increased risk of robberies and assaults.

It's important to understand that sex workers are highly capable of creating safe and fair workplaces, as they have done in places where sex work is decriminalized. Sex workers do the same things as other service industry workers to improve their workplaces, like talking to other workers about their problems with the boss, organizing for better conditions and demanding basic health and safety precautions. But under criminalization, almost all of their potential avenues to keep their workplaces safe are illegal. Working together instead of independently, sharing information about clients and bosses, leaving a bad boss and opening their own business, communicating their boundaries regarding the sexual services in their advertisements, discussing any of these topics over the phone or with their own colleagues and bosses, choosing where they can work most safely (such as in well-lit, populated areas), and even just using a bank account to keep their cash safe are not legal avenues and put them at risk of detection by law enforcement. Abuse and exploitation thrive in any sector where workers are legally prevented from defending themselves.

EXPLOITATION AND ABUSE AT HOME

Intimate partner violence (IPV) is the most common form of physical, sexual, and economic violence against women—and those risks increase when the survivor is marginalized and criminalized, as migrant sex workers are. Abusive partners and family members know that migrant sex workers are at risk of arrest, deportation, eviction, and having their children taken by child welfare services, and they use this to increase their control over the sex worker.

Criminalization makes it hard for migrant sex workers to get help for IPV and family abuse because it might lead to an investigation, arrest, charges, detention, and deportation. Many migrant sex workers do not want to report abuse or even to seek help from social services or a facility like a hospital, whose staff might then contact the police. Some sex workers choose to deal with the problem themselves rather than take the risk that things would get worse for them (sometimes much worse) if they speak to anyone about their experiences. The need to keep their work hidden keeps sex workers isolated and cut off from external support from friends, family, and social and medical services, decreasing their protection against abuse and support.

ECONOMIC ABUSE

Controlling a partner's access to money, forcing them to turn over their earnings, spending all the partner's money against their will, and preventing a partner from earning (or keeping) enough money to be able to leave the relationship are all types of economic abuse. It is extremely common—over 90 percent of domestic abusers commit economic abuse. Sex workers are at a heightened risk of economic abuse because of their marginalization. For example, some abusers force their partners to sell sex or sell sexual services in ways they don't want to (such as working with unwanted clients). But it is also economic abuse when abusers keep their partner *out* of the sex industry so that the survivor is isolated in the home, away from support systems associated with their work (like colleagues, work friends, or good clients), and can't earn enough money to escape. But when sex workers experience economic abuse as part of IPV, it is often labeled sex trafficking. This has obscured the actual crisis of violence against women and the overlooked issue of economic abuse. And again, when IPV against sex workers is investigated as sex trafficking, this can lead not to supporting the survivor but criminalizing them, and potentially their family. Sex workers who report IPV (including economic abuse) can be subject to criminal and immigration investigations, and so can their family members and support system.

INSTITUTIONAL DISCRIMINATION AND EXPLOITATION

The state contributes to discrimination within the institutions that govern nearly every aspect of migrant sex workers' lives: housing and labor, health care, the courts, child custody, banking, employment law, education, and social services. For example, under federal sex work and human trafficking laws in the US and Canada, landlords cannot knowingly rent a home or worksite to migrant sex workers, and must evict the tenants if they are engaged in such work.

This kind of institutional discrimination creates barriers that migrant sex workers deal with by relying on help from others—lawyers or immigration consultants, for example. But the people involved in those systems can take advantage of migrant sex workers' vulnerability and exploit them. Consultants can charge double or triple the prices that they charge other clients, for instance, and landlords can extort bribes or sexual services from migrant sex workers in exchange for not reporting them to the authorities.

VIGILANTE VIOLENCE

"It was filthy. . . . There was just a state of disorder and it was clear: There was prostitution."[9] This was how, in 2023, New York City mayor Eric Adams described a visit he made to the predominantly Asian sex work district in Queens, New York—the same borough where Yang Song was killed during an NYPD police raid in 2017. Adams had visited the district in response to a conservative news story that complained of brothels in the area, blaming them on reduced police enforcement and "immigration surges."[10]

The state fosters vigilante violence against migrant sex workers by framing them as evidence of filth and disorder, as subhuman social problems, victims and slaves without human agency, undeserving "illegal" immigrants, vectors of disease, permanent outsiders from dangerous cultures, naive and damaged women who are also hyper-sexual deviants, a threat to children, marriages, families, national identity, borders, and security. Through laws and law enforcement, the state justifies control, containment, and punishment of migrant sex workers as necessary for protecting the public. This encourages people outside of the state to see their own violence against migrant sex workers as justified and even helpful to (white) society too.

The 2021 Atlanta shootings are the most well-known recent instance of this, committed by a twenty-one-year-old evangelical man who killed eight people in three massage businesses, six of them Asian women between the ages of forty-four and seventy-four.[11] Speaking on the shooter's motives, Cherokee County Sheriff Department officials recounted that the killer blamed the massage parlors for providing an outlet for his "addiction to sex," and that he had had "a really bad day . . . and this is what he did," reflecting the way that some police view vigilante violence against women in the sex industry as understandable—if not authorized.[12]

The Atlanta shootings were not the only instance of this kind of vigilante violence against workers in massage businesses. In February 2020, a seventeen-year-old young man who identified as a "proud incel" walked into a massage business in Toronto and stabbed two women—the business owner and the receptionist—the latter of whom was twenty-four-year-old Ashley Arzaga, a mother who died from her injuries. The killer used a sword engraved with the words "thot slayer" (a reference to the slang term that means "That Hoe Over There") and, to one of the women, shouted "Die!," calling her a "stupid whore" as he attacked her.[13] He later said he chose his victims because "I just thought they weren't very clean people."[14]

The media characterized the Atlanta killings as the result of anti-Asian racism and characterized the Toronto attack as misogynist violence against women. This is true, but in both cases, the perpetrators also specifically targeted businesses associated with sex work, espousing whorephobic ideologies that align with the state's view of sex workers as filth to be "cleaned up." In both cases, the courts sent the killers to prison, but the role of the state in fostering the conditions for deadly violence was never interrogated. This is because the state does not want to end violence against migrant sex workers—it simply wants a monopoly on that violence.

STATE VIOLENCE AND MIGRANT TRANSGENDER SEX WORKERS

Migrant sex workers, particularly those who are racialized, are also targeted and abused by police. However, there are important differences in how migrant trans sex workers and migrant cisgender sex workers experience criminalization and state violence. From our conversations with community organizers working with migrant trans sex workers, including Nora Butler Burke, who has worked extensively with a trans health organization in Montreal, we learned that police officers are more likely to claim that migrant trans sex workers were acting as dangerous aggressors, not helpless victims. This framing increases police officers' ability to justify serious charges, such as "armed assault" for carrying items of self-defense such as mace, physical assault for defending themselves against an attacker (including a police officer), and drug offenses. It also increases officers' ability to justify assaulting trans migrant sex workers as "self-protection."

The following is speculative and warrants further research, but what we notice is that when the police characterize migrant trans sex workers as dangerous aggressors they justify increased physical abuse, charges, and fines related to violence, weapons, or drugs. These kinds of charges make it very difficult for trans women to leave the sex industry and get jobs in other sectors. Many employers discriminate against people with these types of convictions. Also, such punishments may be more likely to prevent trans women from getting access to secure immigration status, including citizenship, without which many of them cannot access public services such as state-provided health insurance. This leaves them paying for their own health care, including expensive gender-affirming care like surgery and hormones.

We can't say if this is intentional or by design; we can simply look at the effects of state violence. And what we see is that the state is more likely to target trans migrant sex workers for a cycle of repeated criminalization, formal labor market exclusion, and exclusion from state recognition and services, than for coercive "rescue and rehabilitation" forms of state control. In other words, the state is more likely to push cisgender migrant sex workers out of the sex industry (and into more sanctioned forms of labor and sexuality) but to keep migrant trans women locked into the sex industry, unable to get other work. From trans women's experiences we can better understand the system as a whole—how the capitalist state selectively characterizes some sex workers as helpless victims who can be rescued while positioning others as "dangerous offenders" who are beyond rehabilitation, based on what advances their economic and political agendas.[15]

ALL VIOLENCE AGAINST MIGRANT SEX WORKERS IS STATE-FACILITATED VIOLENCE

Violence against migrant sex workers is a policy choice. Migrant sex workers are not too naive, weak, or vulnerable to effectively protect themselves. They are *experts* at protecting themselves. And migration and sex work are not too "high risk" to ever be safe. The problem is that migrant sex workers live at the intersection of multiple systems of oppression, and the state enables and fosters violence against them. They are pushed away from sources of power, protection, and support—their families, neighbors, colleagues, and friends. They are denied social inclusion, labor protections, migrant rights like the right to legal immigration status, and access to emergency support services and community and advocacy organizations. When they are pushed out of the sex industry or their homes, they lose two of the most powerful safeguards against violence against women—good wages and housing stability. The state abandons them to aggressors—from predatory thieves, rapists, and exploitative bosses to unscrupulous landlords, lawyers, and abusive spouses—who target them because they know they can get away with it. The harms they experience are manufactured. The criminalization of migrant sex work is not about "rescuing" anybody or bringing down nebulously defined international sex-trafficking rings. It is about facilitating violence.

WHY DOES THE STATE PUNISH MIGRANT SEX WORKERS?

Why would the state want to control and punish migrant sex workers? We can't say for sure and there are likely many reasons. But as organizers within the community, we have an intimate understanding of how the state benefits from its violence against migrant sex workers. It is through looking at these benefits that we can offer some theories about the state's interest in controlling low-income, racialized migrant women's work and their movement.

Migrant women use sex work to resist punitive, low-paying, highly surveilled work. They use sex work to resist state control over their movement, getting across borders, and going where they want undetected by the state, outside of migrant worker programs. They also use sex work to control their sexuality, to benefit from it personally rather than keeping it restricted to marriage, where their husband is the sole beneficiary of their sexuality. Low-income, racialized women use migration and sex work to resist three major structural forms of oppression—control over the international flow of migration, the racially hierarchical organization of labor, and the appropriation of women's sexuality in service of the heteropatriarchal family. State violence forces migrant sex workers back under the control of each of these institutions.

The capitalist class and corporations benefit from access to a large supply of cheap, exploitable, rightless workers who can be coerced into doing the most work for the lowest wages. The largest and most underpaid group of workers in the world are low-income, racialized women from the Global South, who are relegated to hyper-exploitative and underprotected labor sectors like farming, factories, and domestic work. This is true internationally as well, where massive US multinational corporations rely on the labor of this same group. The sex industry interferes with this arrangement by providing an alternative. State violence limits sex work as a viable labor alternative and forces migrant women back into lower-paying work.

Migrant sex work interferes with the surveillance and management of racialized women's movement. Migrant worker programs allow the state and corporations to track, control, and restrict the movement of racialized workers, keeping them out entirely, or allowing them in only under programs where they cannot leave their employer and are tied to one location. Sex work provides migrants with a way to earn a living and move across borders without registering their migration across a border and without restrictions on their location. State violence restricts sex workers' ability to move freely. They are either immobilized and unable to migrate or can only migrate under conditions that track and control their movement.

Finally, the state and the capitalist class have an interest in controlling women's sexuality. Sexuality is valuable for many reasons. First, sex is for the most part, how the next generation of humans is reproduced. Second, sex can provide people with pleasure, joy, and emotional and physical well-being. It can offer relief from pain, sadness, anxiety, or loneliness. In that way, sex can be a type of reproductive labor—the work that sustains and nourishes human life. Third, sex is also closely tied with other forms of reproductive labor, such as cooking, cleaning, and taking care of children and elders, since this work is usually performed by the primary sexual partner–wives.

Sexuality is important because life depends on the reproduction of humans and their care. But profit depends on it too. Capitalist economies couldn't exist without workers and consumers, and the capitalist class couldn't make a profit if they had to pay for the actual value of reproductive labor including pleasure, childbearing, and housework. It is in their interest to control which kinds of human life are reproduced, and to make sure that women keep providing reproductive labor—for free. Heteropatriarchal marriage provides the capitalist class with much of this control. Heteropatriarchal marriage is an institution where women are expected to restrict their sexuality to the marriage or be heavily punished, to provide pleasure to their husbands, bear legally recognized children, and to take care of the house and family, being paid nothing for this labor. It is a sexist institution that exploits women as it limits their sexual autonomy and extracts unpaid reproductive labor that it devalues as "non-work." But many low-income women must enter into the institution of heteropatriarchal marriage, in spite of its downsides, because they cannot economically survive without a man's income, especially if they become mothers.

Sex work can provide low-income women (and especially low-income mothers) with an economic alternative to economic dependence on a husband. Sex workers harness one of the benefits of their sexuality—its ability to provide pleasure, joy, and well-being—and they use this to benefit themselves (not their husbands), by making money from selling it. The higher wages of sex work can provide low-income women with more financial independence and therefore more choice around their decision to marry. They are less likely to have to enter into a heteropatriarchal marriage to get themselves and their children out of poverty. State violence against sex workers eliminates this economic alternative and pushes women back into heteropatriarchal marriage.

COVER FOR GLOBAL INEQUALITY AND ECONOMIC EXPLOITATION

Measures, programs, and policies that punish migrant sex workers under the guise of "combatting human trafficking" also provide the state with a way to export and impose its economic and political agenda on foreign countries' governmental and nongovernmental policies. To illustrate this, we're going to use the example of an important annual report called the *Trafficking in Persons Report*. The *TIP Report* grades countries on their compliance with US-defined standards for combating human trafficking around the world. It was authorized by the Trafficking Victims Protection Act (TVPA), and it is published by the US Department of State. The State Department claims that the *TIP Report* assesses the efforts of foreign governments to prevent trafficking, prosecute traffickers, and protect victims. However, these standards are based on the ideologies of the modern slavery panic, thus the report doesn't address any of the real causes of labor exploitation, coercion, and violence, like social and economic injustice or access to safe migration and labor protections. Instead, surveilling, criminalizing, and prosecuting sex workers are defined as human trafficking prevention.

For example, in 2008, after the US State Department had repeatedly ranked Cambodia poorly on its efforts to combat human trafficking, the Cambodian government responded by passing the Law on the Suppression of Human Trafficking and Sexual Exploitation. Sex work was already illegal in Cambodia, but the new human trafficking law increased the criminalization of sex workers, leading to more police raids on sex work businesses, a rise in physical violence and rape by police and prison officers, and an increase in HIV/AIDS transmission among sex workers.[16]

The consequences of international human trafficking policy are significant and extend far beyond the grave harms they cause to sex workers. The US government is required by law to deny anti-humanitarian aid to countries it has ranked poorly in the *TIP Report* and US representatives at the International Monetary Fund and the World Bank are instructed to deny loans to these poorly ranked states. Creating economic suffering by withholding aid and loans provides the US government with the leverage to influence foreign policy, especially in countries that rely on the US as a major trading partner or for aid.

The US also uses human trafficking measures to influence international nongovernmental policy. For example, in 2003, then US president George W. Bush introduced a policy known as the Anti-Prostitution Pledge. Any nonprofit organization that received anti-trafficking funding from the US had to agree to explicitly oppose the decriminalization of prostitution. "No funds made available to carry out this act . . . may be used to provide assistance to any group or organization that does not have a policy explicitly opposing prostitution and sex trafficking."[17] The criminalization of sex work significantly increases HIV infections among sex workers, but organizations dependent on US funding had to either stop their advocacy for sex workers or close. As of 2013, the Anti-Prostitution Pledge no longer applies to US-based organizations, but it remains in place for non-US-based organizations where the US can continue to use it to exert control over foreign nongovernmental policy.[18]

Why would the US government want to pressure other countries to increase the criminalization of sex workers through anti-trafficking measures, especially when they cause such demonstrable harm? The example of US interference in Cambodia is again instructive. Cambodia plays an important role in the $380 billion garment trade with the US.[19] The large profits of US-based multinational apparel corporations rely on the exploitation of cheapened Cambodian labor. Garment workers—90 percent of whom are women—work in factory conditions that have been described as analogous to slavery—ten hours a day, six days a week, in temperatures up to 99 degrees (37 Celsius), without adequate access to food, water, toilets, or rest.[20] Workers report mass fainting, workplace fires, contagious diseases, and sexual abuse from male coworkers and bosses.[21] In the year that the Cambodian government cracked down on sex workers at the behest of the US government, the minimum wage for Cambodian garment workers was only $50 USD per month.[22] Not surprisingly, for some Cambodian women (both cisgender and transgender), the sex industry provides a better alternative to economically and sexually exploitative garment factory jobs. Criminalizing sex workers is a way for the state to arrest women out of the sex industry and push them back into the garment factories, maintaining the supply of workers available for US apparel companies to profitably exploit. Criminalizing sex work also keeps overall wages for Cambodian women low, by eliminating a higher wage alternative.

Anti-trafficking NGOs are an important part of corporate control and exploitation of Cambodian women's labor. Their "sex-trafficking prevention" and "rehabilitation" programs often include training arrested sex workers to sew so they can be employed in garment factories—workplaces that many of them have left for the sex industry. Some Cambodian anti-trafficking NGOs even run their own factories and employ arrested sex workers, directly supplying Cambodian women's labor to apparel corporations. The corporations win—they get cheap labor—but so do the NGOs. Large apparel corporations are among the largest funders of the anti-trafficking NGO sector in Cambodia and in other countries in the Global South where they exploit the labor of racialized poor people. "The garment industry supports the arrests of, and finances the supposed rehabilitation of, women who leave the garment trade (for sex work) forcing them to return to these low-paying, high-risk jobs that more often than not include a likelihood of sexual exploitation. This happens all over the world as a matter of the course of fast fashion."[23] This is reflected in one of the iconic slogans to come out of Southeast Asian sex workers rights organizing: "Don't talk to me about sewing machines, talk to me about workers' rights."[24]

The US government dominates international governmental and nongovernmental policy related to sex work because this protects the economic interests of corporations. Criminalizing sex work and punishing sex workers helps corporations to control the cost and availability of the labor of poor racialized women. We believe that this mirrors the motivation for the criminalization of migrant sex workers within the US and Canada as well. Criminalizing migrant sex workers pushes women out of the sex industry and into cheaper and more highly controlled work on farms, factories, private homes, and processing facilities.

Is this intentional and deliberate? Sometimes it is explicit, such as when politicians say that closing massage businesses will address the shortage of caregivers in local nursing homes and care facilities. But often it's not explicit or deliberate. It doesn't have to be. The oppression of migrant sex workers is structural and is not about individual intentions or enforcement. State violence against migrant sex workers is designed so that it will control the labor, mobility, and sexuality of low-income racialized migrant women by cutting off sex work as an alternative way of working, moving across borders, and forming family. In the next section, we look more closely at how the state manufactures consent to state violence through the laws, policies, and narratives related to "sex trafficking" and "modern slavery."

PART II

MIGRANT SEX WORKERS AND STATE VIOLENCE

INTRODUCING THE ANTI-TRAFFICKING INDUSTRY

CHAPTER 4

"WHITE SLAVERY" AND THE ROOTS OF THE "MODERN SLAVERY" PANIC

A great commercialized vice ring reaches around the world, it is systematized, its organization is strength itself. A girl is missing today in Chicago or New York, a month later she is found in some remote American city or in the dives of the Orient, or worse yet, she is never found nor heard of again.
—Jean Turner Zimmermann[1]

The slavery of black women is abolished in America; but the slavery of white women continues in Europe.
—Victor Hugo, letter to white British feminist Josephine Butler[2]

The "modern slavery" panic isn't so modern. Its roots go back to nineteenth-century Europe and North America and the "white slavery" panic. Reaching its zenith in the early twentieth century, the white slavery panic was a widespread expression of terror about racialized migration and the movement of poor European women into cities and into sex work. It entailed an international campaign promoting baseless claims that gangs of "foreign-born" men were preying on white virgins of England and America, luring them to the city with false promises of work or marriage, only to make them captives in an underworld of sex slavery.

In this chapter, we'll look specifically at how the white slavery panic operated in the US and Canada from the late 1800s to the 1930s. During that time, thousands of newspaper reports, magazine articles, pamphlets, theater productions, and sermons, doctors, ministers, politicians, social movement leaders, journalists, and artists whipped up a mass panic by claiming that they had discovered a new type of slavery—forced prostitution committed by migrant Asian, Arab, and Jewish men. With titles like "White Slave in Hell," and "Social Menace of the Orient," the stories were highly sensationalized, fictional accounts of the grim horrors that befell white women in the sex industry as a result of the "foreign menace"—Asian and other racialized men. The myth that nonwhite men pose a threat to white women's sexual purity is perhaps as old as America and core to how the US colonists and enslavers justified white-supremacist domination, colonization, chattel slavery, lynching, and imperial wars. The white slavery panic put the mythology of white purity and racialized sexual danger to work in justifying the subjugation and exclusion of racialized migrants, spreading lies that migrant men were kidnapping innocent white girls and women, trafficking them across international borders, and sexually victimizing them.[3]

Implied in the term *white slavery* is the idea that only certain (innocent) white women matter, and that nonwhites are their enslavers. White slavery campaigners wanted to protect the innocent white women from the foreign enslaver, but they also wanted to protect white men and the white nation from what they saw as the dangerous foreign woman in the sex industry. Asian sex work was understood within the broader framework of racist ideologies like the "Yellow Peril" that constructed Asian migrants as dangerous, uncivilized, dirty, immoral, permanent outsiders, and bad workers whose presence undermined the building of the US nation—and therefore required surveillance, containment, and exclusion. Sex work was viewed as a contagious "moral disease" that spread through Asian cultures because of their lower level of development and patriarchal subjugation of women.

In reality, white and Asian sex workers faced very diverse circumstances depending on what period in history we look at, their geographic location, their access to rights and resources, and many other factors. Some were better off than their sisters in other forms of work, and used sex work to achieve a kind of economic stability that was otherwise impossible for Asian migrant women. But most of them worked under the same oppressive conditions as other Asian migrant workers, with few rights and protections. They experienced serious problems like exploitation, coercion, and abuse. White sex workers were largely poor and working-class mothers who chose sex work to supplement other work, because of its higher wages. Then, as today, their working lives were not the result of sex slavery, but a rational means for surviving the impoverishment of women and the white supremacist exploitation of racialized labor.

White American suffragettes were heavily implicated in the white slavery scare, stoking racist fears about Asian men to build support for their campaigns for political power and the vote. They presented themselves as angels of salvation who, if given the vote, would put it to good use by fighting Asian immigration and thwarting growing Asian political power. In their 1907 book *Heathen Slaves and Christian Rulers*, Elizabeth Wheeler Andrew and Katharine C. Bushnell wrote: "We must realize what may happen to American women if almond-eyed citizens, bent on exploiting women for gain, obtain the ballot in advance of educated American women. We must realize how impossible it is to throttle this monster, Oriental Brothel-Slavery. . . . Beside the peril arising directly from the flood of Orientals who are accustomed to dealing with women as chattels, there will be the peril from a debased American manhood."[4]

Another white suffragette, Rose Livingston, gave lectures across the US about New York City's Chinatown, depicting Chinese men as sexual threats to white women and casting herself as the "Angel of Chinatown." Historians attribute her activism as a contributing factor in the push to get the Chinese Exclusion Act passed. The white slavery panic attracted popular support among white people because it drew on myths that were and remain deeply rooted in white supremacist US culture—the sexual danger of racialized men to white women and the danger of Asian women who tempt and corrupt white men.[5]

Most historical interpretations of the white slavery moral panic focus heavily on how the white ruling class used its false claims about white women's sexual virtue and racialized "sex slavers" to regulate sexuality and gender. But less has been written about the way the white slavery panic was also about the regulation of race, class, and labor. Its proponents used the white slavery panic to control the labor of Asian migrants and protect white ruling-class wealth and political power.

Following the Civil War, the labor system in the US went through a cataclysmic transformation, in part because of the formal abolition of chattel slavery. Wealthy industrialists and landowners relied on tens of thousands of migrant workers from China, India, and other parts of Asia to replace enslaved workers and to fill roles in a rapidly growing economy. Migrant workers' conditions were hyper-exploitative, dangerous, and unfree. Many were locked into indentureship contracts and forced to perform years of grueling and dangerous labor. Some Chinese workers were in debt bondage, forced to work for no wages as they paid down debts and whipped if they tried to escape. But over time, migrant Asian workers began to gain some economic independence and community power in North America. They founded community associations, advocated for their political and human rights, built businesses, and started their own families with children who could claim a right to remain in the US. They were an increasing threat to ruling-class white control over land and resources. Meanwhile, the building of the transcontinental railroad had been completed and capitalists' desire for cheap Asian labor was in decline.

While chattel slavery had been outlawed, many of the institutions created by the slave-owning establishment in the US remained intact or were adjusted so that the white ruling class retained full control of the political and economic systems. The wealthy continued to profit from the extreme exploitation of Black and Asian labor through racist, but legal, labor practices, such as sharecropping, indentureship, and the convict leasing system. And much of the massive, unprecedented accumulation of wealth that white, ruling-class American families had accrued through enslaved Black labor remained in their hands. Chattel slavery had been outlawed, but in many ways, it lived on through structural racism and extreme economic inequality. The white slavery panic offered the white ruling class a means to take control over the *meaning* of slavery and their perceived relationship to it. By presenting chattel slavery as "over" because it was no longer legal, the white ruling class could indemnify themselves against accountability to formerly enslaved people, their descendants, and the ongoing legacy of slavery. According to them, they had abolished it.

Second, the concept of white slavery allowed the white ruling class to position themselves as the "new victims" of slavery and racialized people as the new enslavers. Chattel slavery was something that white people and white society did to Black people. It involved forcing people to work and often forcing them to move, such as being kidnapped, transported to plantations or sold to faraway enslavers, and separated from their families. The white slavery panic reversed these roles to position white people as the victims. This new form of slavery was characterized as something that racialized people did to white society. Stories of white slavery focused on racialized, migrant men who forced women to work in the sex industry, and the stories often featured some form of forced movement (e.g., white virgins being kidnapped and transported to faraway lands). This granted the white ruling class political cover to attack their alleged perpetrators—migrants and workers—and justify this as self-protection. They used white slavery to justify their campaigns to end Asian migration into the US, and restrict Asian social and political power in the country by claiming this as a necessary form of protection against "foreign enslavers." The white slavery panic—as part of the broader anti-Asian Yellow Peril panic—led to the first US federal immigration exclusion law based on race: the Page Act of 1875.

THE PAGE ACT AND THE TRAVEL BAN ON CHINESE WOMEN

The Chinese Exclusion Act of 1882 is often cited as the first federal immigration ban based on race in the US, but it was preceded by the Page Act, which became law in 1875. US politicians sold it to the public as an anti-trafficking measure, but its main function was to ban Chinese women. In the history of racist immigration policies, the Page Act is largely ignored for the important role it played: it banned unfree indentured labor and formerly incarcerated workers as well as Chinese women who were seen as entering the US "for the purposes of prostitution" or other "lewd" and "immoral purposes." The act was justified on the basis of the perceived close associations between Chinese sex workers and slavery, corruption, and disease. Chinese women who wished to immigrate were forced to submit a statement affirming they had suitable sexual morals, and to undergo repeated questioning by US officials about whether they had ever engaged in prostitution or lived in a house of prostitution. US border officials were granted total authority to determine who was or was not admissible based on this policy of exclusion. They used it to exclude nearly all Chinese women seeking entry, by rarely enforcing the Page Act's prohibitions against the entry of forced labor while aggressively enforcing its anti-trafficking/anti-prostitution provision.[6] In early 1882, during the few months immediately *preceding* the implementation of the Chinese Exclusion Act, only 136 of the 39,579 Chinese people who entered the United States were women.[7] Thus, years before the notorious Chinese Exclusion Act, the US government had already found a way to restrict Chinese migration into the US—by banning women under the pretext of protecting them from sex slavery. Yet the racist and sexist discrimination of the Page Act is commonly overlooked, perhaps because even today the immigration exclusion of Chinese women is seen as less important than the exclusion of men.

The Page Act claimed to be protect Asian migrants from coercion and exploitation by prohibiting unfree migrant labor and labor that was assumed to be unfree—prostitution. We argue that the real purpose of the Page Act can be seen in its key effects—the de facto ban on Chinese women and the precedent it set for a more explicit ban on Asian migration, through the Chinese Exclusion Act. The Page Act was written by and named after a Republican representative, Horace Page, who had been advocating for years (and failing to get support from the US Congress) to ban Asian people from entering the US. Page and others had been unsuccessful because "corporate interests, trade agreements and treaties with China did not permit the United States to altogether ban Chinese immigration at that time, and race-based immigration exclusion was legally and morally unprecedented. So legislators had to use different tactics to disenfranchise and exclude Chinese immigrants."[8] The Page Act, as an "anti-trafficking" law, was the tactic that worked. It was only one of hundreds of anti-migrant measures of the time, and it demonstrates how Asian migrant sex workers have been constructed as dangerous bodies, how the state uses anti-trafficking as a cover for racist border policies, and why migration rights are so important to migrant sex worker justice.

The US government also used the white slavery panic to pass the White Slave Traffic Act (also known as the Mann Act) in 1910, which criminalized the movement of women across state lines for the purposes of prostitution or other purposes deemed sexually immoral. It is considered the first US "domestic sex-trafficking" law, and it remains in effect, although the phrase "white slave" has been dropped from the law's name. The law was enacted in the first year of the Great Migration, when millions of Black people began to move out of the rural South to other parts of the US to escape the Jim Crow segregation laws. Although the police used the White Slave Traffic Act to criminalize many kinds of unsanctioned behavior, they most notoriously used it to criminalize Black mobility across internal US borders, as well as Black people's work and sexuality. Black people could be charged with white slavery offenses for any movement that was considered suspicious, especially if it involved white women and sex.[9]

THE END OF THE WHITE SLAVE

By the 1930s and 1940s, stories about foreign enslavers abducting white women began to disappear, and the racial element of the issue was stated less explicitly. In 1949, the United Nations passed an anti-trafficking law that refrained from using the term *white*. While white slavery has ceased to be the subject of moral panic, its ideas, laws, and policies live on and the enforcement of the laws remain racialized.[10] People of color are still targeted or excluded from entry into countries through white slavery laws and policies that have been re-named without a direct reference to whiteness.

Historians typically attribute the end of the white slavery moral panic to a lack of evidence. But the white slavery panic was never based on evidence. It was created to serve the social, racial, and economic agendas of the ruling class. We think a more likely explanation is that the myths of white slavery didn't really disappear; they just evolved as the agenda of the ruling class changed in the 1930s and 1940s. In 1942, the US became military allies with China, which was considered critical to US military action against Japan. Just a year later, the government repealed the Chinese Exclusion Act, and Chinese people already living in the US were permitted to become citizens. Improved US-China relations may have led the US ruling establishment to reduce its aggressive promotion of Yellow Peril stereotypes about "Oriental brothel-monsters" and sex slaves. But these attitudes certainly did not disappear from the US, whose approaches to China continued to be guided by racist ideologies and restrictive immigration policies. For example, the US retained an extremely strict quota on Chinese migration and later banned members of the Chinese Communist Party.

The second development that we suspect accounts for the decline of the white slavery panic were changing attitudes toward women's sexuality. By the 1930s and 1940s, the view that women's sexuality should be governed by Christian morality was being supplanted by eugenics-based scientific and medical approaches to social issues. Social control over sex was justified, less as a matter of being Godly and Christian, but as a matter of health and the "fitness of the race." Within this framework, sex workers were increasingly constructed not as "fallen women" whose moral character had been soiled through sex work, but as unhygienic vectors of disease and a danger to public health.

Together, these two historical developments—shifting relations with China and the movement away from explicitly Christian moralistic approaches toward governing sexuality—may have led to the decline and temporary disappearance of the white slavery panic. We can see through the trajectory of the white slavery panic how immigration law and policy—and human trafficking policy—are related to the moral, social, economic, and political interests of the US.

WHITE FEMINISM REDISCOVERS THE "WHITE SLAVE"

In her 1979 book *Female Sexual Slavery,* sociologist Kathleen Barry wrote, "Several thousand teenage girls disappear from Paris every year. The police know but cannot prove that many are destined for Arab harems. An eyewitness reports that auctions have been held in Zanzibar, where European women were sold to Arab customers.[11] A few years later, Barry compared sex work to slavery, stating that "[prostitution] is like black slavery in the 19th century." These claims were part of a resurgence that gave white-slavery stories and their tropes new life through second-wave white feminism.[12]

In the early 1970s, radical, racialized, and poor women were fighting for their liberation, for abortion rights, political rights, and economic rights like equal pay. This included activist campaigns against patriarchal control over women's sexuality and for sex workers' rights. In 1975, hundreds of sex workers in Lyon, France, occupied a church to demand an end to arrests, police abuse, the courts' apprehension of sex workers' children, and other forms of state violence, spurring hundreds more actions like it and support from France's two largest unions.[13] Sex workers participated in feminist campaigns for welfare reform and wages for housework, and in the late 1970s, activist Carol Leigh coined the term *sex work.*

But a small number of white women with positions in academia, government, law, and publishing began to use feminist movements for sexual autonomy to oppose sex work. They considered women (defined only as cisgender women) naturally incapable of giving consent to sex work and defined sex workers as exploited, even as the new chattel slaves. Barry's *Female Sexual Slavery* was the landmark text of anti–sex work feminism, and it laid out a version of the white slavery panic nearly identical to the original one. It opens with Barry walking into a neighborhood of Paris that she describes as North African and "dangerous for women at any time of day or night." She writes with growing tension about seeing three hundred North African men, crowded onto narrow streets, who are "frantic, pushing and shoving." She then discovers another frightening crowd of "100 North Africans . . . pushing body-to-body" to get near the neighborhood brothel. The brothel, she tells us, contains "enslaved prostitutes" who are subjected to "terrorism," held captive, raped, and tortured, leaving them "passive and apathetic."[14] To her horror, French police officers stand nearby, looking on and doing nothing—smiling even.

Barry hits all the plot points in the white slavery story, the same one that white suffragettes used to build support for their political power. Visceral storytelling designed to paint a picture of white cities surging with beastly foreign men, abducting European girls into sexual slavery, as white men merely look on, too sexually corrupt to do anything about it. She positions herself and other white feminists like her as courageous crusaders leading the slaves out of bondage. This part of the story has not changed either, the implicit claim that (virtuous and enlightened) Western white women are defenders of the white nation, the only ones who can stop hordes of predatory foreign men from bringing sexual deviance and slavery to the West.

The influence of anti–sex work feminism grew through the 1980s as its sexual and racial conservatism aligned with the right-wing Christian movement. Anti–sex work feminist professors, journalists, and lawyers worked with the Christian right and US Republicans on attempts to criminalize pornography and sex work. By the 1990s, crusades to outlaw pornography had largely failed and this alliance was in decline. Sex workers' power was advancing. Dancers at the Lusty Lady peep show in San Francisco made international news when they formed a union that was affiliated with the largest US federation of labor unions, the AFL-CIO. Sex work was exploding through emerging internet technologies, and more and more sex workers began to speak for themselves, start their own businesses, and organize to improve the conditions in the sex industry. The ideas of white slavery persisted but did not amount to a moral panic. Enter US Republicans.

THE WHITE SLAVE BECOMES THE MODERN SLAVE

Between 1995 and 2000, Republican strategists reunited carceral white feminists with right-wing Christians and generated what they claimed was a new humanitarian crisis of unprecedented proportions—"modern slavery"—whose targets were Eastern European and Asian women. Hundreds of news stories, reports, US and European government pronouncements, Christian sermons, statements, and articles in the feminist press emerged about the growing horde of Eastern European and Asian women being sold off by their patriarchal families, abducted by predatory men (who were coded as racialized and migrant), and brought to the US as their corrupt, backward governments looked away. Evidence for these claims were scant, but proof wasn't necessary, as the tropes of "modern slavery" drew on deep-seated historical white fears about the sexual dangers racialized men posed to innocent white women.

Historians of this era have speculated that in the early phases of the "modern slavery" panic, Eastern Europe figured centrally because, after the fall of the Soviet Union, labor migration among poor and working-class Eastern Europeans was exploding. There was also growing Asian labor migration, spurred by the increased globalization of capitalism. The capitalist class and the governments of the US, Canada, and Europe were anxious to increase their control over the mobility of tens of millions of Eastern European and Asian migrants.

The birth of the anti-trafficking industry revived the failed evangelical–white feminist collaborations of the 1980s under a new rubric by introducing anti-migrant xenophobia into the mix. These activists were no longer anti-porn scolds: now they were sex-trafficking experts fighting "modern slavery." Writing for the US Department of Justice in 2001, "feminist" anti–sex work / anti-trafficking scholar, Donna Hughes claimed:

> In the last decade, hundreds of thousands of women
> have been trafficked from Central and Eastern Europe
> and the republics of the former Soviet Union into prosti-
> tution throughout the world. The U.S. State Department
> estimates that 50,000 to 100,000 women and children
> are trafficked into the United States each year for la-
> bor or sexual exploitation, primarily from Southeast
> Asia, the newly independent states of the former Soviet
> Union, and Eastern Europe. . . . These illegal activities
> and related crimes not only harm the women involved;
> they also undermine the social, political, and economic
> fabric of the nations where they occur.[15]

Casting Eastern European women as the new white slaves was a
strategic choice. They were white enough to be seen by white voters
as innocent women whom the US should take action to protect. At
the same time, the culture and men of Eastern Europe were seen as
inferior, coming from countries with lower levels of democracy and
legal freedoms for women. Thus, they were a threat the US should
guard *against*. Asian women, meanwhile, were cast as they had been
throughout US history—as both inherently docile and dangerous
criminal temptations, originating from uncivilized cultures where
families sell women and girls.[16]

The first big policy win of the "modern slavery" panic in the US
was the passage of the Trafficking Victims Protection Act (TVPA) in
2000. The TVPA enhanced the state's ability to track, ban, detain, and
deport migrants in a number of ways. In a remarkable parallel to the
Page Act, the TVPA authorized immigration agents to refuse migrant
women work permits if they were deemed at risk of sex trafficking.
Hailed as the first major US legislation to combat international sex
trafficking, it passed with unanimous support from Republicans and
Democrats.

CHAPTER 5

"RED FLAGS"

HOW THE ANTI-TRAFFICKING INDUSTRY SUPPORTS STATE VIOLENCE AGAINST MIGRANT SEX WORKERS

The passage of the Trafficking Victims Protection Act of 2000 heralded a new era in the US criminalization of migrant sex workers. Travel bans, surveillance, racial profiling, police raids, detentions, deportations, theft, and physical and sexual assault by law enforcement were increasingly justified as part of the protection of women and children against human traffickers. As the US state advanced its agenda, a massive infrastructure of anti-trafficking organizations and agencies began to spring up. The US state is powerful, but it could not effectively target migrant sex workers without an extended infrastructure providing it with material and ideological support. State violence against migrant sex workers is supported, funded, morally justified, and exported through its champions in anti-trafficking nonprofit organizations.

WHAT ARE ANTI-TRAFFICKING NONPROFITS?

As concern about international human trafficking has grown, there has been an explosion of advocacy organizations, social service agencies, research centers, think tanks, school clubs, Christian charities, academic journals, and foundations across the US (and the world) that profess a dedication to combating human trafficking, sex trafficking, or "modern slavery." These organizations develop human trafficking law and policy for the state, advise the state on human trafficking policy, and lobby members of local, regional, federal, and international bodies to enforce human trafficking laws and policy. They lead public education ("awareness raising") campaigns about human trafficking, provide services (such as hotlines) to those suspected of being victims of human trafficking, and develop research on human trafficking. At least, that's what they say they do.

In reality, anti-trafficking nonprofits do not combat human trafficking, violence, exploitation, and coercion in the sex industry; they facilitate, enhance, and expand state violence. They are aligned not with a social justice movement fighting gender-based violence and "modern slavery," but with right-wing and carceral feminist movements that are opposed to racial, social, and economic justice.[1]

To illuminate the role between these nonprofits and state violence, we'll share an imagined scenario that brings together all the elements we've witnessed play out in cities across North America in advance of major sporting events (and detailed in Gregory Mitchell's book *Panics without Borders: How Global Sporting Events Drive Myths about Sex Trafficking*).[2] In this fictional city that we'll call Surveillance City, local anti-trafficking nonprofits claim that their research predicts that there will be a spike in sex trafficking in advance of an upcoming major sporting event. Their research is not based on reports of exploitation or violence, but on the evidence of increased sex work—especially that involving poor and/or racialized workers—such as an increase in the number of advertisements placed by Asian massage and sex work businesses in that city. These advertisements are an indicator of sex work, not violence, but the conflation goes unquestioned, because multiple national anti-trafficking organizations (and many other sources) have already claimed that massage businesses are "known sites of sex trafficking." The local organization releases its research as a report on "Trends in Sex Trafficking" and shares it with the local police department. The organization and the local police have a formal working relationship because they are both on a regional anti-trafficking task force that coordinates on information sharing, training, and policy advocacy.

The police in Surveillance City then use the findings of the anti-trafficking organization's report to justify conducting raids on migrant sex work businesses. They monitor the online ads for Asian sex workers or Asian massage businesses, focusing on businesses that are near the location of the sporting event, and set up fake appointments with workers. A few days before the event, a heavily armed SWAT team, armed with rifles, breaks down the doors of the business at dawn, screaming orders at the workers who live and work there to come out with their hands up. The police line up the workers along a wall outside the business in view of their neighbors, then search the business and seize hundreds of thousands of dollars (including the massage workers wages and savings), and everyone's phones. They arrest the workers and take them to jail, where they are strip-searched in view of other officers and interrogated. Based on information the police recover from the workers' phones (workers rarely provide information to the police willingly), they begin immigration and criminal investigations into the workers' friends and families. Their businesses are shut down and now, with the arrival of tens of thousands of tourists to the sporting event, there are no Asian massage or sex work businesses in view. The following day, the police hold a press conference announcing that they have rescued "sexually exploited women," when what they have actually done is racially profile an immigrant business, conduct a terrifying raid, then rob the workers and lock them up. The workers are turned over to Immigration and Customs Enforcement, where they are held in detention for months until some are deported, some are charged with criminal offenses, and some are released and must find new work and homes. The police freeze the businesses' banks accounts and seize that money as well. The courts fine each one of the workers thousands of dollars. The police split the money with the local city government and the money is used to fund the police unit that conducted the raid.

The local news media report that the police have broken up a sex-trafficking ring run by Chinese organized crime gangs who are "importing women into America." The stories all mention of the nationalities of those who have been arrested and detained. The anti-trafficking organization counts every woman who was arrested in its data as a sex-trafficking victim and puts these numbers into its annual impact report, which it uses to fundraise. The city grants the lead police investigator and the executive director of the organization an award for human rights leadership. Finally, a European anti-trafficking coalition invites the organization to collaborate on the coalition's campaign to rescue women from the sex industry and get them into "rehabilitation programs," where they learn to sew clothing for companies that work with US garment retailers.

This is a typical example of how anti-trafficking nonprofits work with the state to facilitate violence against migrant sex workers—by spreading a moral panic about migrant sex work, collaborating with the police to find clandestine migrant sex workers, and providing the state with the moral cover for violence through anti-trafficking law, policy, and services.

WHY ANTI-TRAFFICKING NONPROFITS EXIST

The state has many resources at its disposal, including billions of dollars, laws, surveillance, and police and immigration control agents. But this is still insufficient to catch, control, and punish migrant sex workers. First, because the state can't abuse people that it can't find. Like all criminalized people, migrant sex workers are skilled at staying under the radar as they go about their lives. And although police officers and police surveillance are entering more and more places in our lives (like schools and public transportation), they still aren't everywhere. So migrant sex workers can evade them.

The second problem for the state is public consensus. The police operate with some level of public consensus that they have an important and necessary job to do in protecting public safety. Some members of the public would object if they understood migrant sex workers as workers who are being criminalized and abused by the police, not sex-trafficking victims who are being protected or rescued by them. Third, although the state benefits from control over sex work, migration, and human trafficking policy internationally, it lacks direct authority over other countries' laws and law enforcement. And US power internationally is somewhat contingent on there being a consensus that it is a modern democracy, a moral leader, and defender of human rights. In short, to control migrant sex workers, the US state needs help finding and catching them, it needs to manufacture consent for its violence, and it needs a way to extend its influence to foreign laws, border policies, and law enforcement while appearing democratic and fair.

This is where the anti-trafficking nonprofit world comes in. These nonprofits are the evangelists of the movement against human trafficking. They spearhead the moral panic through sensationalistic stories and imagery that link racialized sex work to "modern-day slavery" while obscuring (or defending) the real causes of violence and exploitation in the sex industry. They expand surveillance (such as in hospitals and schools); collaborate with the police on investigations into migrant sex workers; lead advocacy campaigns to further criminalize migrant sex workers and organize against migrant sex worker campaigns; develop policies that strip migrant sex workers of access to rights and services (such as banking); and they promote the US state's interests abroad.

They advocate for the criminalization of migrant sex work at the local, national, and international level, and for larger police budgets and more agencies devoted to enforcement. They directly consult on the laws and policies that criminalize migrant sex workers, and sometimes even draft them themselves. Multinational corporations sit on the boards of anti-trafficking nonprofits, where they can influence government border policy and criminal law. Anti-trafficking nonprofits lead campaigns to harass migrant massage businesses and have them shut down. They run public education mass media campaigns that train individuals on how to spot the signs of sex trafficking— which, again, are too often merely the indicators of migrant sex work. They encourage people to report migrant sex workers to the police, or they provide a way to do so indirectly, via their anti-trafficking hotlines. They share information they gather about migrant sex workers with the police, collaborating with them and immigration control on investigations, prosecutions, and deportations. They conduct biased research that generates misinformation about migrant sex workers.

They run social service programs that deter women from engaging in sex work, often directing them into lower-paid, service-sector work. Anti-trafficking nonprofits provide members of the ruling class—business owners, progressive and right-wing evangelicals, wealthy white carceral feminists, politicians—with the social status of being seen as crusading social justice heroes as they promote their anti-worker, anti-migrant, and anti–sex work rights agenda.

Were it not for anti-trafficking nonprofits, state violence against racialized migrant sex workers might not be possible (or it at least would be drastically reduced). There have been strong criticisms of the anti-trafficking industry since its inception, largely focused on its harmful impacts on poor and racialized sex workers. Many critics describe the harms of anti-trafficking policies as "unintended"—that the motives behind them are good. Anti-trafficking laws are viewed as unintentionally failing at their intended purpose—combating human trafficking. We disagree. The history of the anti-trafficking industry and its practices suggest that the harms it causes are achieved by design. This industry is not broken or failed. It is incredibly successful in realizing its actual aims. This becomes clearer when we reflect on where anti-trafficking ideas and policies come from, as we examined in the last chapter.

WHAT ANTI-TRAFFICKING NONPROFITS ACTUALLY DO

Despite presenting itself in progressive terms, as a social justice movement fighting for freedom from slavery, the anti-trafficking industry brings together the full spectrum of the right—white supremacist Republicans; giant, union-busting multinational corporations; cops; Immigration and Customs Enforcement (ICE) and Homeland Security officials; homophobic Catholics and evangelicals; weapons manufacturers; and TERFs (trans-exclusionary radical feminists). Most of the funding for anti-trafficking nonprofits comes from the state or from corporate foundations and right-wing Christian foundations. The International Justice Mission, more commonly known as IJM, is the largest anti-trafficking nonprofit in North America, with a revenue of $140 million in 2021.[3] Its board is made up of executives from Amazon, Walmart, the Boeing company, and Shell Oil and Gas. Polaris Project, which runs the US national human trafficking hotline, and boasted a revenue of $22 million in 2021, proudly partners with Amazon, as well as with Palantir, a tech firm founded by a billionaire whose clients include the world's largest weapons and defense companies in the world. Palantir "developed mass-surveillance technology for the U.S. military in Afghanistan and Iraq . . . [and] provided the technology that allows for racist gang databases by law enforcement which were later used by ICE to locate people without documents."[4] Polaris Project's board is made up of people with connections to the US Department of Justice and law enforcement.

The anti-trafficking industry includes some of the more extremist conservative Christian groups. The National Center on Sexual Exploitation (NCOSE) is a good example. Formed by far-right white Christians in 1962, NCOSE was initially named Morality in Media until it rebranded to give itself the appearance of a social justice organization. NCOSE advocates for the prohibition of all forms of sex work, and also for the prohibition of sex education in schools, sex toy stores (which it considers "a slow-moving cancer"), gay marriage (which it claims has caused mass shootings), and, of course, abortion.[5] It reported a revenue of over $5 million in 2021 and is led by the former chief of the US Department of Justice's Child Exploitation and Obscenity Section. In addition to its association with US law enforcement, its board is stacked with anti-porn and anti-abortion Catholic advocates and Ivy League professors, including anti–sex work and anti-trans feminist Donna Hughes, one of the architects of the TVPA.[6]

Feminist anti-trafficking organizations work with these extremist anti-abortion, anti-LGBTQ groups and with anti-trans feminists. One of the larger feminist, anti-trafficking and anti–sex work organizations in the US is World Without Exploitation (WWE), which leads campaigns against the decriminalization of sex work across the country and works in coalition with far-right Christian organizations, including NCOSE and Exodus Cry (whose founder describes Planned Parenthood as "Planned Assassination").[7] WWE is a US-based project of the Coalition Against the Trafficking of Women, the first anti-trafficking NGO of the modern era, which was shaped and formerly led by Janice Raymond, one of the leading architects of both trans-exclusive feminism and sex work–exclusive feminism. Raymond is the author of *The Transsexual Empire: The Making of the She-Male*, a landmark anti-trans text where she claims that "all transsexuals rape women's bodies by reducing the real female form to an artifact, appropriating this body for themselves," and proposes that "the problem with transsexualism would be best served by morally mandating it out of existence."[8]

Anti-trafficking nonprofits make money off the criminalization of sex workers. It is billion-dollar industry, and it can be easy for nonprofits to get a piece of it through fundraising campaigns that promise to "rescue the sex slaves," and by providing training to civilians, government, and corporations. Virtually anyone can start an anti-trafficking organization and brand themselves a "human trafficking expert" without any knowledge or expertise of the actual causes of violence against poor, racialized migrant workers (such as the criminalization of migration). People who get paid to criminalize the sex industry, or who profit off that criminalization, are not knowledgeable about the sex industry. But anti-trafficking nonprofits don't need this expertise because their trainings consist largely of misinformation about sex work and migration, and their "strategies to combat human trafficking" just direct people to collaborate with law enforcement or nonprofit agencies, who ultimately ally themselves with police forces. Some anti-trafficking nonprofits make money by providing court-mandated services to arrested sex workers who have been forced into anti-trafficking programs as a condition of avoiding prosecution or jail time.

The boards and funders of anti-trafficking nonprofits—even the small, local ones—are typically made up of those in powerful positions—business owners, corporate community leaders, conservative church leaders. The leadership of anti-trafficking nonprofits promote themselves as the experts on human trafficking and sex trafficking, but what we see are wealthy and connected people who benefit from the status quo and could not be more removed from the problems facing oppressed workers. Perhaps the only thing that anti-trafficking leadership know about labor exploitation, abuse, and violence is how to perpetrate it. And yet, their websites are full of pictures showing happy Black and brown people, with smiles conveying their gratitude to their rich white saviors for rescuing them from slavery.

Anti-trafficking nonprofits claim that their strategies are based on the United Nation's "4 P's paradigm" of combating human trafficking, which are: prevention of trafficking, protection of victims, prosecution of traffickers, and partnerships. What they actually do is use the 4 P's as a cover for their real, hidden agenda, which consists of three duplicitous plans of action.

1. CREATE VICTIMS IN NEED OF PROTECTING

Perhaps the most important role of the anti-trafficking industry is to generate the appearance of evidence. For there to be a crisis of "modern slavery," there needs to be victims—millions of women and children held in captivity by gangs of sex traffickers. But there has never been evidence for this, just as there wasn't evidence for the "white slavery" panic. This isn't because there aren't major social problems. There are. But most abuse against women and children occurs in the home, and most exploitation and violence faced by workers occurs outside of the sex industry, in workplaces like factories and farms. And when people do experience abuse in the sex industry, it is rarely due to human traffickers. More commonly, when people in the sex industry experience abuse it is due to poor working conditions that result from their complete exclusion from labor protections, or it is at the hand of an abusive romantic partner. The anti-trafficking industry twists or obscures these social problems (worker abuse and intimate partner violence) to generate the appearance of millions of sex-trafficking victims.

They do this through emotionally evocative imagery that visually links migration and sex work to extreme violence, and secondly, through pseudoscience that generates false data about the prevalence of modern slavery to make it appear common and increasing. Their imagery, stories, and false data confuse sex work and migration with exploitation and violence, so that sex workers (and especially migrant sex workers) can be easily labelled as victims.

SENSATIONALIST IMAGERY

Anti-trafficking nonprofit materials typically use graphic, sensationalist imagery of extreme violence against women and children, such as rape, slavery, and assault, to create a strong emotional reaction against sex work, and sometimes against migrant sex work in particular. Anti-trafficking public education and promotional materials feature staged photos of young white girls, alone, covered in bruises, crying, with rough ropes or chains around them, locked into shipping containers, or shown with a man's shadow in the background. When anti-trafficking organizations are involved in police raids where adult women sex workers are beaten by police and imprisoned, some anti-trafficking agencies will use photos of crying children in their media campaigns to describe the raid as a sex trafficking rescue.[9] The setting of the photos sometimes show signs of poverty like darkened alleyways, or a torn bed mattress, to suggest squalor and filth. In some cases, the danger of sex work is explicitly linked to the immigrant massage sector through staged photos of a crying, bruised, or chained Asian girl or young woman trapped behind bars and a neon sign for a massage business. These images are designed to evoke fear, anxiety, and disgust about sex work and racialized sex work, in particular.

Thousands of these images have been published in the past two decades, creating a strong negative emotional association around sex work and a consensus that violence must be widespread and inherent to the sex industry. In our advocacy work, the public's feelings about sex work are far more powerful in guiding sex work policy than any actual evidence. It is very difficult for sex work advocates to win support for their campaigns for improved working conditions when the public has been trained to imagine beaten and bruised women and children inside massage businesses and to feel a powerful sense of fear and horror.

This is why anti-trafficking organizations like the Texas-based Center to End the Trafficking and Exploitation of Children can publish a report that warns in all caps, "35,000+ TEXAS CHILDREN ATTEND PUBLIC SCHOOLS THAT ARE WITHIN 1,000 FEET OF A SUSPECTED ILLEGAL MASSAGE BUSINESS."[10] This suggests that massage businesses (which are illegal because of the sex work and migrants working there), pose some kind of grave danger to children. The Center produced an "illicit massage business toolkit" for law enforcement that describes "sex workers who are unable to speak English" and "women who are unwilling to explain how they came into the United States" as possible signs of human trafficking in an attempt to link being undocumented, racialized, and a non-English speaking sex worker with violence and vice.[11]

FALSE DATA AND RESEARCH

Anti-trafficking nonprofits also produce sex-trafficking victims through biased research that leads to false data about the nature, causes, and solutions to exploitation, abuse, and violence in the sex industry. Their science-y sounding findings counterbalance the overt and empty sensationalism of sex-trafficking imagery, making myths about "modern slavery" appear as neutral evidence-based facts. Research on exploitation and abuse in the sex industry is important and valuable, but research that focuses on sex trafficking cannot be accurate because the concept itself is biased against migrants and sex workers. "Sex trafficking" conflates every aspect of sex work (including migration), with exploitation and violence. Nearly all anti-trafficking nonprofits define sex work as exploitation and/or violence, and many further single out the massage sector (where the majority of workers are racialized migrants) as a site of sex trafficking. The Canadian Centre to End Human Trafficking for example, describes massage spas as "facades" that conceal their primary business: "sex trafficking and commercial sex exchange."[12] "Commercial sex exchange" (that is, sex work) and immigrant massage spas are not just *linked* to sex trafficking but defined *as* sex trafficking, regardless of the workers consent or self-definition.

Not only do anti-trafficking nonprofits create millions of victims by defining all sex work as sex trafficking, they also define everything related to sex work as trafficking too. When migrant sex workers experience violence in their relationship, anti-trafficking nonprofits register this as human trafficking, not intimate partner violence. When migrant sex workers have a bad boss, they define this as human trafficking, not poor working conditions. If the person helping to smuggle a migrant sex worker across a border is exploitative, nonprofits describe this as an instance of human trafficking, not as unsafe migration. But even when migrant sex workers have a fair boss, a good partner, or a decent smuggler—this, too, is all construed as human trafficking because the concept of sex trafficking nullifies consent. Some anti-trafficking nonprofit organizations even count everyone who they suspect *might ever* sell sex, or everyone living in extreme poverty, to be "at risk" of human trafficking. Other anti-trafficking nonprofits count everyone who has had any contact with their services (such as calling a hotline or speaking to an outreach worker) as a human trafficking victim. Not only is the term *sex trafficking* used to describe child sexual abuse, child marriage, and forced (or coerced) marriage, but also to some (or all) sex work, regardless of consent.

This has allowed anti-trafficking nonprofits to generate an ever-growing number of victims, from early estimates that there were less than a million human trafficking victims in the US in 2000, to ten million and to thirty million today. The richest anti-trafficking organization in the US (IJM) now claims there are fifty million people held in slavery and hundreds of millions more who are "at risk."[13]

Most (if not all) of the frequently quoted statistics about human trafficking are fabrications. Consider two of these statistics—that the average age of entry into prostitution is thirteen and that there are more slaves today than during chattel slavery. Both these claims are false and have been repeatedly debunked.[14] If there are over fifty million slaves (and the average age of entry into prostitution is thirteen), this would mean there are millions of eight-, nine-, and ten-year-olds being held captive in brothels whose families cannot find them, despite twenty years of anti-trafficking measures and billions spent on police and border surveillance, investigations, and raids. These are fabrications generated through the bad faith research of anti-trafficking nonprofits. They create the widespread belief that a very serious danger (violence against women and children), is massive (fifty million victims), encroaching (it's in your neighborhood), and perpetrated by immigrants (the massage parlor). Within a society that is already biased against sex workers and racialized migrants, these are the perfect ingredients for a moral panic that targets migrant sex workers for surveillance, criminalization, and border restrictions. There *are* real and massive social problems of violence against women and children and the exploitation and abuse of workers in all industries. But the myths spread by the human trafficking industry hide the real sources of these problems, instead creating a greater fear of racialized migrants and sex workers.

2. MIMIC SOCIAL JUSTICE MOVEMENTS TO CO-OPT AND WEAKEN THEM

SOCIAL JUSTICE WHITEWASHING

The anti-trafficking industry is a right-wing movement misrepresenting itself as a social justice movement working toward justice, equity, women's equality, slavery abolition, and ending sexual violence against children. It promotes everything that keeps society unequal and unjust—even the movements to address the ongoing legacies of actual chattel slavery. For example, scholar Lyndsey P. Beutin's research argues that "modern slavery" discourse is used by former slaving nations, including the US, to neutralize and subvert global racial justice movements for reparations for chattel slavery in the 1990s and early 2000s. "The anti-trafficking industry uses modern-day slavery rhetoric and imagery to circumvent Western historical responsibility for slavery. In the process of doing so, it creates a parade of characters and slogans that imply Black demands for redress and racial justice in the present are illegitimate."[15]

Corporations can whitewash their responsibility for labor exploitation and abuse by sitting on the boards of anti-trafficking nonprofits. Being part of a major anti-trafficking organization can provide them with a way to get involved in crafting border regulations, labor policy, and criminal laws while skirting any criticism about their influence over public policies that benefit them. The Catholic and evangelical right and carceral feminists use the anti-trafficking industry to find renewed power, legitimacy, and funding by christening themselves "human trafficking experts." In other words, politicians in formerly enslaving nations use the "modern slavery" panic to evade responsibility for legacies of slavery, while the elites in those nations use the discourse to justify social and economic policies that maintain their ability to control, exploit, and coerce migrant labor.

COUNTER-MESSAGING AND PROPAGANDA

Anti-trafficking nonprofits directly target organizing led by sex workers, especially racialized sex workers, and they organize against the measures that racialized and migrant sex worker movements fight for. Some coordinate special projects that specifically focus on opposing the migrant massage sector's fight against criminalization and job loss, such as the Polaris Project, which has extensive resources devoted to surveilling, criminalizing, and closing massage businesses. A national Christian anti-trafficking group in Canada provides civilian advocates with a special toolkit that trains people with a step-by-step guide on how they can use the city's licensure to push massage businesses into closing, such as advocating for increased small administrative rules that the police can then use to target, issue fines against, and charge businesses with until they are forced out of business.

Anti-trafficking organizations vilify sex work organizers as individualistic, selfish, and dangerous pro-slavery advocates, as opposed to the caring, responsible anti-trafficking advocates. When the Atlanta spa shootings occurred in 2021, there was a sudden, unprecedented level of attention surrounding violence toward Asian massage workers and the advocacy of migrant sex work organizations such as

Red Canary Song and Butterfly. NCOSE (the homophobic, Catholic anti-trafficking organization) responded by releasing a statement that doubled down on the criminalization of sex work and referring to Butterfly and RCS as "the pimp lobby" and the "pro sexual exploitation lobby" and accused these grassroots groups that were built entirely by racialized workers of "co-opting social justice." Other anti-trafficking groups try to discredit sex worker organizing through thinly veiled antisemitic conspiracy theories, claiming that pimps and George Soros are behind sex workers' rights movements."[16]

Like other marginalized communities, sex workers have been demanding access to representation and power in policy making. However, the anti-trafficking industry ensures that only certain voices are recognized and heard. Only those who identify as survivors of the sex trade, support criminalizing sex work, and are pro-policing are considered legitimate survivors. They often identify as born-again Christians or are strongly affiliated with faith-based anti-trafficking groups. Some anti-trafficking organizations have started to claim to be "survivor-led" because this is a framework that comes out of feminist, anti-violence movements. But it is more accurate to say that those who agree with the anti-trafficking industry's political analysis get funding and a platform, and those who do not are silenced.

3. COLLABORATE WITH LAW ENFORCEMENT IN POLICING AND IMMIGRATION CONTROL

Anti-trafficking organizations collaborate with law enforcement by providing them with information they have collected about sex workers, partnering with the police in their investigations, raids, research, gatherings, training the police, making direct financial donations to the police, and joining police advocacy campaigns to increase police power and funding to police agencies. Some anti-trafficking nonprofits directly participate in police raids. Operation Underground Railroad (OUR) has a budget of $21 million and was founded by a white former Department of Homeland Security undercover officer and named after the clandestine routes used by enslaved Africans to escape slavery.[17] The anti-trafficking industry claims to be "modern-day abolitionists," appropriating Black struggle as it promotes the structural racism of criminalization, policing and prisons, and racist narratives about migration and sex work.[18] OUR has been reported to take wealthy, high-paying donors, who pay for the privilege of participating in what they believe is a sex-trafficking rescue, into nightclubs in poor countries, where they pose as clients, demanding to hire underage girls. Anti-trafficking nonprofits also collaborate with immigration control. Polaris, which runs the national US anti-trafficking hotline, provides reports to ICE, and their cofounder sits on the advisory council for the Department of Homeland Security—the organization responsible for ICE, immigration control, and deportations.[19] But even when anti-trafficking nonprofits don't work directly with law enforcement, their fake data is used to justify racial profiling, surveillance, raids, and arrests by police and immigration control.

CIVILIAN AND CORPORATE SURVEILLANCE

One of the claims of the moral panic about "modern slavery" is that the reason that no one can find these tens of millions of human trafficking victims is because they are being hidden by super-powerful criminal syndicates operating in every neighborhood and in every massage business. The solution, we are told, is that every public and private industry should be involved in ferreting out suspected sex trafficking and reporting it to the authorities. Anti-trafficking organizations partner with private industry and the media to present stories that promote support for more surveillance, especially public spaces that sex workers use to travel (such as buses, trains, and airports); spaces where they do business (such as banks); and their actual workplaces—massage businesses and motels. In a recent news article about the Canadian government's claims that increasing banking surveillance of the massage sector will combat human trafficking, the journalist stated, "Although sex trafficking has long been narrowly viewed as a law enforcement issue, it's much bigger than that. In fact, the perils of this crime also create risks for industries including banking, technology, telecommunications, airlines, trucking, hospitality and health care—and all have a role in solving the problem. . . . The collaboration involves the sharing of general information about potential red flags for criminal activity."[20] In reality, increasing surveillance of the massage sector makes it harder for massage workers to use banks, travel, or access health care without the risk of being reported to the authorities. This pushes them underground and away from help. Increasing banking surveillance of the massage sector would be the perfect plan if you wanted to *punish* migrant sex workers, by increasing their isolation and abuse, not if you wanted to help them. Accompanying the text of the article is the typical, sensationalist image that plays on the tropes of the "modern slavery" panic. It is a staged photo of a thin young woman, naked except for a bra, with visible bruises on her body and the shadow of a large man's hand on her back. The photo serves as a visual reinforcement for the false claim that increased surveillance of the massage sector and reporting of "red flags" to the police is helpful—heroic even—because the massage sector is full of young, beaten, and enslaved girls praying to be rescued.

In reality, migrant sex workers work very hard to stay hidden from the police and immigration control and they are quite adept at it. Thankfully, law enforcement isn't present in most of our daily spaces—homes, workplaces, schools, the bus, the bank, or in social services and health care offices. But civilians are present in those spaces, and they can be trained to watch for migrant sex workers—or any racialized mobility and sexuality that seems out of place—and report it to the police, or to an agency that works with the police. This is where the "awareness campaigns," human trafficking hotlines, and professional trainings on "red flags" come in.

PUBLIC EDUCATION "AWARENESS CAMPAIGNS"

Awareness campaigns claim to help the public identify potential human trafficking victims through information about how to spot the "indicators" or "red flags" and help the victims to get support. But the causes of labor exploitation, abuse, and violence, including in the sex industry, are visible, legal, and structural. They include the conditions we outlined in the introduction—such as the state's total assault on racialized migrant sex workers, making every aspect of their movement and work illegal, and even criminalizing aid and self-defense. Awareness campaigns do not address those problems. Instead, they train the public on how to spot the "red flags" of racialized and migrant sex work and report it to the police. In its "typology of modern slavery" report, Polaris claims that "victims of illicit massage businesses are women from the mid-thirties to late fifties from China and South Korea" encouraging civilians to view Asian women working in massage businesses as modern slaves.[21] They recommend calling their national human trafficking hotline, which works with the police and ICE. The following is from another report by the Polaris Project: "Indicators that a massage parlor is engaging in commercial sex and potential human (sex or labor) trafficking include:

- Prices significantly below market level (e.g., $40 for a one-hour massage where $80 is the norm)
- Serves primarily or only male clientele
- Locked front door; customers can only enter if buzzed in, or enter through back or side doors that are more discreet
- Windows are covered so passersby cannot see into the establishment
- Women appear to be living in the establishment"[22]

These are all indicators of migrant sex work and criminalization. Migrant workers' wages tend to be lower than those of white people for the same work because of structural racism. Sex industry clientele are primarily male. Front doors are locked or private to protect sex workers against being the target of thieves and to delay law enforcement raids. Windows are covered for the privacy of the workers, the clients, and to avoid detection by law enforcement or neighbors who might report them. Other supposed indicators of sex trafficking include how a worker "avoids eye contact," "seems nervous around law enforcement," and "uses cash." Again, these are indicators of sex work by criminalized migrants. Some migrant sex workers live at their workplace because it is better for them financially. Sex workers prefer cash to avoid detection by banks, and they avoid eye contact and law enforcement because they are trying to avoid having their lives ruined by being reported and arrested.

Anyone who has taken a flight or train ride in the US in recent years has seen the human trafficking awareness campaign posters that blanket US airports and transit centers. The Department of Homeland Security runs an anti-trafficking awareness campaign it claims is "designed to educate the public, law enforcement, and other industry partners to recognize the indicators of human trafficking, and how to appropriately respond to possible cases." They train those in transportation (trains, planes, buses, and ships) and those in retail establishments how to "See. Call. Save." But the campaign teaches people to "see" things like "living in substandard housing" as an indicator of human trafficking, then to call a hotline that is literally spelled out as "1-866-DHS-2-ICE," reflecting how the hotline collaborates with police and immigration control, insisting that this will "save a human trafficking victim," when what it really does is recruit the public to help law enforcement identify and capture poor migrants.

Anti-trafficking awareness campaigns claim that sites of transportation such as airports, bus stations, truck stops, motels, and so on are common sites of human trafficking. Transportation does not cause violence. Instead, what the focus on transportation does is encourage civilian surveillance over the movement of working-class racialized people who seem "out of place." For example, many airlines have agreements with anti-trafficking organizations that require their staff to attend human trafficking prevention trainings where they are taught to "spot the red flags" of human trafficking and to report suspected cases to the police.

Here are some situations where airline staff have contacted the police for suspected sex trafficking: An Asian woman traveling with her Puerto Rican boyfriend; a white man sharing his cup of orange juice with his Asian wife (this act was seen as an indicator that his wife was "under his control"); a white single mother traveling with her mixed-race, Black child; a white father traveling with his Black son. None of these instances involved human trafficking and none of them led to an arrest. But they all involve two elements: some type of movement by a person of color, and the perception of sexuality that violates white supremacist norms, such as those against interracial relationships and families. Human trafficking laws don't need to result in an arrest or a conviction for them to increase state scrutiny and harassment for racialized people whose movement and perceived sexuality seem "out of place" to white people.

ANTI-TRAFFICKING HOTLINES

Anti-trafficking organizations in the US and Canada operate human trafficking hotlines that claim to "connect victims and survivors of sex and labor trafficking with services and supports to get help and stay safe." Survivors of labor exploitation, abuse, and violence do not get the help they need through these services. First, most labor exploitation is legal or the laws in place are unenforceable, especially if the workers are undocumented. Anti-trafficking hotlines do not address these problems. Second, at most nonprofits, the vast majority of the funding goes into the organization's salaries, not into the community or toward survivor's economic support. Little or none of the money gets into the hands of survivors who need services such as housing, mental health support, medical and legal accompaniment, or support dealing with intimate partner violence.

Instead, these hotlines serve as a conduit between civilians and the police. First, anti-trafficking organizations teach civilians how to detect racialized migrant sex workers through "awareness campaigns." Then the hotline serves essentially as a tipline, collecting information about migrant sex workers such as their location, worksites, family members and colleagues, the websites they use to advertise, home countries, immigration status, and more. Anti-trafficking hotlines claim to be confidential, but they also openly work with law enforcement as their central anti-trafficking strategy. The Canadian Human Trafficking hotline boasts how it "is focused on working with law enforcement in communities across Canada. . . . The hotline also aims to facilitate collaboration among law enforcement agencies across the country at the municipal, provincial, and national level."[23]

CORPORATE BANKING SURVEILLANCE

As we have mentioned, migrant sex workers are not legally permitted to use banks to conduct business. Anti-trafficking organizations increasingly work with banks and credit card companies to assist with banking surveillance, regulation, and reporting of migrant sex workers to the police. For example, Polaris and the Canadian Centre to End Human Trafficking both work with private corporations to surveil Asian massage businesses' finances.[24] As a result, more migrant sex workers have been barred from using bank accounts or had their accounts frozen and funds seized by banking institutions. Imagine for a moment not being able to use a bank or living with the risk that you could have every dollar taken from you. Add to this that most migrant sex workers are also parents or supporting other family members. Imagine how complex it is to conduct your life, your work, your travel, your health care, education, family support, and so on without banking.

Living without banking is very difficult—many aspects of modern life are impossible without it—so many migrant sex workers must rely on a spouse or close friend to hold their money for them, in their accounts. This opens the worker up to the risk that the spouse or friend will keep the money. The migrant sex worker has no recourse in this situation. The spouse or friend who keeps money earned from sex work in their own bank account can also be charged with multiple serious criminal and immigration offenses. This introduces the risk of many kinds of abuse, such as extortion, bribery, and theft. This is an example of how anti-trafficking regulations—not just laws—increase migrant sex workers' risk of exploitation and abuse.

STIGMATIZE AND DETER SEX WORK

Some anti-trafficking nonprofits that offer "rehabilitation" services and "exit programs" claim to support human trafficking survivors, but these programs attempt to deter sex work through a variety of means, such as stigmatizing sex work, gatekeeping essential social services, sharing information with the police, and in some cases, directly reporting people who return to sex work to the police or immigration enforcement.

Anti–sex work stigma is built into the goals and structure of anti-trafficking nonprofits. For example, Exit Doors Here: Helping Sex Workers Leave Prostitution is a $5 million government-funded program for women sex workers and "trafficked sex workers (both Canadian and migrant)." This is typical. Because of the association between women, sex work, and violence, women sex workers are assumed to be the same as women survivors of violence. The program's goals include that women will "adopt a non-prostitution identity." This locates the source of any harm the woman may have experienced as her fault—it's because of her "identity" as a prostitute—therefore, ending that identity will help her.

Exit Doors is typical in that it offers services that poor women in the sex industry cannot access or afford, such as mental health counseling, legal support due to criminalization (like help getting a pardon or a record expungement), food vouchers, and small amounts of money. But to get this help, they must be defined as victims of violence, have that blamed on their identity, endure stigma, and be counted as a trafficking survivor in the organization's data—data that is used to justify more policing and more criminalization of the sex industry, which increases violence against sex workers.

Funding for Exit Doors comes from the Canadian federal body responsible for the national police, prisons, immigration control, and the spy agency, which raises another serious issue with anti-trafficking nonprofits. Not only do they adopt the agenda of the carceral state to deter sex work, but many of them also collect data on sex workers and share this with the state, or their data is used to inform the policing of sex workers. Some anti-trafficking nonprofits are funded by the state to provide services to arrested sex workers who are mandated to participate in involuntary counseling as part of their "rehabilitation"—counseling that deters sex work. But if they violate the terms of their discharge, such as not attending their counseling or engaging in sex work, the anti-trafficking nonprofits may report them to the authorities, meaning the sex worker could then face jail time. Anti-trafficking social service programs are intimately tied up with the criminalization of sex workers through stigma, surveillance, and reporting.

INTERLUDES III

LINDA'S STORY[25]

Linda was a stay-at-home mother in a major Asian city. Her husband was well connected and wealthy, so she had little experience with paid work, but felt financially secure. Due to political conflict, though, her husband was arrested. To keep herself and her son safe, she had to divorce him and flee the country with her son. She came to Canada on a tourist visa and made a refugee claim. An immigration agent and lawyer said he could help with her refugee claim and charged her a steep fee—$10,000 just to take her case. He advised her on what to say for her refugee claim. She was uncomfortable with his advice, but she was even more worried that if she told the refugee board her real situation, it would endanger her ex-husband who was still in prison at home. Every time she met with the agent, he would ask her for money—each meeting was another $500 or $1,000. Sometimes when she received a letter, he would charge her $500 to tell her what the letter said. Linda used up all her money for the refugee claim and her husband's legal fees, but then her refugee claim was rejected, and she and her son faced deportation. She was told the only way she could get immigration status would be to marry someone with citizenship and apply for sponsorship.

She had no marriage prospects, but she met a man who said he was willing to help her out. She borrowed money from her friends and family to pay him $20,000 for the marriage arrangement. In the meantime, she tried to find work, but because she did not have a work permit and did not speak fluent English, it was difficult for her to find anything decent. She had to take what she could find. Employers knew that she was working illegally, so they took advantage of her. She worked in a factory for ten hours a day and was paid three dollars less per hour than every other worker. She worked in a restaurant and was sexually harassed by the boss and, again, was paid less than the other workers. She was too scared to tell anyone and instead just left to work in a grocery store. She was injured because she had to work very long hours, standing and lifting heavy boxes.

Eventually Linda started working in massage parlors and found the working conditions to be better. In the first parlor she worked at, the client paid $30 per half hour and she kept 50 percent of the fee. In the next parlor, the boss kept all of the client's base fee, and she kept all of the money she earned for providing "extras"—sexual services. This added up to a much better income. Also, Linda had injured her back doing regular massages, so she welcomed the opportunity to earn more through sexual services that were easier on her body than providing massage. Linda worked long hours, seven days a week, but at least she could sit and read when she waited for customers. The money was critical in helping her to pay for the legal fees, and working in the parlors reduced her isolation in her new home, introducing her to more people.

Linda went ahead with her marital arrangement and her new "husband" asked her to stay with him, claiming that this would help them to avoid any problems with immigration. But shortly after, he began abusing her. Linda thought it was just a "paper marriage" for both of them. But her new "husband" knew that her work in the parlors could get her and her son deported—and that she earned good money. He physically and sexually assaulted Linda and demanded more money, up to $1,000 or $2,000 per week. Her abuser installed a hidden camera at her workplace and kept videos of her providing sexual services with the clients. He threatened her that if she did not give him money, he would kill her son, stop his sponsorship of her immigration, and report her to immigration authorities. To protect the safety of her son, Linda sent him to a private boarding school. It was expensive, but she was afraid that her abuser would hurt him too. She also wanted her son to get a better education so that he could have a better future.

People in Linda's community told her that even if she left her "husband," she could still get immigration status because she was a victim of domestic violence. But she did not want to take any risk of losing her immigration status and being deported. And she didn't want to risk having her son and family find out that she worked in a massage parlor offering sexual services. She decided that she would pay whatever it took to stay.

In an attempt to stop the abuse, Linda told her abuser that she would give him more money. He agreed that she could live on her own, but even after that, he kept harassing and threatening her. She felt that the legal system could not help her and that her only option to protect herself, her son, and her immigration status was to keep paying him. She paid him another $60,000 and she put $40,000 toward her legal fees. She never took a day off work because she wanted to earn as much money as possible. To earn more money, she decided to be less selective about which clients she saw. Sometimes she had the sense that a client would be pushy or mean to her, but she took those clients anyway.

After three years, the immigration authorities told Linda that she had earned her permanent residency card. She was so excited but afraid to believe it. She still feared that something could go wrong. Even though it might not have been necessary, she still paid a final $1,000 to her immigration lawyer. At the moment she held her residency card, she broke down sobbing. Even though it had cost her so much—all the suffering, all the money, and all the pain and violence—she felt relieved to have given herself and her son an opportunity and a future. With her new immigration status, she was able to divorce her abuser.

Linda continued to work in massage parlors but, without the additional financial burdens, she could be more selective about which clients she accepted. Eventually, she opened her own massage parlors and stopped providing sexual services to clients. Things for her were still up and down, though, because the city council wanted to shut down the massage parlors. They claimed that the women working in parlors like Linda's were sex-trafficking victims. Anti-trafficking groups were trying to shut her business down to "rescue" Linda and the women she employed. Linda joined Butterfly and fought to keep the parlors open. She didn't lose her business and was able to buy her own house and support her son to go to a good school. She was proud to have achieved this when she started with so little. When the pandemic hit in 2020, Linda's business took a nosedive and she went back to offering sexual services. For her whole life, Linda had felt that she needed to rely on others—from her first husband, to the lawyer, to the second "husband." But now she felt proud of herself for being strong enough to rely on herself and survive.

DM'S STORY[26]

I'm an Asian woman who successfully supported myself and my family for many years through working in the sex industry. I was living and working as a migrant, traveling to different countries and choosing the gigs that offered the best rate; I'd be a domme in Berlin or an escort in New York. But that ended after I was stopped at the US border and denied entry for being a sex worker. I already wanted to leave sex work because the stigma of whorephobia had gotten to be too much. Being targeted at the border and denied access to one of my biggest sources of income only made it worse. It compounded all of my anxieties, affected my mental health, and left me in an incredibly compromising position. Like all sex workers, I was also additionally dealing with the criminalization of it. I was in a relationship at the time with someone who really shamed me for my work. And I was growing further distant from my own family because I can't be out to them about my sex work. I spent so much of my life in fear of them finding out about my work. There was a snowballing effect of having to hide parts of myself from my loved ones and being criminalized. I felt the weight of all of this and found myself wanting some "legitimate" work, even though, for me, sex work offered me more financial sustainability and flexibility. I'm trying to get out of poverty, I'm trying to support my mom, and I'm trying to do it in a way that works with my needs.

I got into sex work for the classic reasons—I needed money, and straight jobs can be so draining and demoralizing. I wasn't making enough money at my last retail job, and I'm disabled. I wanted to be able to focus on taking care of my family and my health needs. If only I had enough resources—which is really what I want for all poor and traumatized people, especially poor migrant people of color. But, of course, sex work is hard too. Performing pleasure with someone you don't want to have sex with, pretending to be interested in their stories, not calling out ignorantly offensive offhanded comments is hard emotional labor; especially when you're burnt out. That was when I saw a poster for a social services program that read, "Looking to Exit Sex Work?" It featured the stereotypical illustration of a femme's legs in fishnet stockings and red high heels, seen from only the thighs down. It was run by an organization whose mission is to support women impacted by the criminal justice system.

The weekly program was attended by a mix of sex workers and maybe some sex-trafficking survivors. We weren't supposed to talk about our personal experiences in the sex trade, so we never knew who identified as a sex worker, or if anyone experienced being trafficked. They never defined what trafficking even meant. It was strange to mix us together. That's the problem with conflating trafficking and prostitution. Our experiences are already too nuanced and diverse to be flattened in this way. Putting us together is not the issue, but if you can't tell your own story, it gets told to you.

The bulk of the program was made up of weekly "information sessions" that began with a check-in. I saw how this was helpful for some people to be able to talk about what was going on for them that week, to have community (even though it wasn't OK to bring your whole story). Then there would be a guest speaker. One week they had an anti-trafficking organization give us a list of resources on human trafficking, which included Hollywood movies. I wish I was joking. Another anti-trafficking group ran a consent workshop that felt both condescending and wholly inadequate. It was like they assumed we— the ones from the sex industry—had no skills or knowledge managing sexual consent. When in fact, managing sexual consent is something we navigate regularly.

Prostitution felt like this elephant in the room. We were not supposed to talk about our experiences in the sex industry—or about sex at all—because the assumption was we'd all been victimized by it and it would therefore be triggering. But I came to realize that this was because the counselors were unequipped to talk about the complexities of sex work and consent. They didn't have any personal experience in the sex industry, and so lacked this point of view. If they let us speak to each other as experts on our own experiences, it would have revealed how unqualified they were. We needed to be "good" victims, for them to play the part of our savior. This organization always viewed our clients, the men, as the perpetrators and exploiters and themselves as the rescuers. Never adequately taking into account the racism, the whorephobia, the ableism, and the crushing capitalism, all under criminalization, that we were dealing with. And they couldn't help me at all with the things I actually needed.

When I'm with other sex workers, we can vent about our calls, commiserate about lousy clients and be real about burnout. But if we talk about those things to non–sex workers, they're like, "Oh my god, prostitution is killing your soul!!" No—it's everything else that's killing me. But rescue-based organizations are biased to draw out "the correct story"—to be their perfect victim. Their ideas about our victimization showed up in all kinds of direct and indirect ways. First, they thought that it would be a step-up for me to take a minimum-wage job. The only financial help they could offer me as an alternative to sex work was a retail job or a factory job for minimum wage, which would never pay enough. Second, this was a factory that produced highly scented products, and I would get sick. I'm disabled; I can't do those jobs. No minimum-wage work is ever going to be enough to support me and my mom, and I didn't have the energy to work the number of hours it would require to meet my needs. They couldn't address the economic reasons for why I was in sex work. If I'm trying to take care of my health and my mental health, then I can't go work in a demeaning job that would make me physically sick. Sex work, despite all the stigma it came with, still gave me more self-determination and flexibility to mostly choose my own working conditions and hours at a good rate. I didn't want them to help me apply for welfare because I didn't understand all the ways it could compromise my future ability to qualify for loans.

As part of the exit program, I'd have meetings with a social worker. One time, she asked me about my week, and I told her that I was going to be working that night. And I was grateful for the gig! It was during COVID, and I was relieved to still have this one client. I couldn't get myself sick or my mom sick so I had to be extra careful, since we're both immunocompromised. The social worker could have asked me about my COVID precautions. Instead, she said, "Oh, no! You still have to go to work?" Of course, I still have to go to work! Did she think she'd given me anything that gave me an option not to work? I'm excited and happy to see this client because I really need the cash flow. It's a win for me.

Then she said, "Well, after you see him, I just ask you to maybe try to sit with it. See if you feel anything icky, inside." That's the exact word she used: *icky*. See if you feel icky?? I did want to exit sex work, but not because my work was making me feel "icky." It's because the world is making me feel so goddamn icky. And I wouldn't use the word *icky* honestly. How infantilizing. Is this their model? To have people realize how gross we are for doing sex work? What was that? A degradation tactic?

I said, "I'm not gonna 'sit with it.' I'm probably going to cheer because I feel really good about having cash in my hand." Because whatever, who cares, we have some sex. For this client, it's an escape from real life. It can be an escape for me too. Afterwards, I'm relieved. I feel happy because of the cash on my counter. That money buys me a week or two that I get relief from anxiety. If anything, right after I work, I feel affirmed in my work choice. I am good at this, and it makes me decent money. And surprise! I *don't* feel icky.

They say the program is about trauma recovery—which is needed. I want access to those services. But in order to be effective, I also need economic stability to do the work of healing from my trauma which started long before my sex work. From the beginning I said I needed a financial alternative. I wanted economic support while I received training or developed another business. They helped me write a letter to apply for a small grant to help me pay for my health insurance so I could get my prescriptions and pay for therapy. But the grant was provided by an anti–sex work organization so in order to qualify, I would have to position myself as a victim and exaggerate all the ways I was in immediate danger of being exploited by sex work. So I lied which of course I shouldn't have to do just to get needed support.

Instead of helping me economically, they were actually extracting money through us. I came to learn the program received five million dollars in grants to fund their admin costs and salaries, for a program which is hardly being used. On average five people attended our weekly meetings. Sometimes more, if they were giving out food vouchers because people need food. They even had us lead some of the weekly sessions when there was no external guest speaker and if we were paid, it would be another grocery gift card.

Instead of helping us financially, they'd try to funnel us into companies for low wage work. Or they would use us as research. At least three times we were asked to comment on their research findings. Just by being in the program, I was counted as a sex-trafficking survivor in their data, which is not accurate.

All this and the organization didn't even support decriminalization of sex work! Don't claim to be supporting me by criminalizing my clients, which still puts me under criminalization. And especially because this organization is supposed to help women who've been through the justice system. But rather than work towards our decriminalization, you just catch me on the way out. They had information sessions on how to get a pardon. We wouldn't need a pardon if we weren't criminalized in the first place.

Instead of playing your victim, I want to see an organization that can acknowledge and appreciate all of the skills that I must have to do sex work. Such as putting nervous people at ease or being a companion to a diverse range of individuals. I honed and learned my consent skills by being with clients. Anyone who does this work knows there's so much more involved than just sex. I'm able to decenter my own emotional needs and make space for someone else, which requires a level of emotional capacity and intelligence. It would have been helpful to validate my many transferable skills.

It's okay to want to exit. I wish we could be honest about the reasons we want to exit. It's why in a group of my own peers, I can be safe to complain about clients or complain about what things about this job are getting to be too much. And maybe troubleshoot, resource-share and figure out how to fill in those gaps. And it's not just "leave it all behind," because then it's not acknowledging what I do get from it.

If you shame me out of it, then you're just relegating me to poverty, without a real way out. That's not helpful. Their "abstinence"-like approach to sex work doesn't consider that I might want to slowly transition to other work or just mix in other work and not exit at all or that I might need the income that sex work was providing me. This approach assumes I felt shame and experienced psychological harm from every session, therefore, exiting was paramount. What I needed was realistic help transitioning from the flexibility, higher pay, and independence of sex work to something else. And I needed help improving my current circumstances within sex work while I'm still relying on it as my main source of income.

I would have wanted a space to be honest about our experiences of sex work and support each other. What if we could talk about what we each were facing? What we each needed for better working conditions? How we were isolated? Then we would see it was about more than just sex work itself. We would see how stigmatization and systemic barriers made our lives more difficult to navigate. I would have liked to talk about those things. Why were we not given the opportunity to talk about these things and instead prevented from doing so?

Another reason that these rescue organizations don't want sex workers and trafficking survivors to talk to each other openly about the industry is because they don't want the survivors to decide to become sex workers on their own terms. Women who were exploited for their labor by someone else, often figure out how to work for themselves, and then sex work becomes their exit. The way I experienced prostitution might be an exit strategy for someone who never got to work for themselves. And we could support each other in working safer, how to work for yourself, and how to make more cash. I would be honest that I am also trying to exit. I'm not saying this is some glorious thing. But sex work is a stepping stone for a lot of survivors.

But in the end, the program didn't help me exit. I left with new ways to feel ashamed of my work than I had before I reached out to the program. I'm having a harder time posting a sex work ad—which I guess was their goal. So it kind of worked. But it has affected my income and livelihood. The organization described their program as empowering. But they didn't do anything to make me feel empowered for the choices I have made with my labor and my survival. They only talked about how prostitution is something disempowering. They needed me to be their victim. And in the end, I still didn't have a job. I didn't have access to more resources. The only reason I stayed in the program was because they were paying fifty bucks a week and giving me grocery gift cards. I needed the grocery gift cards bad enough that I let them disempower me. Isn't this funny? They think that trading sex for resources is so dire. But I let them victimize me for those gift cards.

I see why it's very tempting for sex workers to tell rescue organizations a victim story—you can get hired and turned into a hero. It's a ticket. You tell them your harrowing victim story and then these rescue organizations pimp your story out. They create the demand for human trafficking victim stories. They say they want to save us from exploitation, but too often I've seen our stories being used more for their benefit than our own. I'd like to get a chance to tell my whole story for real, from my perspective.

That's why I feel it's so dangerous. These programs contribute to the stigma and criminalization of sex work. Then they destabilize our lives by giving us even lower-paying jobs and telling us we're traumatized, but without having the skills to support us. That's not just misunderstanding us, it's being irresponsible with people who are dealing with a lot.

Today I work with other migrant sex workers, and I'm an educator. I speak to social worker and service organizations like gender-based-violence agencies to help people understand the complexity of sexual consent, the potential harms and exploitation of anti–sex work, anti-trafficking organizations, and how sex workers need labor and migrant rights, housing, and health support like any other worker trying to keep their head above water. And, I'm still trying to exit sex work. I aspire to create the support network that I need to actually exit in a way that takes into account the realities of my circumstances. A network of my peers so that we can all come up together.

CHAPTER 6

"CONSENT IS NOT RELEVANT"

CRIMINALIZING MIGRANT SEX WORKERS

O nce the public has been whipped up into a frenzy with stories that the sex industry is a cover for massive international networks of sex traffickers (who are presented as rapist immigrants) and their helpless victims, the state can translate those fears into public policy that targets migrants and sex workers, while counting on enthusiastic support from across the political spectrum. Constructing racialized migrant sex workers as victims in the public imagination, serves as the pretext for an expansive web of surveillance, policing, border exclusion, and punishment that claims to protect them. In this chapter, we look specifically at how laws and policies related to sex trafficking operate as tools to surveil, criminalize, exclude, and deport racialized migrant sex workers.

ANTI-TRAFFICKING SEX WORK LAWS

The criminal laws regarding sex work vary in many respects from state to state in the US and between the US and Canada, but they do share one important similarity: in every US and Canadian jurisdiction, migrants and their associates can be arrested, charged, and incarcerated and deported for engaging in sex work, in any role, including in cleaning, reception, management, and security.

Since the late 1990s and early 2000s, human trafficking approaches have had an enormous impact on the policing of sex work, as police forces increasingly characterize their arrests of sex workers as key elements of "anti-trafficking investigations." By the 1990s, state punishment of sex workers had become increasingly unpopular. The anti-trafficking industry is far more effective at building support for criminalization by masking its true objective—the punishment of sex workers—as the protection of victims. The anti-trafficking industry has helped popularize a model of sex work criminalization that it refers to as "End Demand," also known as the Nordic (or Swedish) model, which has been implemented in Canada and in Maine. Liberal feminists tend to be the biggest proponents of these laws, claiming that they are punitive toward the purchasers of sex (stereotyped as inherently exploitative and abusive) but protective of "prostituted/exploited women." However, in this model sex workers are still charged, as they often play multiple roles in the sex industry—working with other sex workers, referring clients, renting their space to other workers, answering phones, providing advice on where to travel for work, and so on. These are all criminal activities under "End Demand" laws. Migrant sex workers (and their clients) are still deported under "End Demand" model laws for infractions as minor as a prostitution misdemeanour. We assert that the anti-migrant effects of "End Demand" (and other anti–sex work laws) is not incidental, but essential to their actual purpose. Co-opting the language of sex workers' rights movements, "End Demand" campaigns have increasingly described themselves as "partial decriminalization" initiatives. But these laws are simply the new way of criminalizing sex workers but packaging it as "feminist." The terms have changed, the criminalization has not.

In this next section, we'll break down how sex work and human trafficking laws are written so that the state can use them to criminalize sex workers, their clients, and their entire support networks, including their colleagues, friends, and family, while claiming that the laws are protective. The crucial element in the criminalization of migrant sex workers is the conflation of sex work and migration for sex work with human trafficking. Laws against sex trafficking and human trafficking define sex work and migration for sex work as exploitation or violence. The conflation of human trafficking with sex work is not an accident. In our over twenty years of global advocacy, we have never seen an anti-trafficking law that does not conflate it with sex work and does not criminalize sex workers and their support networks.[1]

Let's look at one example, the Canadian federal criminal law prohibiting sex work. The law was introduced through the "Protection of Communities and Exploited Persons Act" (PCEPA). Its ostensible purpose is in the name—protection against exploitation. This is how the language of this law authorizes the police to arrest sex workers, their associates, and their support:

> Everyone who procures a person to offer or provide sexual services for consideration *or*, for the purpose of facilitating an offense under subsection 286.1(1), recruits, holds, conceals or harbours a person who offers or provides sexual services for consideration, *or* exercises control, direction or influence over the movements of that person, is guilty of an indictable offense and liable to imprisonment for a term not more than fourteen years.

People who "procure" someone to provide a sexual service are sex workers' clients. In other words, their source of income. People who "recruit" a person to offer sexual services are managers who hire sex workers or sex workers who help a friend to get hired where they work. People who "hold, conceal or harbour" a person who offers sexual services includes roommates and family members who live with a sex worker. These laws punish people with a prison term of up to fourteen years.

The third section of this portion of PCEPA criminalizes those who control, direct, or influence the *movement* of someone who provides sexual services. This part of the law criminalizes migration for sex work. "Influencing" the movement of someone who provides sexual services could include sharing an ad for a sex work job that is another city and "influencing" the worker to move to that city. "Control" over a sex worker's movements could include being paid by a sex worker to smuggle them across a border. Other portions of PCEPA (and many other sex work laws like it) criminalize earning any money from a sex worker. These laws are sometimes called "anti-pimping" laws, but they include anyone who conducts business with sex workers, such as receptionists who answer the phones and screen out potential bad clients and sex workers who rent their apartment out to other workers. People who are simply associates, clients, colleagues, bosses, family members, friends, landlords, smugglers, advertisers, and so on are criminalized because they have been defined as participants in exploitation. This is typical of "protective" anti–sex work laws. They criminalize the actual sources of sex workers' support and protection—their source of income (like clients and workplaces) and their own community, like friends, family, and colleagues.

HUMAN TRAFFICKING LAW AND POLICY—THE US TRAFFICKING VICTIMS PROTECTION ACT

For the remainder of this chapter, we survey a sampling of other laws and policies related to human trafficking—including federal anti-trafficking law in the US and an international United Nations human trafficking policy—to show how they are crafted so that the state can use them to criminalize racialized migrant sex workers. This is not meant to be comprehensive, but to help readers understand the basic ideologies and principles of anti-trafficking laws and policies, such as how they construct human trafficking as a crime and conflate it with sex work and migration.

We'll start by looking at the US Trafficking Victims Protection Act (TVPA) of 2000, considered the most influential law for combating human trafficking both in the US and globally. The TVPA authorized the establishment of federal human trafficking authorities, and also established standards for how other countries were expected to approach human trafficking. The basic premises, definitions, and approaches of the TVPA have been copied around the world. The text of the TVPA (and its enforcement) conflates human trafficking with sex work. The text constructs human trafficking as a crime committed by rogue individuals (not as a problem stemming from social and economic injustice). It criminalizes sex work and all activities that aid sex workers. It fabricates "modern slavery" as the product of people of color's "inferior" culture. It constructs the default victim of slavery to be a white or Asian girl (or a childlike woman). And it normalizes the status quo and justifies state carceral control. We'll first look closely at the wording of the TVPA, and then at how its framework has been adapted into other laws, policies, human trafficking police units, courts, immigration policy, international policy, and city licensing in the US and Canada.

THE REDEFINITION OF EXPLOITATION, ABUSE, AND SLAVERY AS SEX WORK

The TVPA uses the language of exploitation, abuse, and slavery in ways that are so broad and vague that the law can be interpreted as prohibiting sex work. According to the TVPA, the legal definition of sex trafficking is "the recruitment, harboring, transportation, provision, or obtaining of a person for the purpose of a commercial sex act." Note that in this section, it does not yet mention force, coercion, or violence. Sex trafficking only requires "transportation for the purpose of a commercial sex act," A *commercial sex act* is defined very broadly as "any sex act on account of which anything of value is given to or received by any person," which would include legal forms of sex work, such as pornography. Later in the TVPA, we see "severe sex trafficking" defined as commercial sex involving "force, fraud, or coercion, or in which the person induced to perform such act has not attained 18 years of age." But the presence of coercion, force or the involvement of minors slips in and out of the text of the TVPA, so that the law can be interpreted as prohibiting adult sex work. And the definition of "severe sex trafficking" is also still so broad and vague that it can be used to define sex workers as sex trafficking victims. For example, some police departments conduct sex work arrests by claiming that selling sex out of the need to make an income constitutes coercion, and is therefore sex trafficking. But if needing to work for money is coercion, then nearly all workers in every sector are in this situation and the problem isn't human trafficking, the problem is that capitalism compels us to work to survive. The vagueness of the TVPA allows for this conflation of sex work with slavery.

According to the TVPA's definition, sex workers are exploited or are slaves or both. It provides no separate legal category for sex workers, no distinction between those who are forced and those who consent. However, the TVPA does differentiate between the "good" and "bad" slaves. The TVPA reauthorization of 2013 specifically extends special immigration protections only to victims of "severe" sex-trafficking victims, not to "regular" sex-trafficking victims—in other words, those who could be seen as voluntary sex workers. Sex workers are the bad kind of slave—the kind that chose it voluntarily and therefore is unworthy of immigration status.

Because the text of the TVPA blurs the line between sex work and sex trafficking, it also allows the state to define activities that aid sex workers as aiding sex trafficking. The TVPA can be used to criminalize virtually everything that sex workers do to ensure their safety as sex trafficking offenses. It is a sex-trafficking offense for migrant sex workers to communicate openly with clients about sexual services, prices, limits, and boundaries; to help another migrant sex worker to cross a border safely or to share information about migrant sex work jobs, bosses, and clients. Forms of community defense, such as working with other sex workers and sharing a workspace, are also sex-trafficking offenses.

SEX TRAFFICKING VS. LABOR TRAFFICKING

One of the most important legal and discursive elements of the TVPA is its construction of a false binary between sex trafficking and "labor trafficking." This eliminates the reference to "work" or "labor" within the sex industry, delegitimizing sex work as real work and thereby segregating it from other labor sectors. It ensures that those who are defined as "labor trafficking" victims can be considered eligible for labor regulations and immigration protections in instances of poor working conditions, exploitation, or abuse at work—but sex worker victims cannot access the same immigration or labor protections, because they are defined as neither workers nor labor migrants.

THE NEW PERPETRATOR, VICTIM, AND RESCUER

The TVPA promotes a false conception of exploitation, abuse, and slavery that absolves those in power of responsibility. Within the text of the TVPA, exploitation, abuse, and slavery are defined as a new kind of international sex crime, committed *by* racialized men from the Global South against innocent, childlike women, rather than problems that are caused by the wealthy who exploit and dominate poor and undocumented migrant workers. Immediately prior to the passage of the TVPA, US representative Chris Smith, a Republican from New Jersey, presided over a hearing to investigate the TVPA for its ability to combat what he called "the trafficking of women and children for the international sex trade." Smith's language is just one example of how the US state has framed the problem of trafficking as inherently connected to the sex industry and violence against women and children, from the earliest days of the "modern slavery" panic.

The TVPA also uses racist language as a dog whistle, associating racialized migrants with sexual violence that has now become commonplace. Human traffickers are described as bad actors outside the US, operating "worldwide organized, sophisticated criminal enterprises" from countries with "corrupt" governments and villainous poor families who hold archaic, uncivilized views about women ("the low status of women in many parts of the world has contributed to a burgeoning of the trafficking industry"), and who sell their own children ("traffickers also buy children from poor families and sell them into prostitution or into various types of forced or bonded labor.")[2] In the TVPA and in discussions surrounding it, sex traffickers are described using terms with thinly veiled racist connotations—"pimps," "gangs," and "illegal" immigrants. In other words, slavery is no longer a crime associated with white people. "Modern slavery" is caused by the inferior culture of racialized people—vulnerable, childlike women, sexually predatory men, greedy, uncaring families, and corrupt governments. In the TVPA, the United States represents the land of equality, freedom, and justice, and the police and immigration control represent protection against dangerous outsiders and their slavery-prone cultures.

ANTI-TRAFFICKING INTERNATIONAL POLICY—THE PALERMO PROTOCOL

In many people's conception, the United Nations' "Protocol to Prevent, Suppress and Punish Trafficking in Persons Especially Women and Children, supplementing the United Nations Convention against Transnational Organized Crime," also known as the Palermo Protocol, is the comprehensive (and objective) international definition of human trafficking, agreed upon by the UN's member states. But it is actually far from objective, and the process that led to its ratification comprised several years of concerted struggle between conservative Christians, anti–sex work feminists, and human rights organizations advocating for sex workers' labor and migration rights.[3] Like the TVPA, the protocol also defines migrant sex work as a form of human trafficking, and it criminalizes assisting migrant sex workers. The protocol states:

(a) "Trafficking in persons" shall mean the recruitment, transportation, transfer, harbouring, or receipt of persons, by means of the threat or use of force or other forms of coercion, of abduction, of fraud, of deception, of the abuse of power or of a position of vulnerability or of the giving or receiving of payments over another person, of benefits to achieve the consent of a person having control over another person for the purpose of exploitation. Exploitation shall include, at a minimum, the exploitation of the prostitution of others or other forms of sexual exploitation, forced labour or services, slavery or practices similar to slavery, servitude or the removal of organs;

(b) **The consent** of a victim of trafficking in persons to the intended exploitation set forth in subparagraph (a) of this article **shall be irrelevant** where any of the means set forth in subparagraph (a) have been used [emphases added].

The protocol defines sexual exploitation as a type of human trafficking associated with prostitution. Most people reasonably assume that this (and all anti-trafficking) policy addresses situations of force, fraud, or coercion. In fact, the opposite is true—the Palermo Protocol explicitly states that consent is "not relevant" to a finding of human trafficking. Human trafficking can exist even where full consent is present—full consent to work, full consent to sex, full consent to movement. Once consent is not relevant, the legal category of sex worker disappears, and all that remains, legally speaking, is a slave. The nullification of consent in policies like the Palermo Protocol means that states can define sex work as inherently violent, and all working relationships with sex workers (good or bad) can be defined as exploitative. As with the TVPA, all forms of aid and community defense are criminalized. Two sex workers who share a workspace are "exploiting the prostitution of another." A receptionist screening clients at a brothel is doing the same. A client is likewise exploiting "the prostitution of another," as is any manager of a sex work business. States that signed the protocol can use the nullification of consent to criminalize sex work while claiming they are only criminalizing human trafficking. They are technically able to do so because sex work and human trafficking have been legally conflated. Policies like the Palermo Protocol also allow states to define actual violence as not being violence. If abuse and violence are legally constructed as inherent to and inseparable from sex work, then this provides a way for states to refuse to address violence against sex workers, by claiming that the violence is indistinguishable from work itself.

TRAVEL BANS—ANTI-TRAFFICKING BORDER POLICY

Anti-trafficking immigration policies focus on controlling sex workers' movement through exclusion, surveillance, detention, and deportation. In this section, we'll use a Canadian policy—the Immigration and Refugee Protection Regulations (IRPR)—to illustrate how this works. The IRPR explicitly prohibit anyone but citizens or permanent residents from working in any job in any part of the sex industry, making migrant sex workers subject to deportation.

As we mentioned in the introduction, it is not legal to enter either the US or Canada for the purposes of working in the sex industry. US regulations declare that "any alien who is coming to the United States solely, principally, or incidentally to engage in prostitution, or has engaged in prostitution within 10 years of the date of application for a visa, admission, or adjustment of status . . . is inadmissible." It is also not legal for anyone who has received "proceeds of prostitution" to enter the US, meaning that migrant sex workers' family members, spouses, and children may be banned as well.

Canadian regulations are harsh in a slightly different way—they ban temporary migrants from engaging in *all* forms of sex work, in any role, not just prostitution. As a condition of entry, temporary migrants to Canada must agree not to work for "an employer who, on a regular basis, offers striptease, erotic dance, escort services, or erotic massages." This prohibits migrants from taking any job in the sex industry, including nonsexual jobs such as a receptionist, janitor, waitress, cashier, or bookkeeper. Self-employment in the sex industry is also prohibited.

The Canadian government describes this rule as part of its plan for "protecting foreign nationals from the risk of abuse and exploitation," yet the policy makes no mention of force, fraud, coercion, or minors. And the policy offers no measures that promote the rights and safety of migrant workers in the sex industry—or in nonsexual labor for that matter—such as access to support or the legal mechanism to report employers who deny them wages. Instead, the policy simply refuses entry to all those who make a living in any part of the sex industry. It is nothing more than a travel ban—a discriminatory restriction on movement, aimed at migrant sex workers, all their associates, and anyone whom immigration control suspects of being a sex worker. Both Canadian and US border agents are authorized to ban people at an entry point based only on the suspicion of participation in sex work.

ANTI-TRAFFICKING CITY LICENSING

For reasons we've discussed, Asian migrant sex workers are significantly more likely to work in massage businesses. And since the early 2010s, many cities and towns in the US and Canada have introduced plans to increase investigations and prosecutions of massage parlors as a direct result of the advocacy of anti-trafficking organizations. This has resulted in dramatically increased surveillance, harassment, and criminalization of the Asian migrant massage sector.

Anti-trafficking licensing regulations are more extensive, invasive, and covert than anti-trafficking laws. For example, licensing law enforcement investigations usually do not require that law enforcement have a warrant, and the standard of proof for a licensing infraction is far lower than that of a criminal court case. Because of the conflation between migrant sex work and sex trafficking, many jurisdictions have introduced regulations that restrict massage licenses to only those with formal, English-language massage certification, based on the argument that formal massage certifications will drive out the sex workers (and therefore the sex trafficking). These licensure changes often exclude Asian sex work and massage businesses because the English-language educational programs to obtain these kinds of certifications are expensive and a full-time commitment. This makes them practically impossible for working-class, non-English-speaking Asian women to complete. Workers can either quit, or if they want to continue working in massage, they get pushed underground where they must hide from law enforcement for working without a license. Through these kinds of anti-trafficking policies, cities can easily render Asian and migrant sex workers illegal and deportable.

Another strategy to criminalize Asian and migrant sex workers is the introduction (or sudden enforcement) of hundreds of broad, trivial, contradictory administrative regulations. More rules mean more illegality, giving the police the power to ticket, harass, and arrest these business owners, workers, and managers. Speaking to media about his police department's crackdown on massage businesses, Armand La Barge, former police chief of York, Ontario, explained why his department decided to rely on city-licensing regulations when they wanted to eradicate the massage sector in his city:

> We realized too when we had an explosion of massage parlors, that . . . to try to eradicate these enterprises—which were fronts for prostitution in our communities—we couldn't use the criminal code. That's why we went into municipalities and we enacted—uh, we had them enact—bylaws that regulated where they were, regulated their hours, regulated the age of attendants, regulated things that also made it easier for us to investigate that there were no violations of them. And none of them were complying with that. We went from 150 massage parlors in York region in 2002 to six today.[4]

Police can openly harass migrant enterprises out of business through municipal regulations—and pass this off as protecting the public. Also, take note of the officer's description of an "explosion" of businesses associated with racialized migrants, evoking fears about surging or "exploding" immigrant populations. Another way that cities conflate migrant sex work with sex trafficking at the municipal level is the imposition of discriminatory administrative regulations against the massage sector that seriously endanger migrant sex workers' safety at work. Some examples of rules that cities impose on the migrant massage sector include prohibiting massage workers (and only massage workers) from locking the doors of their treatment rooms and forcing massage businesses to operate in isolated industrial areas that are poorly lit. These regulations increase the likelihood of being targeted by thieves and violent aggressors who know that workers are isolated and cannot lock themselves in a room for protection. But they are justified as a way to prevent sex trafficking by keeping sex work businesses away from children and families (without any evidence that massage businesses pose a risk to children or families) and as a way to ensure that city inspectors can visit sex work businesses unannounced, even though this means workers cannot protect themselves during a robbery.

ANTI-TRAFFICKING POLICE UNITS

Many cities in the US and Canada have poured millions of public funds into special new human trafficking police units, or have rebranded their "vice" units as "human trafficking units," reflecting how the anti-trafficking industry is just a repackaging of sex work criminalization. For example, the Metropolitan Police Department (MPD) in Washington, DC, runs a dedicated Human Trafficking Unit, but in 2016, 98 percent of the unit's arrests were for prostitution-related offenses.[5] And most of those arrested for prostitution were Black. Human Trafficking Units do not actually deal with labor exploitation or forced labor—for example, the rapidly growing presence of child laborers in dangerous trades. And they do not even address abuse in the sex industry. Human trafficking police units like this one, arrest people of color in the sex industry, and market this is as freedom. The city-funded report that details the arrests made by the MPD Human Trafficking Unit features a cover illustration of two hands held up to the sun, breaking free from slave manacles, conflating state violence against Black sex workers with liberation from slavery.

ANTI-TRAFFICKING COURTS

The anti-trafficking industry's effects can be seen in the court system as judges increasingly frame sex workers as sex trafficking victims yet *still put them on trial* and convict them of crimes, justifying such punishments as protective. Take, for example, New York City's Human Trafficking Intervention Courts, or HTICs. In the early 2010s, the Unified Court System of New York State pioneered what they claimed was an innovative new form of court that would "promote a just and compassionate resolution to cases involving prostitution, treating those defendants as trafficking victims"—language that makes explicit how the HTIC conflates sex work with trafficking. The so-called compassion of the HTICs did not stop the criminalization of sex workers in New York City. As detailed in the report *Criminal, Victim or Worker? The Effects of New York's Human Trafficking Intervention Courts on Adults Charged with Prostitution Related Offenses*, sex workers are still arrested, put on trial, convicted, and sentenced to prison by Human Trafficking Intervention Courts. And not just any sex workers. Women of color sex workers are significantly overrepresented among those who are dragged before an HTIC judge. The reports' researchers observed that the overwhelming majority of those being processed through the court appeared to be racialized (87–89 percent) and women (98–99 percent).[6] Sex workers who are convicted in human trafficking courts are forced to participate in "rehabilitative" programs that deter sex work, but if they fail to comply with these strict requirements, they can receive additional forms of punishment, such as incarceration. Specialized human trafficking courts like those in NYC have an overall effect of increasing state surveillance, control, and violence against women of color in the sex industry.[7]

THE WEB OF CRIMINALIZATION

Each of these state carceral institutions work together to trap racialized migrant sex workers in a web of criminalization. Here is a scenario to help imagine how that web works: Law enforcement can use licensing regulations to justify conducting surveillance and repeated investigations into Asian massage businesses because they have been stereotyped as "known sites of human trafficking." Prosecutors rarely find any evidence of human trafficking, but they *can* bring criminal charges related to sex work laws, and police can seize the workers' earnings. Once charged, the sex workers can be forced to attend a special human trafficking court, sentenced to mandatory programs, which involve high levels of state surveillance and threatened with incarceration if they fail to comply. In some human trafficking courts, immigration control agents sit in wait, ready to arrest migrant sex workers for being in violation of their immigration permits, to take them into detention and start the deportation process. In the next chapter we look at how these laws, policies, and regulations are enforced in the lives and workplaces of migrant sex workers. This is what we call the "punishment" side of the state's agenda to "control and punish" racialized migrant sex workers.

INTERLUDE IV

YI'S STORY[8]

Yi was an escort in her forties working in Canada. As part of her business, she would regularly tour various small cities, where she would place ads and see clients for a few days before moving on to a new city. She was once sexually assaulted at work by a man who pretended to be a client, but there was nothing she felt that she could do about it except continue working. Reporting it to the police would have meant disclosing her sex work.

One day while she was working in a small city in the prairies, the police raided Yi's hotel room in what they claimed was an anti-trafficking investigation. They interrogated Yi, demanding to know who had trafficked her. Yi insisted that she was not a trafficking victim, so instead the police began to investigate her for immigration offenses. Under questioning, Yi mentioned that she had helped other sex workers to transfer money to their families. Under Canadian laws, this is a human trafficking offense (it would be an offense under federal US anti-trafficking laws as well). She also disclosed the sexual assault, but the police were not interested in the violence she experienced. Instead, they used Yi's sexual assault at work as evidence that she was engaging in sex work—a violation of her immigration visa that specifically bars her from any work in the sex industry. The police contacted border security to report her. Because the town she was in did not have an immigration detention center, the police chained Yi up and held her in jail. She was refused bail and held in detention for almost two months.

Yi was able to connect to the hotline run by Butterfly: Asian and Migrant Sex Workers Support Network and speak to someone in her language about what was happening to her and to request help. Butterfly's staff worked hard to find someone who could help Yi and reached out to the local chapter of the Elizabeth Fry Society

(EFry), an organization that supports incarcerated women. The local EFry chapter was willing to offer support by connecting Yi to a shelter so she could finally get released on bail. Butterfly raised the money for her bail and Yi was released, but she described the shelter as one of the most horrible experiences of her life. She was bullied, intimidated, and robbed. Yi's friend Yuki came to visit to check in on her and stayed at a nearby hotel. Yuki and Yi visited the Elizabeth Fry Society and took photos together with the organization's director.

That night the local police raided Yuki's hotel in yet another "anti-trafficking investigation." This raid was likely also spurred by the presence of an Asian migrant woman in an overwhelmingly white town. The police searched all of Yuki's personal belongings and went through her phone, where they found photos of Yi with Yuki and the director of the EFry chapter. The police accused Yuki of being Yi's trafficker, and they arrested Yuki for organized crime offenses. Sex work is an illegal business and if two people work together in an illegal business, this is considered an organized crime ring. The director of the EFry chapter, who was also in the photos with Yi, was never considered a party to any illegal activity or questioned about whether she, too, was a human trafficker.

Butterfly found them a lawyer and reached out to EFry on behalf of Yuki, but their staff stopped answering calls and refused to help anymore. Eventually, one of the EFry staff members told Yuki's support person at Butterfly that because Yuki and Yi were suspected of working together in the sex industry, EFry also considered them both to be part of organized crime, as did the police. The organization left both women on their own, in jail, unable to get bail.

Butterfly requested information about what evidence the police used to define Yi as a suspected sex-trafficking victim. They refused, so Butterfly reviewed Yi's immigration documents and found out that the local police anti-trafficking unit's method for identifying suspected trafficking victims was to visit the current online sex work ads for their town and target the Asian women. This confirmed that the police had identified Yi as a human trafficking victim and conducted an investigation that led to her arrest based on her race and gender. The police never laid charges against Yi and Yuki, but the evidence found in their criminal investigation was used to deport them both.

CHAPTER 7

THE POLICE ARE THE PREDATORS

I n an October 26, 2022, opinion piece in the *Toronto Star* about the moral panic over sex work, Shree Paradkar shared this account of former sex worker Jane Li:

> Numerous police ripped out the door to [Li's] place and piled in. Was she a sex worker, they asked. She used to be one, but not any more due to health issues. Instead, she used her meagre English skills to take phone calls for other workers who spoke no English at all, and describe the services they offered and the rates they charged. Say $50 or $60. She takes a cut—20 to 30 percent. Is that exploitation or mutual co-operation? Li can't work. Her co-workers asked her to help. She has enough experience to suss out the untrustworthy and she needs sustenance. . . . Li was arrested, led out in handcuffs and eventually convicted, leading to time in prison.[1]

Li was arrested under the provisions of the Protection of Communities and Exploited Persons Act (PCEPA), a law that the Canadian government claimed would remove legal penalties for "exploited persons" in the sex industry. But Li—who is in her sixties—is still criminalized as an "exploiter" through the PCEPA.

Because the public has been fed so many stories and images that romanticize the role of police and government as migrant women's "rescuers" or that hide the real story, there's little awareness of just how violent anti-trafficking investigations are. The police and immigration control have the authority—or the legal cover—to smash down the doors of migrant sex work businesses with guns drawn, line women up against the wall, terrorize them, sexually harass and assault them, force them to strip, rob them of all their money, cut them off from contact with their family and friends, and strip them of their jobs, their homes, and their freedom by caging and deporting them. And they can do all of this to migrant sex workers' friends and family, too.

We should think of an anti-trafficking raid as a state-authorized armed robbery. Massage business raids can be an incredibly lucrative way for the police to make money off migrant workers through asset forfeiture laws or through theft. As we discussed in earlier chapters, police get away with robbing migrant sex workers during their investigations.[2] But police don't have to steal from migrant sex workers secretly, they can do it in broad daylight, at gunpoint, with full legal authorization. In the US, forty-one states and the District of Columbia have laws that authorize the police to seize assets, including cash, bank account funds, cars, and homes for suspected involvement in prostitution-related offenses.[3] Some states do not require a conviction or even charges prior to the seizure. To give you a sense of the economic scale of this tactic, police in New Jersey were able to net over $550,000 in assets from one series of raids on massage businesses in a single suburb—raids that the police department described as part of "cleaning up" its town.[4] In another series of raids on three massage businesses in Rhode Island, Pawtucket police seized $650,000 in cash and assets.[5] When the Department of Homeland Security and NYPD officers raided the homes of the CEO and other employees of the male escort site RentBoy.com (again, at gunpoint), they seized the entire operating budget of the company—$1.4 million.[6] Police get to keep all the funds they seize through unauthorized theft, but they usually retain all or some of the funds seized through legal seizure as well. In the Pawtucket raids, the police department and the local attorney general's office split the seized funds 80–20.

This illustrates some of the reasons why the most dangerous gang in the sex industry is law enforcement. The police are not just the *wrong solution* to the problems facing migrant sex workers—they are the *most urgent problem* facing migrant sex workers. This is why migrant sex workers reject the argument that increasing policing would make them safer, even in cases where they have been targeted for violence.[7]

In this chapter we describe what the enforcement of human trafficking laws, border regulations, and municipal licensing rules looks like, from the perspective of the workers who are targeted by them. We cover the first wave of the modern era of anti-trafficking raids in the late 1990s to the present. Take care as you read this chapter. In it, we share migrant sex workers' stories of abuse, including terror, assault, sexual abuse and rape, theft, impoverishment, detention, and deportation. We've tried to strike a balance between sharing the truth about how anti-trafficking enforcement harms migrant sex workers with showing sensitivity for how painful these stories can be to read.

COPS—CRIMINAL LAW ENFORCEMENT

The late 1990s saw the first wave of police raids on migrant sex work businesses in the US and Canada, which were characterized by journalists and the police as rescue operations of Asian "sex slaves" or human trafficking victims. In prior decades, police had regularly framed migrant sex workers as criminals ("illegal" immigrants and sexual deviants), not as helpless human trafficking victims. The key change was that now state violence was increasingly framed as offering care and protection.

In 1998, a group of law enforcement agencies in Toronto and the surrounding areas raided several Asian migrant massage businesses in what they claimed was a human trafficking investigation. The result? Police laid 750 charges of prostitution and immigration offenses against sixty-eight Asian migrants—mostly Thai and Malaysian women—whom they described as "poor (and) uneducated." Media coverage of the raid declared that police had "uncovered a sex slave ring." One of the police investigators was quoted as saying, "White slavery is something that's traditionally [associated with] Third World countries. Suddenly it's here, in our backyards," and claimed that similar operations exist "anywhere there's a significant

Asian community." When reporters asked the police about their decision to arrest women they'd described as "slaves," the investigator deflected the question, responding that the prosecutor could decide whether to prosecute the arrested women.[8] Note how here, in the earliest stages of the "modern slavery" scare, Asian migrant sex workers were still characterized as "white slaves" and had not yet been labeled "modern slaves."

Researchers from community-based organizations were able to speak with more than twenty-five of the women involved and found that none of them had been forced into Canada or into sex work. None identified as trafficking victims. But as undocumented migrants in a criminalized sector, they *were* facing serious problems, including exploitative and poor working conditions, including debt bondage. They needed support and access to labor protections but instead were the target of police terror. Here is how one of the women described the ordeal in a report prepared by the community-based organizations:

> When I realized that they were the police, I was trembling and frozen with fear. I was so frightened that I could not think clearly. I could not focus on the questions I was asked. . . . I could not even remember my name. As I have never been arrested before, I was overwhelmed. The police asked how I had come to be here; I could not speak because my mind had gone blank. They asked me about my passport, but I could not answer because I did not speak English. It was almost impossible for me to even understand them. I could not even go to the washroom. After a while, they called us inside the massage room for a strip search. They told us to take off our clothes.
>
> They used a baton during the search. We were not allowed to talk to one another. I was very scared because I could not speak the language. I was scolded many times because I did not understand the questions they

asked. They did not let me ask a friend next to me or allow me to sit close [to her]. I was so scared that I was about to cry but had to hold back the tears. After the questions, we were handcuffed. I felt nothing except fear. They videotaped everything that happened. Then we were transported by police cars to an unknown destination. I focused on my parents in order to calm myself. We were all brought to a police station, but I did not know where. There were a number of reporters and journalists waiting for us and they gathered around the car as soon as we arrived. We had to cover ourselves while entering the station.[9]

Police seized the women's money, passports, wallets, photos, letters, and address books. Their conduct mirrored the behavior that human traffickers are believed to engage in—using terror and violence to force women into captivity, stealing all their wages, and withholding their passports. Later, the women were able to get some of their belongings back—but not their money. The courts imposed bail conditions on them that prohibited them from associating with each other, returning to their workplaces, or working in any kind of massage business. The women lived at work, so the bail conditions ended their livelihood, rendered them homeless, and made it illegal for them to seek support from each other. The courts also deported many of them. The women went from a situation where they were experiencing harmful labor exploitation to one where the state seized all their wages, their possessions, their jobs, and their homes. Asian and migrant sex workers today continue to be terrorized, arrested, robbed, and reported to immigration control under the auspices of protection against human traffickers in raids, such as the notorious Orchids of Asia Day Spa raid in Florida, which ensnared the billionaire owner of a professional sports team, Robert Kraft. Within months, all criminal charges were dropped against Kraft. In contrast, four of the spa's low-wage Chinese workers, who were in their forties, fifties, and sixties, had to pay $45,000 each in fines, lost their employment, and now had criminal records. Also, several were turned over to immigration control and detained for months.[10]

CITY ENFORCEMENT—LICENSING AND ZONING REGULATIONS

The danger that police pose to racialized migrant sex workers is well known, but there is less awareness about just how discriminatory and dangerous city-level licensing regulations (and their enforcement) are to racialized migrant sex workers. In this section, we use Toronto as a case study to illustrate how municipal anti-trafficking regulations governing massage businesses led to an increase in harassment, abuse, and physical and sexual violence against migrant sex workers, from the state and from individuals, after Toronto introduced its first city-level plan to combat human trafficking.

Municipal regulations and enforcement vary between cities and regions and between the US and Canada. No single case study can tell us everything. However, this case study has the advantage of our access to records, data, and accounts from workers who describe their experiences before and after the introduction of the city's anti-trafficking plan. From this we have learned a great deal about how city licensing and enforcement regimes harm migrant sex workers, the strategies of this system of power (including how it cloaks itself), and how to recognize and support worker resistance.

In 2013, the city of Toronto's Municipal Licensing and Standards Office issued a report with a plan for "strengthening the protection of vulnerable women, children and all persons from human traffickers." The singling out of women and children communicated that the policy would focus not on labor exploitation and abuse, which occurs in a range of unprotected labor sectors, but instead on surveilling the industry that has been repeatedly associated with "violence against women and children"—the sex industry. And not just any part of the sex industry: the sex industry is vast and diverse, but Toronto's city council passed a motion calling specifically for increased human trafficking investigations into the city's massage businesses, which were staffed largely by Asian migrant women. One of us (Chanelle) was part of a sex work organization that objected to the new plan, on the basis that it was founded on misinformation and would lead to increased law enforcement abuse, especially of those most strongly linked to sex trafficking in the public imagination. Multiple sex work advocates and organizations submitted recommendations that the city not adopt the proposal and instead use evidence-based approaches to combating exploitation, coercion, and abuse in a range of labor sectors, including the sex industry. But the recommendations went ignored by the city council members, who instead followed the guidance of a number of anti–sex work / anti-trafficking nonprofits that had met with the city and helped to inform and develop its plan. The following section is based on Butterfly's research about the plan's impact on migrant sex workers.

TARGETED INVESTIGATIONS, EXCESSIVE CHARGES

After the introduction of the city's anti-trafficking plan, licensing enforcement began to descend on the racialized massage sector, conducting constant and lengthy investigations on massage businesses that resulted in a dramatic spike in fines and prosecutions.[11] Between 2013 and 2017, law enforcement investigations of four hundred massage businesses in Toronto skyrocketed from just over three thousand per year to *over twenty thousand investigations* in a single year.

Not only were the police saturating the massage sector with constant investigations, they seemed intent on making life difficult for the workers. Workers reported that licensing enforcement officers were spending one to two hours in the spas and seemed determined to find an offense. They began to issue citations for trivial infractions (such as having a scratch mark on a massage table or not having a city-issued license number on a business card). Another worker who had put a thimbleful of liquor on a small prayer altar for deities was charged with violating the laws against open liquor. Other workers reported being investigated over twenty times in a single month and enduring investigations that involved as many as seven officers at a time.

In interviews with Butterfly, workers described these inspections as frightening, abusive, and disruptive. Here is one example: "They [law enforcement] searched for an hour and could not find anything. Finally, they found a minor issue that they believed warranted giving me a ticket. They refuse to leave until they can find a reason to give you a ticket." During investigations, police would burst into the workers' closed treatment rooms, shower areas, and private changing areas where women were changing or undressed. Some workers were terrified, thinking that a robbery was under way. Some officers forced workers to stand or not to move for the full length of the questioning. Each officer enforced the regulations differently, and they frequently would not explain the charges and fines they were issuing or would present the information in English only. Consequently, some workers could not understand what they were being charged with.

Licensing officers also began to more frequently enforce regulations that put workers in danger. For instance, workers in Toronto massage businesses are prohibited from locking the doors to their treatment rooms and installing their own closed-circuit cameras, and they must post their license with their full legal name and home address somewhere that is visible to customers. These discriminatory regulations put workers' personal safety at risk, especially for women working alone at night in isolated areas. Some predators know that massage businesses are likely to have cash on hand and are legally forced to keep their doors unlocked, without any cameras in place. Workers are safer if their clients do not have their personal information. Before 2013, most city-licensing officers did not enforce these rules—something that workers appreciated.

This changed, however, after the introduction of the city's anti-trafficking plan, with licensing officers increasingly motivated to prosecute any infraction they could find, including the rules that endangered workers' safety. Massage workers were forced to make a choice—leave their doors open and risk a robbery or a serious assault, or lock the doors and risk getting charges and fines. A business that racked up a certain number of these charges and fines could lose its license, meaning all the workers in that establishment could lose their jobs. The city's human trafficking policies and enforcement thus forcibly made racialized migrant sex workers vulnerable to workplace violence.

Police also began to issue fines that were up to five times higher than what other businesses faced for similar infractions. Some workers tried to fight back against the excessive investigations and false charges by contesting the charges in court. But when they did, the police would retaliate, increasing the number of investigations and the size of the fines. In one case in which a worker tried to fight her fine, the police punished her by levying seven fines in short succession.

ABUSE DURING INVESTIGATIONS

After 2013, workers reported that the tone of their interactions with police changed dramatically. Police became suspicious and hostile and began to more frequently harass migrant sex workers and treat them in a degrading manner. In research conducted by Butterfly in 2018 on Toronto's migrant massage sector, 33 percent of the women working in massage parlors reported discrimination, harassment, or abuse by law enforcement, including different forms of sexual abuse.[12] More police officers began to demand sex in exchange for reduced charges and fines, and to punish workers who refused those demands. One worker stated:

> The police[man] . . . he came to check my shop every day. Our shop was not in his jurisdiction. I had a fight with him. . . . I offended one of the cops, and he checks on me all the time. I knew he was police when he came to my shop. He requested an extra, such as a blowjob. I refused. Then he got pissed off. So this guy began to check up on me all the time. I asked him, "Why do you come check my shop so often? I didn't break any laws. My shop is not in your jurisdiction, you can have other police check." After that, he came back three more times.[13]

Officers increasingly demanded that the workers remove their clothing. In addition to forcing them to undress, some officers would order workers to sing, dance, and entertain them. One worker shared, "Four police officers and bylaw officers came together. They were extremely violent and rude. They ordered us to face the wall, and we were not allowed to talk. They treated me like a criminal as they searched my place, including all the drawers, wallets—even my underwear—without a warrant. They left the room in a mess."[14]

SEARCH, SEIZURE, AND DESTRUCTION OF PROPERTY

Workers reported being searched repeatedly by city enforcement officers without a warrant and that the police were more likely to officially seize their money and property or to steal it outright than they had been prior to the implementation of the city's anti-trafficking plan. Four women said that police took money from each of them in amounts ranging from $2,000 to $50,000. Police claimed they were seizing money as part of their investigation, but the workers received no record of the seizure and were never able to recover the funds.

COLLABORATION WITH IMMIGRATION CONTROL

Recalling an investigation of the establishment where she worked, Wendy Liu, a Butterfly member, said, "One day, a police officer pretended to be a client and set up a date with me.

"When I opened the door, more police arrived. They asked me if I had a boss or if someone took my money. They asked if I was being trafficked. I said no. After that, they asked me for my passport. They also forced me to unlock my phone and looked through my messages and photos. The police called the Canadian Border Services Agency, and I was arrested and deported after being detained for one month."[15] Toronto's anti-trafficking plan led to expanded collaboration between the city and immigration authorities, even when this violated the city's own human rights policies. Workers reported that after 2013, officers became more likely to demand that they show proof of immigration status, or officers would contact the Canadian immigration control agency to check on a worker's immigration status or turn them over to immigration control. Some police would say to workers, "If I see you here again, I'll call CBSA." Some officers would simply bring immigration control agents into an investigation. The city's administrative staff also became increasingly likely to report migrant workers to immigration control. One massage worker related that in the process of renewing her massage business license at the municipal offices, a city staff member that she was dealing with called immigration control to have her investigated.

WORKPLACE VIOLENCE AND CRIMINALIZING SURVIVORS

"A white guy came in and started choking me with his hands," a worker named Nana recounted. "He hit my head against the wall. I was really afraid. I gave him what I had earned on that day."[16] After the introduction of the city's anti-trafficking plan, workers reported an increase in violent attacks like that suffered by Nana, as well as an increase in intimate partner violence. As we reported in chapter 3, in a 2016 survey of the migrant sex workers surveyed in Toronto, 60 percent reported having experienced violence, including robberies, sexual and physical assault, and state violence. Workers who were interviewed for the report described this a significant increase from before the introduction of the city's anti-trafficking plan.[17] Some workers told Butterfly that after they reported a robbery to the police, the police would keep coming back—not to help them but to conduct investigations *on* them, using the initial report merely as a pretext to begin the investigation. As a result, workers became more afraid to report robberies out of fear that the police would call immigration. In one case a worker had managed to get a photo of the robber and showed the police the picture when she reported the robbery. But all they did in response was charge *her* for locking the door of her treatment room. Another worker reported a brutal sexual assault, but the police only charged her with breaking a city regulation that controls the type of clothing massage workers are permitted to wear at work. This is Niki's story:

> Not long after the spa opened, a man came in and chose the forty-dollar massage. I started the massage, and when I'd almost finished, he suddenly got up and pressed me to the massage table. He tore off my clothes until I was almost naked, and then he tried to rape me.

It took all my effort to get out and run outside. I ran to the convenience store next to the spa. Since I had nothing with me, I asked the store owner to help me call 911, but he was afraid of getting in trouble. He didn't want his business to be affected, so he refused. After I begged him, he finally let me use his phone to call my friend. I asked my friend to call 911 for me right away. While I was waiting for the police, that man who had assaulted me came in and asked me to return the payment because I hadn't finished the massage. When the police arrived, they confronted the man. Now I had to face the other nightmare that I never expected. The female police officer who was on duty hinted to me in Chinese that I should give up and withdraw my case, as the odds were against me in the sense that the judge would not believe or sympathize with my words because I was a holistic practitioner. Later on, I heard that the man was released the next day. Additionally, I received a ticket for not being properly dressed at work. Even when I explained the reason why, no one believed me. It is evident from this situation that the heavy discrimination against my profession by law enforcement officers makes me reluctant and afraid to call the police even when I am in danger.[18]

Some aggressors, like the one that Niki faced, plan to harm workers from the beginning. But in others cases, the conflicts with clients owe to miscommunication. Under criminalization, sex workers cannot easily communicate or negotiate services or boundaries, which means that clients are more likely to become frustrated and feel cheated. This increases conflict. Criminalization also increases client violence against migrant sex workers because it scares off the good quality clients. Clients who are respectful and considerate and supportive are usually the kind of people who do not want to risk being arrested during a raid on a massage business. They stop coming to massage businesses. The clients who continue coming are those who are not scared off by the risk of an arrest, and these tend to be lower-quality clients who are more likely to be difficult, get into conflicts with workers, or be abusive.

BARRIERS TO SUPPORTIVE COMMUNITY AND SERVICES

After the increase in police harassment in the massage businesses, some workers also became more wary about connecting with their community or support services. Workers who were scared to be reported by neighbors and didn't want their domestic partners or family members investigated became more reluctant to ask for help, seek support, or even seek health care because they knew that the police and courts assume sex workers' partners and family members are traffickers, especially if they are not white. Survivors of abuse who seek help risk being reported to the authorities as a suspected trafficking victim, leading to an anti-trafficking police investigation into the survivor. An anti-trafficking investigation not only will look with suspicion at a sex worker, but also can quickly expand to their family, colleagues, and friends. During an anti-trafficking investigation, police will often search and seize workers' phones. This makes some workers reluctant to text or call people in their community when they need help, because the police could use those records to drag someone into a police investigation. This goes both ways. In Toronto, increased police harassment made some community members who knew migrant sex workers more hesitant to help them because of the fear that it could lead to an investigation into human trafficking or immigration violations.

Workers who had been injured and assaulted at work or at home, sometimes seriously, reported feeling unable to access medical, mental health, or legal help because of the fear that health care providers, legal support services, or sexual assault support lines might report them to the police as suspected sex-trafficking victims. Reaching out for any kind of help could mean losing everything—their money, their housing, their employment, and their freedom. To protect themselves against further loss, migrant sex workers increasingly went without support.

NEW POLICE POWER AND INCREASED FUNDING

The increase in policing in the massage sector led to the false appearance of an increase in illegal massage businesses. After descending on massage businesses with thousands of inspections that generated hundreds of fines and charges, law enforcement used that very large number of charges to claim that it needed to increase its manpower and funding. The city agreed and increased funding, creating an entire "adult services" enforcement team, a ten-person outfit whose mandate was to police massage and sex work businesses. This is how targeted policing works. When a community is subject to heavy policing and faces constant investigations and charges, the police will claim it's because that community is crime-ridden, not cop-ridden. This is what happened in Toronto, and it meant the diversion of more money out of the community and into law enforcement.

ABOLITION IS MORE THAN DECRIMINALIZATION

Looking at the various ways that policing harms migrant sex workers reminds us that the problem is not just badly written laws that conflate migrant sex work with exploitation and violence. The problem is bigger than that—it is the power of the state to criminalize and the power of the police over those who are criminalized. To reduce the harms of policing on migrant sex workers, we work to reduce the presence and power of police in their lives. *We do not work to improve relationships between the police and migrant sex workers.* This is an abolitionist approach—resistance to the power of the state and society to define some people as criminals, and resistance to the use of state force through police and immigration control to control and punish people. Abolition is more than decriminalization—the overturning of harmful laws, policies, and regulations. The decriminalization of sex work and migration for sex work are important steps. But these steps alone will not end state violence or state-facilitated violence against racialized migrant sex workers. If the state and the police are reformed but still retain the same amount of power, they'll just use different laws, policies, and regulations to control and abuse migrant sex workers. The problem is that the state and law enforcement have so much power that they can use *any* law (or policy or regulation) to oppress migrant sex workers and other marginalized communities. Were human trafficking laws ever overturned, the police would still carry out its repressive agenda by simply employing other weapons, such as housing laws and zoning regulations—or no laws at all. The police can do nearly anything they want. They have been known to report sex workers to their landlords and tell the landlords to evict them. They will work with banks and financial regulators to investigate migrant sex workers by framing their work as criminal activity. They will use public health regulations such as COVID lockdowns as a pretext to target migrant sex worker businesses for investigations, fines, and charges. They will work with professional bodies such as registered massage therapist associations to ensure massage workers are excluded from professional associations. They will present themselves as part of "wraparound services" and "trauma-informed practice" for human trafficking victims so they can conceal the violence they do under the guise of social work.

Systems of domination are responsive and will take whatever form helps them to retain power, including incorporating the language and frameworks of their opposition. This is similar to the way that so many police forces are rebranding their searches of people's homes and businesses as "wellness checks," when actually, what they are doing is racial profiling and surveillance. These are what threaten people's wellness and safety. Dressing up policing as part of support services can grant officers greater access to incriminating information about sex workers, as in Yi's story about the "victim-support team" she thought she was speaking to. The police don't even need laws to hide behind. Many police regularly engage in illegal forms of surveillance, theft, and abuse because their power allows them to do so with impunity. There is no safe version of policing for migrant sex workers, and "better human trafficking laws and policies" or "better-educated police" would not stop this. The problem is much bigger than the harms of specific laws, regulations, or policies, and addressing it requires reducing the power of the state and the police.

BUT WHAT ABOUT THE CHILDREN?

The myth that the sex industry is full of drugged and abducted thirteen-year-olds plays a key part in the moral panic about "modern slavery" because it is used to criminalize adult racialized migrant sex workers. The anti-trafficking industry constantly promotes misinformation that links adult migrant sex work with child abuse. Campaigns to shut down migrant sex and massage businesses refer to "women and children" jointly in a way that conflates adult sex work with child sexual abuse: they spread the myth that the average age of entry into prostitution is thirteen, their public education materials heavily use images of children, and they conduct and disseminate research on "child sex trafficking" whose data set may include individuals who are in their twenties and even as old as thirty-five.

It's important to remember that in terms of age range, migrant sex workers tend to be in their thirties, forties, or fifties. They are more likely to be seniors than minors. In research conducted on Asian migrant sex workers in Toronto, Butterfly identified zero minors under eighteen, but 15 percent were over fifty-five years old. It is racist and sexist to conflate migrant sex workers with vulnerable children. It stokes fear and disgust in order to crush their campaigns for the legal and workplace rights they need and deserve. Fearmongering about "children's safety" is an empty strategy. It does not protect children—it is used to direct funding into law enforcement and raids on migrant massage businesses, rather than into services that actually address the structural causes of sexual violence against children and young people, inside and outside the sex industry, such as poverty and homelessness.

But what about the young people who *are* in sex work? What can be done to protect them? There is a great deal of research on this issue that we can't do justice to here, but we'll summarize it by saying that the anti-trafficking industry misleads us about young people and the sex industry. Research shows that young people in the sex industry are typically sixteen to seventeen, and 91 to 96 percent were not forced or recruited into sex work through violence or coercion. They are often poor and precariously housed, having run away from unsafe housing—either their own home or some sort of institutional setting, such as foster care or a group home. A high percentage are LGBTQ+ and dealing with multiple forms of discrimination, including racism. They are discriminated against in other jobs or school, they can't stay in their unsafe housing, and they sell sex for the same reasons as adults—they need money.[19]

The idea that human trafficking laws and their enforcement will protect young people is based on a deadly misunderstanding about the function of the state. The police can and do use human trafficking laws to criminalize youth, especially poor and racialized youth. A human trafficking framework provides the police with even more power over the lives of young people than it does over adults. In 2015 and 2016, a young woman in the Oakland area reported that up to twenty-nine police officers from seven different police departments had had sex with her in exchange for protection, money, drugs, and information about raids and investigations, many of them while she was still a minor.[20] This is not a bug in the system—it is by design. We need to listen to young people in the sex trade who tell us what they need. But this, too, has been criminalized under human trafficking legislation. In 2013, the only US group led by and for young people of color in the sex trade—Young Women's Empowerment Project (YWEP)—was forced to close because anti-trafficking legislation had criminalized some of the harm reduction services that YWEP provided.[21]

The anti-trafficking industry has led to state violence against racialized workers, the passage of hundreds of new laws, expanded police powers, hardened borders, millions in public funds diverted into policing and border security, opposition to nearly every social and economic justice movement, and the criminalization of young people. Given how harmful carceral approaches are, why do so many people support them when they should be supporting migrant sex workers and advocating to end the harms of policing and immigration control in their lives?

PART III
MIGRANT SEX WORKERS FIGHTING FOR POWER

CHAPTER 8

THE LEFT AND MIGRANT SEX WORKERS

In late 2019, members of AF3IRM, an anti-trafficking group that describes itself as a "transnational feminist, anti-imperialist organization of women dedicated to the struggle for women's liberation" posted a photo of what they called "guerilla action" to X, then known as Twitter. The night before, on Halloween, they had vandalized the doors of the Sawadee Thai Massage Center in Honolulu with a pentagram, saying they had "hexed" the building—a high-rise tower called the Century Center, which they described as "the largest vertical brothel in the United States and a symbol of state hatred of Pacific Islander and Asian women."[1] It wasn't the only time AF3IRM has targeted the migrant sex and massage businesses in Century Center, and its members have conducted similar harassment campaigns in other cities that encourage people to report suspected sex trafficking to the Polaris national human trafficking hotline (which works with ICE).

At the time that AF3IRM targeted Sawadee, the workers in Century Center businesses, some of whom were undocumented, were under significant threat. Between early 2019 and May 2020, Honolulu police raided seventeen massage businesses in the Century City building alone.[2] Police seized money, laid charges for prostitution, charged at least one woman with immigration offenses, and closed over a dozen workplaces. The Century Center condo board relentlessly harassed the massage businesses, too, going so far as to hire its own attorneys and private investigator and to contact the FBI in an effort to "chase them away."

It was during this time of intense surveillance, raids, seizure of wages, harassment, and job loss that AF3IRM campaigned *not to help any of the workers*, but to make things worse by painting an actual target on the businesses, outing them as sex workers and inviting more discrimination, criminalization, and job loss.

We can't say what impact AF3IRM harassment campaigns had on migrant sex workers in Century Center, but we do know that police continued to raid their workplaces. In 2021, Honolulu prosecutor Steve Alm announced that his administration was switching enforcement tactics. Complaining that police raids had resulted "only" in misdemeanor prostitution arrests (no evidence of human trafficking was ever found), law enforcement's focus would now shift to Homeland Security investigations—in other words, immigration control. Alm claimed this would deal with the "root cause of the problem: Human trafficking."[3] The police thus identified migrant massage businesses as a problem that could be solved through immigration raids. In the media coverage, women from local anti-trafficking organizations spoke approvingly of this change in focus. Hawai'i sex work organizations were not quoted.

Organizations like AF3IRM profess to be leftist feminists opposing imperialism and fetishization, but their work does not align with these politics, and in many cases supports the right's agenda. Their actions invite police, immigration, and civilian harassment of migrants and reflect a refusal to listen to sex workers about how they deal with problems like exploitation, fetishization, and the impacts of imperialism. They are anti–sex work feminists.

ANTI–SEX WORK FEMINISTS

Some sections of the left are highly susceptible to right-wing approaches to migration and sex work in part because anti–sex work feminists have been promoting contempt for sex workers and whitewashing state violence against them (such as criminalization and enforcement) since the 1970s, portraying this stance as "feminist." The "modern slavery" panic is inextricably linked to a powerful subset of the left—conservative feminists who reject the term *sex work* because they believe sex work is violence that women are unable to consent to.

These particular feminists view the sex industry as a product of patriarchy, and sex workers as "enslaved," and they cast themselves as the liberators and "abolitionists." They are whorephobic. They promote ideas and policies that legitimize discrimination, exclusion, exploitation, state violence, and state-facilitated violence against sex workers. They promote cruel rape myths about sex workers, such as the idea that women who choose sex work welcome sexual violence. "To the extent that any woman is assumed to have freely chosen prostitution, then it follows that enjoyment of domination and rape are in her nature," to quote two anti–sex work feminists.[4] They actively work to oppose migrant sex worker organizing, in spite of claims to be radical, leftist "abolitionists of the sex trade."

Anti–sex work feminists are not "abolitionists." They are prohibitionists who advocate for a type of criminalization and law enforcement that they claim is feminist. Anti–sex work feminists are the driving force behind "End Demand" laws, also known as "partial decriminalization" or the Nordic/Swedish model—laws that seek to abolish the sex industry via criminalization. Punishing sex workers has become less popular, which anti–sex work feminists have capitalized on by appropriating the language of the sex workers' rights movement and referring to "End Demand" as "partial decriminalization," thus misleading people into thinking it will promote the safety and human rights of women in the sex industry. The proponents of the "End Demand" model claim that it criminalizes only the sex buyers and exploiters, not sex workers. "End Demand" laws do not decriminalize sex workers or provide immunity. Under these laws, sex workers are still arrested, charged, incarcerated, deported, and placed on sex offender registries. Even if they are not personally charged, sex workers can still be harmed through increased exposure to police. This happens because "End Demand" laws activate the carceral web, increasing sex workers' risk of harms under immigration law, family law (as it relates to child custody, for example), municipal law, housing law (e.g., eviction). "End Demand" laws also force workers into hiding and into much more dangerous circumstances, and criminalize anyone aiding sex workers.

Some anti–sex work feminists promote "End Demand" laws specifically as a solution to violence against racialized and Indigenous sex workers, claiming that this removes penalties for the selling of sex, which disproportionately affects women of color. But under "End Demand" regimes, those who are arrested or subject to raid or detention disproportionately are racialized women. "End Demand" laws are, after all, enforced by cops and immigration agents—armed agents of a racist state who have the power to abuse sex workers with impunity.

Anti–sex work feminism is an anti-worker movement. Its proponents point to the ways that the sex industry can be exploitative and shaped by white supremacy, imperialist wars, colonial extraction, poverty, and misogyny—and many claim that they are the only ones bravely taking a stand against it. Meanwhile, the anti–sex work feminist movement actively opposes organizing against exploitation, abuse, and violence *by the workers themselves*. Most migrant workers in the sex industry are directly impacted by multiple systems of domination and exploitation. The true experts on white supremacy and sex work are racialized sex workers and racialized sex worker organizations. But many anti–sex work feminists discredit racialized sex worker organizers as a privileged minority who support "the pimps and buyers" and do not understand or care about women. Anti–sex work feminists do not join migrant sex workers in their campaigns for fair working conditions or safe migration, but instead organize against those campaigns.

The problem with anti–sex work feminism is not that it is based on negative views about the sex industry. Many workers hold negative views about the industry they work in, including sex workers. That's why they organize for better working conditions, which is not possible in a criminalized sector where workers can be arrested and deported for organizing their workplace. The problem with anti–sex work feminism, then, is that it seeks to abolish sex work by opposing worker-led organizing efforts and criminalizing workplaces, which is fundamentally an anti-worker position.

Anti–sex work feminism is also sexist and anti-migrant because it denies that migrant women are capable of sexual consent, and it endorses state control over their bodies and their labor. Pushing low-income racialized migrant women out of sex work reduces their options for surviving and resisting their circumstances. As Kate Zen, one of the founders of Red Canary Song, put it, "Asian sex workers today are not responsible for the negative associations of the sex trade; neither are we responsible for the global economic structures that make sex work one of the most highly paid ways for a woman without an education to survive. Changing those economic and social structures does not start with violently silencing sex workers."[5]

Finally, anti–sex work feminist politics play into the dehumanizing narrative of migrant sex workers as a rescue project in which whorephobic feminists cast themselves as the saviors "liberating the slaves," whether migrant sex workers like it or not. Calling this "modern slavery abolition" is an appropriation of Black-led movements for the abolition of chattel slavery, in service of an agenda that creates more carceral state violence, including against Black people, through the prohibition of sex work. We think of "sex trade abolitionism" as a kind of "zombie abolitionism." Non-Black carceral forces co-opt and mimic the language, imagery, and heroes of chattel slavery abolitionist movements to cloak state violence—largely against people of color—and declare themselves the next generation of freedom fighters. In practice, anti–sex work feminism plays out in the form of cops pointing guns at racialized women, stealing their savings, caging them in detention centers, and then deporting them. It deals in racialized terror, suffering, and death and calls this abolition and freedom.

WHAT ABOUT PATRIARCHAL AND RACIST ABUSE OF SEX WORKERS?

It is possible to both support migrant sex workers and be critical of the sex industry, including the patriarchal and racist abuse of sex workers, such as at military bases, resource extraction areas, and prisons. If human trafficking laws aren't the answer to these problems in the sex industry, what, then, should be done? It starts with understanding how the conditions facing migrant sex workers reflect what women of color face in broader society. From there, recognizing and respecting different experiences and different forms of resistance that can include sex work. Sometimes migrant women and LGBTQI+ people are using sex work as a way to resist patriarchal and racist abuse in other parts of their lives. That's why our emphasis must be on the need to build collective struggle to end patriarchy and white supremacy—not to end the sex industry.

As in other industries, women of color workers are organizing against abuse in the sex industry. Support for *worker-led* organizing means ending their criminalization and stigma and building up workers' power, not taking it away. Leftists should support migrant sex worker organizing for the same reasons they should support domestic worker, farmworker, and Amazon worker organizing—because doing so is an effective strategy for building the power of oppressed laborers.

SESTA / FOSTA AND LEFTIST COMPLICITY

Some anti–sex work feminists are so committed to their vision of society that they are willing to sacrifice the lives of migrant sex workers to achieve it. We think that most people do not want this. They want to help migrant sex workers. This is why the anti–sex work feminist agenda has been packaged so as to appear in support of human rights, women's rights, and children's rights. This lures in those who want to help, and it is why we have witnessed people from a wide spectrum of political stances, from the anti-capitalist and anti-imperialist left to progressives and center-left feminists, uncritically accept promises that tougher anti-trafficking laws and border policies will protect the vulnerable—even when these false promises come from the far right.

In April 2018, the US Congress passed two sets of laws that its backers claimed would curb sex trafficking. In an editorial, one of the laws' cosponsors, Republican senator Ted Cruz, wrote, "The U.S. Senate passed the Stop Enabling Sex Traffickers Act / Fight Online Sex Trafficking Act, which seeks justice for victims of sex trafficking and ensures that websites which knowingly facilitate this horrible crime can be held liable. And on April 11, President Trump signed our legislation into law. I cosponsored this legislation because it combats a real threat to the most vulnerable members of our society, especially young people, the poor and immigrants."[6] The passage of the Stop Enabling Sex Traffickers Act (SESTA) and Fight Online Sex Trafficking Act (FOSTA) is a recent example of the allegiance of certain progressive, feminist, and leftist groups to the racist far right when it comes to sex work politics. SESTA / FOSTA had nothing to do with protecting young people, the poor, or immigrants. It effectively suspended Section 230 of the Communications Decency Act in cases where online platforms are perceived to be promoting prostitution. Online providers can now be held liable for posts perceived to be advertising sex on their sites. In effect, SESTA / FOSTA made it a crime to carry advertisements for sex work, and forced the shutdown of websites that sex workers used to find and screen clients to ensure their safety. The bill package was vigorously backed by Donald Trump, and its lead sponsor was Representative Ann Wagner, a Midwestern "family values" Christian Republican. All of its proponents framed SESTA / FOSTA as a form of safety and protection.

Republicans did not discover a newfound concern for the safety of migrants, however. Ted Cruz and Donald Trump are notorious racists, after all. They promoted SESTA / FOSTA because it increases the power of the state to surveil and criminalize sex workers and migrants. SESTA / FOSTA targets sex workers' safety strategies, once again criminalizing aid to sex workers and pushing them deeper into poverty, off the internet, into more dangerous street work in search of clients, and into greater dependence on third parties to help them find work, such as old managers they had worked with previously. The laws were opposed by sex work organizations in the US and internationally, including by organizations of sex workers who were survivors of violence, such as Survivors against SESTA.[7] "SESTA will send these women back to the abusive managers, cop violence, rape, and monotonous misery of street work," said organizer Caty Simon, discussing sex workers who are unhoused and use drugs.[8] Sex workers reported having to return to bad managers who had taken advantage of them in the past, but who could help them find clients without the

use of the internet. Others reported that they had to stay with or return to abusive partners because they weren't making enough money
to survive on their own. The painful irony about anti-trafficking laws
is how effectively they put more power into the hands of men (bosses,
boyfriends, the cops) and increase the very patriarchal violence that
they claim to combat.

In spite of the vociferous opposition from people in the sex industry, SESTA / FOSTA passed with near unanimous support from
across the political spectrum. In an illustration of the incredible
power of the "modern slavery" panic, Democrats, progressive poli-
cymakers, feminist anti-violence service providers, and many leftists,
including Bernie Sanders, supported a law that was sponsored by a
white supremacist like Ted Cruz and Donald Trump.

As predicted by sex work organizations, SESTA / FOSTA did not
reduce violence in the sex industry. It did what it was meant to do: it
increased state and interpersonal violence against sex workers, sup-
pressing sex worker organizing. Research on the effects of SESTA /
FOSTA revealed that it worsened working conditions, increased raids
on migrant massage businesses, increased violence against sex workers by 33 percent, and increased their vulnerability to contracting
HIV.[9] In 2019, the largest national sex worker–led conference in the
US canceled its annual gathering, stating that holding it could put the
organizers at risk of human trafficking charges. Other sex worker-led
organizations suspended their critical outreach efforts for the same
reasons.[10] Why would so many leftists and feminists accept, and even
encourage, this kind of harmful and unjust legislation, when they had
ample opportunity to listen to those who would be harmed by it?

THE LEFT'S ADOPTION OF THE "MODERN SLAVERY" PANIC

In our view, much of the left's support for state violence against migrant sex workers is rooted in three problems. First, some leftists don't
know what the anti-trafficking industry is, or what it does to migrant
sex workers—or to social justice movements, more broadly. They
want to support migrant sex workers and believe that human traffick-

ing laws and policies laws help women who are trapped in "modern slavery." The anti-trafficking industry has so thoroughly suppressed and discredited migrant sex worker movements that few on the left include migrant sex workers in their movements. As a result, many leftists don't have connections to migrant sex workers. These leftists don't know who migrant sex workers are, what they face, or that they can—and do—resist the oppression they face. They have heard little to nothing from migrant sex worker organizers about their realities, analyses, and organizing. Even some white-led sex work organizations believe that surveillance, policing, and laws are bad for *themselves* but good for racialized migrant sex workers, whom the white workers assume are being trafficked.

Second, the anti-trafficking industry is effective at co-opting social justice in part because some liberal ideas about justice are heavily influenced by racist, capitalist, militaristic ideologies, and therefore compatible with right-wing ideologies. Take, for example, the myths that the oppressed Asian woman sex worker needs a white savior. Sometimes people on the left fail to support migrant sex workers because of these kinds of biases. This helps explain why many social movements are progressive in some areas but not in others. They reject some aspect of migrant sex workers' experiences or identities due to some combination of racism, classism, whorephobia, sexism, ableism, or anti-migrant xenophobia.

When we speak to people in labor and socialist movements about migrant sex workers, for example, they understand the problem of labor exploitation within capitalist economies. But these activists might assume that migrant sex workers are inherently the *most* exploited type of labor simply because of the nature of their work, regardless of their working conditions or wages. They exceptionalize sex work and treat it as a different, inherently harmful form of labor, rather than treating it as just another form of oppressed labor. This reflects a failure to understand capitalism as the root of sex workers' labor problems, not sex work. Or they don't believe that sex work is "real work" and dismiss sex worker labor concerns, failing to recognize sex worker organizing as *worker* organizing. They remain trapped in a whorephobic view of sex work.

When we speak to white sex worker–led organizations, they clearly understand that sex work is work, but they often fail to understand specific aspects of racialized capitalism. White sex workers often see racialized migrant workers charging less for their services and working long hours, concluding that this means the migrant worker has been trafficked and needs to be rescued from sex work. They fail to see that migrant sex workers share similar problems with other racialized migrant women in every other labor sector. Their problem is not trafficking, but the racial hierarchy within the labor market and the way that racism dictates low wages and poor working conditions.

Many white-dominated feminist, LGBTQ+, and sex work organizations can be racist and xenophobic in their advocacy. For example, these organizations often show little interest in supporting racialized migrants (including sex workers) to achieve migrant rights or build migrant power. Some advocate for stronger policing and prisons, or for hate crime laws, despite the evidence that policing and prisons uphold structural racism and hate crime laws are so often used to charge people of color with offenses, and do not protect them from racial discrimination. Some are swayed to take funding from anti-trafficking initiatives and shift their work from supporting sex workers to "ending human trafficking," even when the anti-trafficking programs they offer harm racialized people.

When we talk to some racial justice organizations, they understand the racial hierarchy of labor, but some support the anti-trafficking industry because supporting migrant sex workers means challenging capitalism, class stratification in the West, and the power of the police. Some mainstream racial justice organizations are drawn to an agenda in which people of color achieve inclusion, wealth, and recognition within the status quo. Some Asian American and Asian Canadian organizations identify with the myth of the model minority and don't want to be associated with poor, criminalized, incarcerated, or undocumented Asian migrants, including sex workers.

When we speak to police reform activists (who are not abolitionist) about the criminalization of migrant sex workers, they understand that police can be violent toward racialized and poor people. But when we try to recruit support for our campaigns against human trafficking laws that would increase police budgets and expand police surveillance and powers, some anti-policing reformers do not support us. They believe that the police could help sex-trafficking victims and ask us, "How can the police do better to support victims?" They do not believe that policing is violent by deliberate design.

Sometimes we talk to feminists who work to end violence against women and we find that they have conservative ideas about sexuality—that it should always be intimate, private, and an expression of love. For many middle-class white women in particular, other forms of sexuality appear to them as exploitative and violent. It can be hard for them to embrace the perspective that there is no one right way to relate to our bodies, sexuality, and work—that these can mean different things and be used in different ways. They only focus on their own way, so they look at migrant sex workers and think they must be naive, lying, ignorant, or confused when they say they consent to sex work.

This thinking overlaps with ableist ideas that sex workers have some kind of mental or emotional pathology that prevents them from being able to govern themselves, that they are "brainwashed" into thinking they consent to sex work because they suffer from a kind of "Stockholm syndrome." Few organizations push back on the ableism of these claims and recognize that sex work is not a pathology, and that sex work can be an important form of economic survival for disabled migrant people. The disability justice movement is an important exception, as from its inception it has respected sex workers as part of their vision of disabled people's art, politics, and community.[11]

The third reason that so few leftists offer support to migrant sex workers is that the "modern slavery" moral panic and the anti-trafficking industry perpetuate anti-Black stereotypes and work counter to Black racial justice movements. Here we'll briefly explain a few ways that the anti-trafficking industry mobilizes an anti-Blackness that is tolerated or endorsed by some on the left.

Though this book primarily addresses the moral panic around "international sex trafficking," the racial construction of the "domestic sex trafficker" has been crucial to the criminalization of sex workers. "Domestic sex-trafficking" tropes draw on the white supremacist association between Black people and violence, especially the myth of the Black rapist. This is evident in the imagery and language that the anti-trafficking industry uses. Anti-trafficking posters, for instance, will use the image of a little white girl with a Black man's hand over her mouth, and some training materials describe sex workers as the slaves of "gorilla pimps" and "urban gangs," and list "gold chains" as indicators of human trafficking. As the Texas anti-trafficking organization SAFE Austin put it: "[Human trafficking] is not just a Black man who is decked out in gold chains and diamond rings."[12] By defining human trafficking as more than "just" Black men, anti-trafficking organizations promote the idea that human trafficking usually includes Black men.

Some leftists are willing to believe the myth that Black men are more dangerous to sex workers than the police. These racist myths belie the fact that the police are the number one danger to sex workers—especially Black sex workers. Black people in the sex industry are more likely to be physically and sexually assaulted by the police than non-Black people, more likely to be viewed as human traffickers for engaging in sex work or sex work management, and more likely to be placed on sex offender registries for sex work and given longer sentences, based on racist assumptions that their association with the sex industry must be of a violent and exploitative nature.[13]

Related to this myth is the belief among some people on the left that police and prisons make people safer and that sex workers, too, would be made safer through anti-trafficking strategies such as border surveillance, special police task forces, and "rescue" raids. They fail to believe the evidence presented by Black organizers and researchers that the carceral state is inherently anti-Black and that its real function is to protect private property and white supremacy. Because anti-trafficking initiatives fund, expand, and legitimize surveillance, policing, and incarceration—which strengthens the state's ability to surveil and police Black communities—the harm they pose to Black communities is clear. Solidarity with migrant sex workers requires that people on the left reject myths about the sources of harm in sex workers' lives and the sources of safety, and instead support Black-led movements to abolish the police, prisons, and other carceral institutions of control and captivity.

UNDERSTANDING EXPLOITATION AND VIOLENCE

People on the left must, and often want to, address the violent conditions faced by migrant sex workers. The conceptual and political tools that they use to understand those conditions are important, though. It is crucial that the left stops viewing sex work (and migration for sex work) as inherently violent and instead recognizes how structures of capitalist domination and state violence underpin every other form of violence experienced by migrant sex workers—such as intimate partner violence and client violence.

When people blame sex work or are uncomfortable with migrant sex workers, they lose their critical analysis and don't see the real problems facing migrant sex workers, such as hierarchical and exploitative labor markets, social inequality, state violence, and borders. It's necessary to uncover all the biases that shape our analysis of migrant sex workers. It's encouraging to us that many people on the left do quickly recognize how their moralistic misunderstanding of sex work has distorted their ability to understand and support migrant sex workers. Often in our work, we see people have an "Aha!" moment when they realize that the best strategies to address labor exploitation and abuse in the sex industry, such as worker protections and establishing legal immigration status for all, are generally the same for other oppressed workers.

LEFT SOLIDARITY AGAINST
THE ANTI-TRAFFICKING INDUSTRY

There are a small but growing number of left organizations showing up for migrant sex workers. Real solidarity means joint struggle for collective liberation among movements that are accountable to each other. Engaging in joint struggle together does not mean tokenistic "representation" of migrant sex workers in leftist organizations. It is a recognition of the strategic importance of migrant sex worker and massage worker organizing. In the remainder of this chapter, we'll briefly profile some grassroots organizing we've witnessed or been a part of where migrant sex workers are meaningfully included in movements to resist policing, gentrification, and state violence against women.

ABOLITIONIST ORGANIZING—THE FIGHT TO STOP
THE "COMBATING HUMAN TRAFFICKING ACT"

In spring 2020, the conservative government of Ontario, Canada's most populous province, introduced a new human trafficking law—Bill 251, which later became the Combating Human Trafficking Act. It entailed a $307 million, five-year investment in an initiative to combat human trafficking and "provide support for survivors by adopting a law enforcement model, increasing surveillance powers for police and ministerially appointed inspectors, and imposing charges and hefty fines for violations."[14] The proposed bill would authorize police to conduct searches without warrants and promised to divert millions out of provincial budgets and into policing at a time when the government was being loudly criticized for cuts to social services like health care, education, and legal aid.

When he introduced it, Premier of Ontario Doug Ford stated that the average age of entry into prostitution was thirteen, using discredited data to make an emotional appeal linking sex work to child abuse. The media published this misinformation as fact. Initially, social and economic justice organizations and community groups did not challenge the new police powers provided by the law, the threat it posed to racialized communities, the diversion of funds out of communities and into policing, or the perpetuation of harmful myths about sex work. Outside of the sex worker movement, there was at that time no precedent for organizing against human trafficking laws.

Bill 251 was a turning point. For years, Butterfly had been building relationships with allies in migrant, worker, racial justice, and violence against women movements and providing education on the issue of migrant sex workers and the harms of human trafficking laws and policies. Through Butterfly's work, more movements came to see that human trafficking laws did not just harm sex workers but also harmed other racialized, migrant, and marginalized people. Based on the view that migrant sex worker justice is a joint struggle, Butterfly brought together an exceptionally broad range of organizations working on issues regarding policing, anti-Black racism, migrants and refugees, violence against women, LGBTQ+ abolitionists, HIV/AIDS, poverty, racial justice, harm reduction, and human rights to inform them about the real impacts of the law and to organize a response.

The first support came from Black and racialized migrant leaders whose communities have a long historical experience of being the targets of state violence, and of organizing their communities to end state violence such as police abuse and migrant detention. We find that abolitionists are more inoculated against the lures and false promises of the anti-trafficking industry and more able to see our work as aligned.

In the end, over a hundred social justice organizations signed onto a petition opposing the human trafficking legislation known as Bill 251.[15] Multiple social justice organizations presented at the public hearings about the bill to demand that the law not be passed. Some of these organizations may not share the same position on sex work, but they organized collectively around their solidarity for racial justice and in opposition to police power. No progressive politicians voted against the law, including those who have been critical of the police and have called for reductions in police budgets—likely because they could not risk being seen as being "pro-trafficking." We were disappointed by this but not surprised. The resistance will come first from social movements and communities; and the progressive politicians will follow.

The Combating Human Trafficking Act passed into law in 2021, but it was one of the only times that we have ever seen non–sex worker organizations join migrant sex workers in opposing human trafficking legislation and misinformation. The campaign punctured the unquestioned belief that such laws and the narratives around them are helpful and fair. Most governments had never before had to contend with the slightest public criticism of anti-trafficking laws, no matter how repressive they are. This organizing encouraged other organizations that have been hesitant to join the resistance to anti-trafficking laws, policies, and misinformation. And it built toward a win. In 2023, a coalition of sex work and allied organizations was able to stop amendments to Canada's federal human trafficking law that would have made it easier for the courts to convict people of human trafficking without evidence of exploitation and without demonstrating any threat to individuals' safety.

ORGANIZING AGAINST GENTRIFICATION—CCED-LA

CCED-LA is a Los Angeles–based organization building the power of low-income and immigrant communities that has collaborated with migrant massage and sex workers in Red Canary Song, rooted in a recognition of joint struggle. Yves Tong Nguyen of Red Canary Song, offers this description of their collaboration:

> Chinatown Community for Equitable Development (CCED)-LA is part of a growing number of organizations that have cross-issue solidarity with migrant sex workers and massage workers. CCED-LA is an all-volunteer, multi-ethnic, intergenerational organization based in Los Angeles Chinatown fighting gentrification through grassroots organizing, education, and mutual help. It has built solidarity with sex workers and massage workers since a 2020 convening of Coast to Coast Chinatowns Against Displacements (C2C) that included Red Canary Song in an effort to understand the relationship that massage workers have to gentrification and displacement. CCED came to understand that migrant sex workers and massage workers are often at the center of narratives for gentrification efforts in Chinatowns across North America. They are framed as morally repugnant

and criminalized by police and housing departments to justify shutting them down and pushing workers out to make space for new developments. Over the past four years CCED-LA has expanded to doing outreach with Asian migrant massage workers and working with the Sex Workers Outreach Project of LA (SWOP-LA).[16]

ORGANIZING AGAINST STATE VIOLENCE AGAINST WOMEN— FEMINIST SUPPORT FOR DECRIMINALIZATION

Another area that we see growing inclusion of migrant sex workers is within feminist organizations that have begun to advocate for the full decriminalization of sex work as part of their opposition to state violence against women. In our experience, the strongest support comes from feminist organizations that are led by and for racialized women, organizations that view racial justice as inherently linked to gender justice. These organizations are less likely to be led by carceral feminists who believe that freedom from gender-based violence will come from the state through surveillance, police, and prisons. Instead of seeing cops and prisons as women's saviors and protectors, they understand them as part of state violence against marginalized women.

Slowly, organizations that have historical ties to white feminism are following suit as they become more intersectional, with explicit commitments to racial justice. In the early 2010s, a number of the most influential national feminist organizations in the US and Canada were either advocating to strengthen the criminalization of sex work or remaining silent about their position. Today we can point to many feminist organizations that have begun to change their positions and publicly support the decriminalization of sex work or are in the process of doing so, such as the Canadian Association of Elizabeth Fry Societies, which advocates for incarcerated women.

We are seeing positive changes, but so much more is needed. Organizations that explicitly claim to support sex workers continue to support harmful anti-trafficking legislation and share information with the police. It remains difficult to assess whether an organization is actually in support of sex workers or whether they are only co-opting the language of sex workers' rights while continuing to support the criminalization of sex workers through anti-trafficking narratives and policies. How can we tell if an organization or an individual is pro– or anti–sex work? This can be complicated because of the large numbers of anti–sex work organizations that hide their real intentions. Some anti–sex work organization adopt feminist language about "protecting women" as they work to strengthen the criminalization of sex work and the power of the police. For example, the Coalition Against the Trafficking of Women (CATW) claim to oppose "the buying and selling of women." But this language is degrading as it implies that women in the sex industry are objects for sale, not humans or workers. And CATW actively works to keep sex work criminalized, which severely harms women. To assess whether an organization actually promotes the interests of sex workers (and is not just pretending to be), we ask these questions:

- Does the organization oppose the full legal immigration status of migrant sex workers and the decriminalization of sex work?
- Does the organization collaborate with police and immigration control? Do they see themselves as "partners" with law enforcement?
- Does the organization aim to end sex work by giving more resources and power to law enforcement, social workers, and the carceral system?
- Does the organization support sex workers to have greater control over their lives, by giving them more power and resources so they can resist the oppression they face?
- Does the organization assume that sex workers have agency and autonomy? Or do they view sex workers as objects to save?

To strengthen movements for justice, the left must understand

how anti-trafficking politics serve as a right-wing recruitment strategy and a smokescreen for carceral, anti-migrant, and anti–sex work
policies. Racial, migrant, gender, and economic justice and abolition
are all intimately connected to migrant sex worker justice. We are
hopeful about the small but growing number of leftist organizations
who see their common ground with migrant sex workers and are
building out a coalitional politics between and across movements by
working to combat the myths, the criminalization, and the targeting
of migrant sex workers.

CHAPTER 9

MIGRANT SEX WORKER JUSTICE

The portrayal of migrant sex workers as sex-trafficking victims or "modern slaves" is wrong, but this does not mean that their experience of migration and sex work is safe, fair, or positive. The majority of them are oppressed workers who are too often targets of exploitation, abuse, and violence in their workplaces and homes. We hope it has become very clear that the solution to these injustices is not rescue; it is justice and power. Justice for migrant sex workers begins with increasing their power over the conditions of their lives. The power to work and move, safely, on their own terms. The power to protect themselves from abusers (including the state), and the power over their working conditions and wages, free from control and state violence.

But what about those who are in crisis right now? What can be done to help protect the safety of migrant sex workers facing exploitation, abuse, and violence? The answer lies, again, with migrant sex workers themselves.

MIGRANT SEX WORKER NETWORKS OF CARE

Migrant sex workers help each other deal with exploitation and abuse through their informal networks of care. Yves Tong Nguyen, an organizer with Red Canary Song, put it this way to us:

> Before Red Canary Song, migrant massage and sex workers in New York were already taking care of each other. They were showing up at the jails for each other; showing up at the trials; when someone is abused, when someone

is trying to escape, when someone is fighting off their client. They were showing up when someone didn't have money to pay rent; when people didn't have money to get food; when people needed child care. That has always been true, though it has been historically overlooked. Every single day, the government and the prison industrial complex tries to isolate people. Yet people have survived for decades and decades and decades. From the moment that migrants—especially those who are undocumented and criminalized—show up in Red Canary Song, they see each other and they're like, "We are all we have."[1]

MIGRANT SEX WORKER–LED CRISIS SUPPORT

Another way that migrant sex workers get help is through community-organized, peer-led, culturally safe crisis support that is not connected to the state. Butterfly organizes a 24/7 multilingual crisis support hotline. The core focus of the crisis support is peer support and providing information, resources, and referrals to workers and their community that can increase their power to end violence and deal with problems themselves. By removing any barriers to resources and information, workers get assistance *from other migrant sex workers in their own language* on how to improve their working conditions, or have more options in their lives, such as learning how to negotiate with bosses or clients and how to work together with colleagues or community members to collectively change the conditions in their workplaces or get out of an abusive situation. They learn about how to navigate legal and social systems, available resources, and advocating for their rights. But they also learn why this is happening, and how they are being marginalized, from others who have gone through a similar experience.

Butterfly's crisis support workers do not use the terms *human trafficking, sex trafficking,* or *"modern slavery"* because these terms make invisible the problems workers are facing, such as bad working conditions or intimate partner violence—problems that may require very different forms of support. Using these terms can undermine support by signaling that the crisis support service does not really understand sex workers and views them as passive slaves with no agency.

MIGRANT SEX WORKER JUSTICE ORGANIZING

Migrant sex worker organizers have developed a vast array of knowledge and creative approaches to collectively protect themselves against exploitation, abuse, and violence, including state violence. These solutions include informal networks of support, community building, and grassroots organizing to defend their safety, advocate for their rights, develop leadership, promote migrant sex workers' voices, and strengthen solidarity within global movements for justice. These are some of the programs that Butterfly organizes to resist the criminalization of migrant massage and sex workers:

RELATIONSHIP BUILDING, COMMUNITY OUTREACH, AND SUPPORT

- Worker-friendly, linguistically accessible, in-person outreach visits to massage businesses, apartment sex work businesses, and hotels
- Massage skills classes to prevent workplace injuries
- Classes on self-defense, women's health, art, and storytelling
- Social events where migrant sex workers can network in a welcoming environment

CRISIS SUPPORT: LEGAL REFERRAL, EMERGENCY, AND SERVICES HOTLINE

- 24/7 crisis support hotline in multiple languages
- Legal referrals
- Court accompaniment, translation assistance, and crisis support after arrests
- Representation in deportation hearings
- Bail assistance

- Referrals to community resources, such as shelter and social services
- Post-deportation support including assistance with housing, finances, and long-distance English classes upon workers' return to their country of origin
- Accompaniment, translation assistance, and advocacy during medical appointments

COMMUNITY ORGANIZING, BUILDING CAPACITY, AND LEADERSHIP

- Leadership skill-building (for example, organizing skills)
- Know Your Rights workshops
- English classes
- Gathering and sharing information (through newsletters, for example)
- Gatherings that provide information related to workplace health and safety issues, culture, and a platform where workers can share their stories

PUBLIC EDUCATION

- Public education (through storytelling and art, for example) about the realities of migrant sex workers
- Trainings for service providers on the needs of migrant sex workers
- Developing networks and partnerships with medical service providers
- Worker-led research that documents migrant sex worker experiences of law enforcement harm, and their resistance to police and other repression

CAMPAIGNS AND ADVOCACY

- Organizing campaigns against repressive laws and policies
- Organizing for better working conditions

- Bringing analysis and leadership to broader migrant justice; racial justice; anti-police; LGBTQ+; gender justice; and sex worker coalitions
- Participating in local, national, and international advocacy related to migration and sex work

More and more migrant sex workers in North America are coming together to provide mutual aid, build community leadership, and challenge the criminalization of their community. Butterfly has also worked with many other organizations to support them in organizing migrant sex workers, such as Red Canary Song in New York City, Massage Parlor Outreach Project and the Coalition for Rights and Safety for People in the Sex Trade in Seattle, and ASTT(e)Q in Montreal. Some organizations, like Empower–Thailand, have been organizing migrant sex worker power for a long time. For this book we were honored to interview a number of organizers including Yves Tong Nguyen, Liz Hilton, and Emi Koyama. Because of length restrictions we couldn't include their full interviews, but want to share how they are inspiring our work.

RED CANARY SONG's organizing strategy is based on advocacy; coalitions with labor, racial justice, and abolitionist movements; base-building; and mutual aid to build migrant sex worker power. Its members have worked in coalition with Asian community organizations against gentrification, community policing, and misogynist sentiments about Asian sex workers. In the US in particular, RCS's work has brought the conditions of migrant massage and sex workers into view and punctured the myth that Asian migrant sex workers cannot speak for themselves. Its on-the-ground understanding of how displacement, migration, criminalization, capitalism, and sex work play out in the everyday lives of Asian migrant sex workers is a crucial counterpoint to the faux-leftism of the anti-trafficking industry.

EMPOWER FOUNDATION—THAILAND has been creatively building the capacity and leadership of sex workers for thirty-seven years, leading to policy wins and the creation of the Can Do Bar, a cooperatively sex worker–owned bar where sex workers can set the terms of their working conditions. As in the West, a large proportion of sex workers in Thailand are migrants who do not have the legal or financial means to travel. To share the voices of migrant sex workers, Empower created the Kumjing dolls, a collection of life-sized papier-mâché dolls that travel with Empower members in their advocacy tours all over the world. The dolls, which stand in for the migrant sex workers themselves, help share the workers' stories and highlight the mobility restrictions they experiences as undocumented migrants. Empower has also built large-scale, cross-sector solidarity by forming a community collective of women human rights defenders, including members of Empower, Indigenous women fighting against mining, and women fighting slum evictions and environmental degradation. They work in coalition with poor women's movements, drawing on their shared experiences as working-class and poor women.

The **MASSAGE PARLOR OUTREACH PROJECT** and **COALITION FOR RIGHTS AND SAFETY FOR PEOPLE IN THE SEX TRADE** work in coalition to bring an abolitionist-democratic strategy to sex worker organizing. Recognizing the challenges that racialized sex workers face, the coalition decided not to focus their work on the decriminalization of the sex industry and more on fully eliminating the presence of police in the lives of people, including youth in the sex trade. This came out of a recognition that removing bad laws does not actually improve the lives of marginalized and criminalized people, because those in power will only do so in a way that maintains the status quo. Through its abolitionist-democratic strategy, the coalition focuses on building a society where people have what they need and do not rely on policing to solve social problems.

A MIGRANT SEX WORKER JUSTICE AGENDA

As the experts on the complex problems they face, migrant sex worker communities and organizers are natural leaders in developing, implementing, and assessing strategic responses to those problems. The next section highlights the structural economic and political changes that are needed to address the root causes of exploitation, coercion, and violence against migrant sex workers.

ABOLITION

Migrant sex worker justice is abolitionist. It requires the abolition of the carceral state, the police, prisons, all sites of detention, and the carceral logic that undergirds social welfare, health care, and child welfare. Abolition is transformative—it is not based on systems of oppression nor does it uphold them.

ABOLITIONIST REFORMS—DECRIMINALIZATION OF SEX WORK

Good working conditions are not possible for workers who are subject to criminalization, arrest, detention, and deportation. This includes sex workers, but it also includes workers with precarious immigration status in every sector. Decent work in the sex industry requires the full decriminalization of sex work including third parties, clients, and those who help sex workers to move across borders, so that police are stripped of one of their tools to surveil, investigate, arrest, and incarcerate.

To show a path forward, we have the example of New Zealand, which in 2003 decriminalized sex work. Although it failed to include *migrant* sex workers in decriminalization, it otherwise provides a model for fair and flexible working conditions in the sex industry. Sex workers were consulted on labor and human rights regulations that would work for them. For example, there is no mandatory registration for sex workers. Decriminalization has reduced police violence against sex workers and therefore should be extended to include all sex workers, including migrants without legal residency.[2]

Decriminalization is not the same as legalization. Legalization of the sex industry often involves very strict and discriminatory regulations, maintaining criminal penalties for sex workers who violate those regulations. It forces sex workers to engage with the state, for example, by registering for a license or only working in "red-light" districts that are highly controlled by sex work business owners and surveilled by the police. Legalization does not protect sex workers from workplace ill-treatment or abuse by cops. Sex workers who can't or won't follow the regulations are criminalized. This is especially a threat to the safety of undocumented, unhoused, and racialized transgender workers, who are profiled, harassed, abused, and criminalized by the police with impunity. As an example of why legalization is a failed strategy, we can look to the state of Nevada, which has legalized prostitution. Legalization has *increased* the criminalization of sex workers, and Nevada has the highest arrest rates for prostitution in the US.[3] Legalization is not an acceptable solution for racialized migrant sex workers because any solution that increases state control over sex workers and interaction with the state will not eliminate the threat of state violence, such as arrest, abuse, theft, and deportation.

DECENT WORKING CONDITIONS

Labor organizations and sex work organizations around the world are fighting for decent working conditions, including fair wages, protection from discrimination, health and safety standards, and control over the policies that make workers vulnerable to exploitation—such as labor regulations that exclude undocumented workers. This is critical: *migrant workers in the sex industry must be able to define decent working conditions and health and safety standards for themselves.* If they do not get to define their own labor standards, regulations imposed on them can easily become tools of surveillance, control, and criminalization.

END MIGRANT SEX WORKER EXCLUSIONS
AND END THE POWER OF IMMIGRATION CONTROL

Migrant sex worker justice requires the repeal of immigration regulations that ban the entry of migrant sex workers into the US and Canada, that prohibit sex work for temporary workers, and that make sex work a deportable offense. Immigration control agencies must be stripped of their power to surveil, investigate, detain, and deport migrants in any part of the sex industry.

SAFE MIGRATION

Migrant sex workers must have control over their movement—and that means the power, resources, and information they need to reduce the risks and vulnerability that accompany different stages of migration. They must have the ability to remain in their home countries if they wish, without being displaced and forced to migrate in search of safety, food, water, work, or other resources. Migrant sex workers must be able to negotiate how and where they migrate, and have free and legal access to information about how to migrate and about jobs in the sex industry. The exploitative migrant labor system should be abolished. No migrant workers, including sex workers, should be forced into exploitative temporary work visas, nor should they have their mobility tied to any employer.

MIGRANT SEX WORKER JUSTICE ON INDIGENOUS LAND

Migrant sex worker justice is inherently linked to the centuries-long struggles of Indigenous nations against colonization. The oppression of migrant sex workers in the US and Canada flows, in large part, from the power of settler states to create and enforce laws, define borders, and control migration. Justice for migrants does not confer on them an automatic right to be settlers on stolen and occupied Indigenous lands. The migrant's "freedom to stay" is not a right to colonize. It means that when we challenge the criminalization of migration and sex work, we must also question the legitimacy of settler states to be the sole authority on laws and borders.

The categories of migrant and Indigenous can also overlap. Many migrant sex workers in the US and Canada are Indigenous people who have been impoverished and displaced through colonial and imperial dispossession or climate destruction of their lands. Others are women and LGBTQ+ people fleeing persecution in the Global South countries whose laws and culture were changed by European colonial powers to be more sexist, homophobic, and transphobic. There is a long history of Indigenous communities supporting excluded and oppressed migrants in North America. These relationships of solidarity between Indigenous and migrant people can help us to redefine migration as not the taking of land but as an ancient, mutually supportive, and nonextractive practice of movement.

ABOLISH THE ANTI-TRAFFICKING INDUSTRY

The anti-trafficking industry must be delegitimized, defunded, and abolished. It is designed for social control, and because it is founded on white supremacy, sexism, and state violence, it cannot be reformed. First, we must challenge the belief that the anti-trafficking industry is a social justice movement, and expose the ways it facilitates state violence against migrant sex worker communities and opposes actual social justice movements. We need to divert the funding it receives back into meeting the needs of communities. This includes defunding nonprofit organizations and programs that facilitate and extend the legitimacy and power of the anti-trafficking industry. We need to dismantle all regimes of surveillance, policing, incarceration, detention, and deportation that target migrant sex workers, as well as the anti-trafficking industry that advocates for and supports those regimes, including those that claim to do it for the good of migrant sex workers.

Migrant sex worker organizing plays an important role in supporting abolitionist movements to recognize the anti-trafficking industry as part of the prison industrial complex, and to recognize how it has effectively disguised itself as a force for safety and protection. Migrant sex workers can lead the reclamation of abolition from those who have co-opted it as a means to prohibit the sex industry and criminalize sex workers.

THE PRESENCE OF EQUALITY AND JUSTICE

Abolition is about presence, not absence. It's about
building life-affirming institutions.
—Ruth Wilson Gilmore

Abolitionist strategy is about transforming the world. Migrant sex worker justice is about more than securing the rights that can prevent violence within the existing systems. Even in a scenario where labor and migration rights were won, migrant sex workers would remain the targets of social and economic inequality and oppression. Migrant sex worker justice is about autonomy and self-determination, full membership in democratic societies, and leadership in transforming our society into one that is fair and just for all oppressed people.

Migrant sex worker justice means an end to the multiple forms of systemic hierarchies of domination that shape migrant sex workers' lives, and it is the presence of freedom—both the freedom for people to stay in their homelands without being pushed out and the freedom for people to stay where they have chosen to migrate. We need a complete transformation in how we understand "work," so that work is not just geared toward the economic exploitation of people and the Earth for profit. This means guaranteed access to basic services such as housing, food, health care, childcare, and education so that people are never coerced into unwanted waged labor. It means the power to be sexually autonomous, as no one should be coerced into trading their sexuality for economic survival and social status, including through heterosexual marriage. It means the end of colonial ideas that position sex workers as deserving of exclusion, isolation, discrimination, and violence. It means a society that values migrant sex workers' lives and lets them live with freedom and dignity.

The migrant sex worker struggle is about generating life-building worlds. This struggle embodies a dream of liberation, freedom, and justice. It is about having a transformative imagination, the creativity to envision new worlds and build new systems; and it is about the relationships between nations that become possible outside of police, prisons, borders, capitalism, and heteropatriarchy. It requires justice for workers, women, and LGBTQ+ people, migrants, people of color, and sex workers, as well as for the natural world.

WHAT MIGRANT SEX WORKER JUSTICE IS NOT

THE ABOLITION OF SEX WORK

Some of those who support migrant sex workers still want to know whether, in a just world without poverty and patriarchy, there would be a sex industry and whether migrants would participate in it. Debates about the sex industry stall the work of building solidarity and subtly engage in victim blaming, by making the problem about the decision to sell sex and migrate, and not about policing, immigration control, the corporate exploitation of migrant labor, and mass containment / displacement through securitized borders. We do not know what would remain of the sex industry in a just world, but we do know that all labor would change beyond recognition, including labor in the sex industry.

The important thing to understand is that sex work and migration are not harms to be reduced or injustices to be abolished but strategies that low-income racialized migrants use to get what they need. In the here and now, migration and sex work help people stay alive and resist their circumstances. Building solidarity means that instead of engaging in theoretical debates about migrant sex work, we work together to transform the social and economic systems that actually oppress migrant sex workers.

REFORMING THE ANTI-TRAFFICKING INDUSTRY

Abolishing the anti-trafficking industry and the ideologies of "modern slavery" will require steady opposition, including reforms that delegitimize, shrink, and reduce its funding. But it's not always so clear which kinds of reforms would actually shrink the anti-trafficking industry and which ones would expand its reach. How can we tell the difference? One reform that we have seen many people advocate for is to shift the focus of the anti-trafficking industry so that it stops doggedly focusing on the sex industry and instead takes on the serious problem of labor exploitation and coercion outside the sex industry, in sectors such as farm labor, factories, and domestic work. We don't agree with the strategy of retaining the concepts, aims, and tools of the anti-trafficking industry but using them to address exploitation and abuse in nonsexual labor sectors. The anti-trafficking industry and its focus on criminalization and law enforcement are not the right tools to address exploitation and abuse in *any* labor sector. The goal must be to stop using anti-trafficking approaches entirely and use other noncarceral tools that can actually address the problem. Labor and migrant rights approaches provide many effective solutions, such as establishing legal immigration status for all. Ensuring that undocumented workers are not deportable would improve their power to resist exploitation, coercion, and abuse without having to involve the state. But reforming anti-trafficking work so that it includes nonsexual labor will not help. It is an anti-abolitionist reform that only expands the scope and legitimacy of the anti-trafficking industry, raising its access to funding, and credibility as a meaningful solution.

What about the good people in anti-trafficking organizations? There are well-intentioned people in anti-trafficking organizations who are fighting to make their organization more supportive of sex workers rights (or at least less harmful). And there are good anti-trafficking organizations that support many of the aims of migrant sex worker justice. Many people in the anti-trafficking industry privately confide to us that they are critical of the industry but remain affiliated with it, in spite of its harms, because leaving would mean risking the loss of their funding and a decision-making role on human trafficking law and policy. Viewing their work as harm reduction within an oppressive industry, they seek to change it from the inside. But the harms of anti-trafficking are structural and by design. Individuals cannot change this. They can, however, help to discredit and defund it. Anti-trafficking organizations should completely end their association with the anti-trafficking industry and instead dedicate themselves to the rights and power of oppressed workers and migrants (including migrant sex workers)—or they should not exist at all.

CONCLUSION

THE BUTTERFLY EFFECT

SOLIDARITY AND THE WORLD WE DREAM OF

Migrant sex workers are like matchsticks. Together they have the potential to become a massive fire that can burn the whole system down. Their creativity and fearlessness can transform society. People think that butterflies are small and insignificant. But because we are all interdependent, small changes can make a huge difference, taking us far from where we started. Change is not linear. By building solidarity, step by step, one person at a time, we can create the world we dream of, a new world where we never need to fight for justice for migrant sex workers.

SOLIDARITY WITH MIGRANT SEX WORKER MOVEMENTS

We've made the case in this book for why the broader left needs migrant sex worker organizing, as the movement's struggle for justice is critical to anti-policing, anti-capitalist, border, gender, and labor politics. We hope that people will see themselves as allies, and that they will also see migrant sex workers as part and parcel of a joint struggle against oppression. Of course, we need to center the voices of migrant sex workers in any work related to them. Also, our lives are connected. We need to fight together, and build movements together, as co-conspirators.

But solidarity does not naturally emerge only from the logical recognition that our fates are tied. It is skilled organizing work that takes support, study, mentorship, and evaluation. It must be built and sustained. This is especially important and difficult under circumstances where solidarity with migrant sex workers may come with intense backlash, including being accused of supporting violence and becoming a target of state repression. We want you to join us in taking action against the exploitation, abuse, and violence against migrant sex workers. And we want you to view migrant sex workers as part of the struggle for a transformed and liberated world. Here are ten ways to deepen your solidarity with migrant sex workers:

1. Start from a place of joint struggle, not saviorism. How does the oppression of migrant sex workers affect you and your community? Does it legitimize policing, immigration control, gentrification, white supremacist ideologies, the punishment of women or migrants who step out of line? Does it disguise the real causes of labor exploitation? Understand your common ground with migrant sex worker struggle and your shared interest in migrant sex worker liberation.

2. Understand before you act. Educate yourself about the diversity, oppression, and resistance of the migrant sex worker community, and particularly seek out the voices of those who are silenced by the mainstream media and social movements. Study the harms of the anti-trafficking industry so you can recognize and avoid replicating those harms.

3. Rethink your existing frameworks and view migrant sex workers through a justice lens. Listen to the stories of migrant sex workers, especially those who are the most marginalized and isolated. Learn their stories—not only their experiences of oppression, but also their power and their fight. Engage in political education about the role that systems of power play in migrant sex workers' lives so you can understand their context.

4. Share this book and the ideas within it with other people. Many people need the grassroots organizing context

and a critical understanding of migrant sex worker justice. The people with power keep dividing us, feeding us misinformation, and co-opting our movements. Keep bringing people into conversations that include migrant sex workers and recognize their importance in our communities and movements.

5.   Include migrant sex workers in activism. Leverage your resources and connections to include migrant sex workers in a wide diversity of social and economic justice movements. For example, campaigns to defund the police could include demands to defund anti-trafficking police units and keep the police out of migrant massage businesses. Include migrant sex workers in labor movements by demanding the decriminalization of sex work and the removal of immigration penalties against migrant sex workers. Include migrant sex workers in climate movements as people displaced by climate chaos and criminalized for their survival.

6.   Support migrant sex worker movements. Ask how you can be of service. For example, could you share office space, offer translation assistance, donate money, invite migrant sex workers to speak and publish on issues related to migration, gender justice, labor, racial justice, climate, or disability? Support migrant sex worker leadership and recognize that there are many forms of it. Support community organizing, mutual aid, and leadership building. Support accountable leaders—not self-appointed, class-privileged leaders but leaders who are actually connected to marginalized people in the community, who will speak up about and work to include the leadership of undocumented people, trans people, and so on. Support the whole leader—their political, economic, social, emotional, and material needs.

7.   Pay attention to power differences and tensions over power within and between communities. Systems of domination

such as white supremacy, colonialism, and class divide people within all movements, including the migrant sex worker movement. For example, be vigilant of the ways that the US and Canadian governments create a binary between the "good migrant" who is a "hard worker" and has legal status, and the "bad migrant" who is undocumented and works in the sex industry. Or consider how few disability community organizations acknowledge migrant sex workers even though the majority of migrant sex workers are disabled, and their sex work is their means of survival. Not recognizing these tensions takes our focus off changing the whole system and instead pits people against each other. By understanding where the tension comes from, we can build solidarity.

8.   Prepare to move outside your comfort zone regarding sex. It is very common for anti–sex work biases to surface among those who are building deeper relationships with sex workers. Ideas that it is "a pity that people have to do sex work" can surface when you view sex work as disgusting, immoral, and a threat to monogamous marriage, something that "no one would want for their own daughter," and so on. Your ideas about sexuality may be transformed by seeing how sex can just be a job.

9.   Build organizing skills. How we do the work is important, and organizing is a set of specific skills. Train in the areas of outreach, mutual aid, building relationships, making calls to politicians, and so on. Learn what to do when a door is closed to you. Exchange knowledge and learn with organizers from other social justice movements.

10.   Be creative and celebrate each small step; celebrate our friendships and connections with each other. Find moments of joy and cultivate a culture of appreciation. But-terfly's organizing is effective because we have so many creative ways to have fun, feel joyful, and break the barriers that people face in coming out about their work,

seeing possibilities, and challenging accepted wisdom about themselves. Creativity lets us challenge the rules, expectations, and practices that we are forced into. It can bring together people from diverse backgrounds to share knowledge with each other and learn.

Even though we have both been in this fight for so long, we still feel passion for this work and hope for change. We are seeing more people recognize the problems of policing and criminalization and join us, bringing imagination, hope, love, care, and transformative justice into our movement. So much of our work has been on the ground, where we see possibilities and imagine something that isn't yet tangible. We want to see more and more migrant sex worker organizing, all over the world. *Not Your Rescue Project* is a call to join migrant sex worker movements in their fight for justice and against state violence. Because our greatest power is when we come together. The migrant sex worker movement cannot be built without sex workers themselves, and it cannot get stronger without allies. We hope this inspires you to build bigger, more powerful movements for justice.

AFTERWORD

Robyn Maynard

This book has been a long time coming. I first met Elene and Chanelle well over a decade ago. It was the heyday of the sex worker–led struggle for decriminalization in Canada. Three sex workers—Terri-Jean Bedford, Amy Leibovitch, and Valerie Scott—were at the helm of a Supreme Court challenge that sought to over-turn three of the central criminal code statutes prohibiting sex work and related activities, on the premise that these laws violated sex workers' access to health, safety, and justice. It was an exciting and exhausting few years; sex workers and allied community and activist groups around the country were in a flurry of activity, ranging from legal education and media advocacy to popular education and end-less demonstrations. Elene and Chanelle, among many others, were tireless in meeting the demands of the moment, playing an import-ant role in drawing some of the crucial analytical and practical links between and across movements, insisting that decriminalization was one part of a much larger struggle to end the carceral webs in po-licing, immigration, and social work that circumscribe the lives of people who sell and trade sex to make a living. They have continued to refine and strengthen this analysis, including working together as Elene founded the incomparable grassroots, Toronto-based organi-zation Butterfly: Asian and Migrant Sex Workers Support Network, and leading and supporting a multitude of grassroots community campaigns with Butterfly members and allies to overturn violent and harmful immigration and criminal justice laws. Elene and Butterfly members have spent years doing outreach, running programming, coordinating services and rapid responses, managing petitions and phone trees and legal strategies, and so much more of the often invisible labor that makes movement work possible.

Readers are now fortunate to have their extensive knowledge articulated with clarity and integrity throughout the pages of this book. *Not Your Rescue Project* marks a crystallization of an incredible accumulation of movement labor and political thought spanning decades. The pages of this book shine with the wisdom gleaned from these years of struggle alongside migrant sex working communities and form a remarkable contribution: a feminist approach to sex worker justice that rejects empire, capitalism, policing, prisons, and the rest of the carceral state.

Not only does this text capture the wisdom gleaned from years of movement and community work, in addition to its trenchant analysis it also weaves firsthand experiences of migrant sex workers—Su, Lisa, Daisy, Blue, among others—into the narrative. These workers' experiences lay out plainly the human impacts of the "rescue" approach to sex work: eviction, loss of livelihood, confiscation of savings, deportation. The high stakes of the struggle at hand are readily apparent, as they draw attention to the lives, relationships, and families that have been violently interrupted by state intervention. And importantly, as the authors have illuminated for us, much of this suffering is inflicted at the behest of a highly dangerous but under-documented moral crusade: the increasingly well-funded behemoth that today calls itself the "anti-trafficking" movement.

Elene and Chanelle are unfortunately not the first to raise their voices against those who deign to "save" women at the barrel of a gun. There is no apparent upper limit to the evils that have been and continue to be justified under the banner of "rescuing" women and children, and some of the great cruelties of our times have been and are still being committed under the imperial guise of rescue. Between 1882 and 1968, white vigilantes lynched thousands of Black men. This brutality, sanctioned by the state, was justified, rationalized, and encouraged by invoking the protection of white women from the figure of the "Black male rapist." Britain's colonization of India, during which an estimated 100 million people died in just forty years, was justified in large part under the logic of rescue, famously described by Gayatri Spivak as "white men saving brown women from brown men."[1]

And post-9/11, Western leaders used the plight of Afghan women and girls to help justify a decades-long occupation of Afghanistan and kick off the Forever Wars on Terror that as of August 2023 have killed 940,000 and displaced 38 million people in and from Afghanistan, Iraq, Pakistan, Yemen, Somalia, the Philippines, Libya, and Syria.[2]

But much as the pattern repeats, the details are different. These differences matter. Elene and Chanelle have produced an important analysis of the growing "anti-trafficking" industry and its role in stoking a moral panic and in advancing legal and political pathways that dramatically expand the reach of policing and migration controls. We ought to be alarmed, the book makes clear, when evangelical Christian, far-right organizations, anti-LGBTQI+ and anti-abortion organizations, funded by the likes of Amazon and Boeing, come together to collectively rebrand as social justice organizations to demand change. The authors' intervention could not be more timely. Because, as they note, if this threat is coming from the right, its discourses and practices are, at times, being uncritically taken up by feminists and others on the left.

As Elene and Chanelle articulate in painstaking detail, today, the invocation of the faceless, nameless, hordes of "modern slavery victims" awaiting rescue relies on obfuscation. These women, spoken about but never speaking, serve as a blank slate through which a conservative social order can be articulated. Yet in *Not Your Rescue Project*, this obfuscation is interrupted. Migrant sex workers, and their struggles for labor rights, citizenship protections, mobility, and the ability to live and work in safety, come to the forefront.

And so, this text is a call for solidarity, and a call for feminist, labor, migrant, and racial justice movements on the left to do more, and to do better when it comes to supporting migrant sex workers, and people who sell and trade sex more broadly.

The authors insist that migrant sex workers' struggles ought to matter to labor organizers. They highlight that if we look beyond Victorian patriarchal morality that rejects migrant sex workers' status as workers, what is revealed is a highly vulnerable class of laborers. Ending criminalization (vis à vis sex work legislation) and illegalization (vis à vis immigration legislation) and supporting sex workers organizing toward workplace protections is a labor issue, and a crucial one at that.

The authors make clear that solidarity with migrant sex workers matters for feminists, particularly antiracist feminists. This is especially the case because so many attacks on sex workers' lives, bodies, and sexual autonomy are advanced *through the mantle of feminism*. Finally, solidarity with migrant sex workers matters for abolitionists. As Elene and Chanelle write:

> We want to challenge the narrative that abusing, caging, and threatening migrant sex workers with death is considered human trafficking when it is committed by non-state actors but legitimate, helpful, and fair when the police do it. . . . It is the police who enter [their] workplaces with guns pointed at their heads. It is the police who are authorized to shoot people to death for resisting an arrest or running from a raid. It is the police who are authorized to seize a sex worker's life savings. It is the police who are authorized to kidnap migrant sex workers and put them into [a cage]—in a prison, jail, or detention center. And it is the police who sexually extort and assault them with impunity.

Their work lays out an understanding of state violence that stands to deepen abolitionist analysis of state power as it traces carceral webs beyond policing that include municipal licensing and zoning regulations, immigration exclusions and travel bans, and the deputization of policing to the health care workers, airport employees, and everyday citizens who are increasingly interpellated by anti-trafficking campaigns to report suspected trafficking victims to the authorities.

It should go without saying that for those who have lived through the age of Ferguson and the Black, queer-led rebellions after the lynching of George Floyd, who have witnessed the mass caging of children and families at the US border, that any rescue project which uncritically begs for carceral state intervention ought to set off alarm bells. In the twenty-first century, there is no compelling argument left to be made, no more plausible reason to believe that any good will come from more policing or more and tighter migration controls, or yet another military intervention. *Not Your Rescue Project* is indeed not only a call for solidarity but a warning for the broader left. The expansion of carceral surveillance, law enforcement, and immigration powers advanced under the mantle of rescue deeply endanger migrant sex workers and will impact us all. This is readily apparent as forms of digital surveillance first used to monitor sex workers are now being applied to criminalize those seeking abortion.

Yet, of course, many of our communities are rightly concerned, as all ought to be, with real issues of sexual and gendered violence, forced labor, wage theft, sexual assault, nonconsensual sex, and degrading and unfree working conditions, in any industry and in any part of our society. So as any decent feminist, leftist, progressive ought to ask oneself, *What is to be done?*

The text does not shy away from this question: the authors are firmly committed to thinking about how to end violence and coercion, *including* that which emerges from or is legitimated by the carceral state. But as they remind us, those most concerned by the forms of oppression that the anti-trafficking crusaders pretend to solve are migrant sex workers themselves. So, if we are paying attention, the question is not so much "What is to be done?" but "How do we support the demands coming from migrant sex workers, and how do we integrate their struggles within our own liberatory imaginations?"

As Elene and Chanelle remind us: we do not need to pull these answers out of the sky. They turn us toward forms of safety and world-building that are already underway, as seen in Butterfly, Red Canary Song, and countless other organizations of workers and communities' self-organizing. They remind us that migrant sex workers have been at the forefront of an extensive array of projects—outreach, storytelling circles, health and legal clinics—that have created collective forms of labor to prevent violence, coercive labor practices, and wage theft, and have come together as workers to unionize. They show us that solidarity looks like supporting sex worker–led projects, including language classes, court support, bail support, decriminalization, status for all, and safe migration routes. It looks like challenging our preconceived notions around sexual and bodily autonomy, labor, and questioning our socially scripted racist and sexist understandings of who does and does not possess political agency. It looks like standing in solidarity with those on the forefront of creating the conditions for decent life.

And so, where we go from here depends on all our collective willingness to reinvigorate our political imaginations. It depends on whether we are willing to take up Elene and Chanelle's call to support migrant sex workers and to "envision new worlds and build new systems; and it is about the relationships between nations that become possible outside of police, prisons, borders, capitalism, and heteropatriarchy."

FURTHER READING

Below is a list of organizations and researchers whose work we recommend reading to understand more about the issues we've raised in *Not Your Rescue Project*. Resources and statements produced by organizations that are led by or support migrant sex workers include:

- Butterfly: Asian and Migrant Sex Workers Support Network (Toronto)
- Red Canary Song (New York City)
- Massage Parlor Outreach Project (Seattle)
- Canadian Alliance of Sex Work Law Reform (Canada)
- TAMPEP (European Network for HIV/STI Prevention and Health Promotion among Migrant Sex Workers)
- Empower Foundation–Thailand
- x:talk (London)
- Asian Migrant Sex Worker Advisory Group, convened by Scarlet Alliance (Australia)
- Migrant Rights Network (Canada)
- Global Network of Sex Worker Projects (www.nswp.org) – this website provides information about international sex worker organizing on every continent.

We also recommend materials written by or featuring (in alphabetical order) Laura Agustin, Lyndsey P. Beutin, Angela Y. Davis, Ann De Shalit, Elya Durisin, Melissa Gira Grant, Mariame Kaba, Julie Kaye Kamala Kempadoo, Emi Koyama, Robyn Maynard, Andrea Ritchie, Katrin Roots, Elena Shih, Emily van der Meulen, Harsha Walia, Ronald Weitzer, and Vincent Wong.

ACKNOWLEDGMENTS

We want to close by acknowledging the migrant sex and massage workers who are working, surviving, and fighting every day to chase a better future. We honor those who have lost their lives due to state violence or state-facilitated violence as we were working on this book. Our movement is filled with blood, tears, love, care, and power. We learn, fight, and struggle with each other. That's why we honor the workers we've met, those we've worked with for a long time, and those who appeared in our lives for just a moment. All of their stories are powerful, their struggle and their resistance move us. It's not easy to be a sex worker, especially a racialized migrant sex worker. There is tremendous stigma, a sense of responsibility for others, and oppression. But our experiences in community with migrant sex workers have shown us that no matter how oppressed people are, they are powerful and will fight for their autonomy and for a better life. Society teaches migrant women to stay put, but migrant sex workers inspire us with their courage and creativity. For us they are all important mentors, sisters, siblings, family and community members.

We'd like to thank the organizations and organizers whose work informs ours, and whom we interviewed for this book: Elena Shih, Esther K, Eunbi Lee, Yves Tong Nguyen, Yin Quan and Yoon Grace Ra of Red Canary Song; Liz Hilton of Empower Foundation–Thailand; Emi Koyama of Massage Parlor Outreach Project; Lyndsey P. Beutin; Nora Butler Burke of Action Santé Travesti(e)s et Transexuel(le)s du Québec (ASTT[e]Q); Purple Rose; and migrant sex worker organizers who wished to remain anonymous. Thank you to Kamala Kempadoo, Emily van der Muelen, Coly Chau, and Kai Cheng Thom for reviewing the manuscript and offering generous feedback.

Appreciations to those who supported us with transcriptions of interviews: Amy Lebovitch, Andrea Werhun, Meenakshi Mannoe, Hannah Harris-Sutro, and Jules Lippe-Klein.

We'd also like to thank the activists, community artists, and researchers who have supported Butterfly: Asian and Migrant Sex Workers Support Network, including Hussan Syed, Bei Xi, Mac Scott, Kelly Lui, Vincent Wong, Sandra Ka Hon Chu, Tara Santini, Loretta Mui, Elena Shih, Amanda De Lisio, Renee Dumaresque, Justin Kong, Brianna Greaves, Mariana Valverde, Jenn Clamen, Jenny Chan, Kara Gillies, Jenny Duffy, Ellie Ade Kur, Monica Forrester, Marcus McCann, Aliah El-houni, Mika Imai, Molly Bannerman, Karen Campbell, Diana Da Silva, Deena Ladd, Loly Rico, Rittika Goel, Patricia Ki, Randi Reynolds, Anna Willats, Anna Malla, Rick Sin, Lorraine Hewitt, Kristyn Wong-Tam, Josh Matlow, Lisa Nussey, Eshan Rafi, Kael, Kennis Lin, Deepa Mattoo, Hannia Cheng, Jessie Tang, Marry Gallatly, Bill Sinclair, Winnie Ng, Blyth Shulan Hunter, Harry Au, Chase Lo, Rain Chan Jessie Tang, Rui Liu, Sandra Wesley, Gemma, Jennifer Hompoth, Annie Chen, Vincent Wong, Amy Casipullai. Ming Zim, Karen Cocq, Sarom Rho, Katie LI, Fei Kuo, Peter, Deniqua Ewards, Karen Campbell, Eddie Fu, Kori, Evelyn Cheung, Israa Islam, Christina, Elaine Coburn, Bjorn Wagenpfeil, Katrin Roots, Ann De Shalit, Kamala Kempadoo, Molly Bannerman, Tracy Gregory, Alison Lam, Alice Cheng, Eric Li, Jared Wei-Yang Ong, Brenda Campbell, Brenda Doner, Jackie Esmonde, Ryan Chan, Rachel Tam, Yubo Wang, Sharon Chow, Rosel Kim, Vivian Leung, Lung Yu, Jasbina Misir, Laura, Bill, Anson, and so many more.

We'd like to thank organizations that have been strong allies to Butterfly from the beginning: Workers Action Centre, Migrant Workers Alliance for Change, HIV Legal Network, the Chinese Canadian National Council–Toronto, Stella-Montréal, Maggie's: Toronto Sex Workers Action Project, Canadian Alliance for Sex Work Law Reform, and the first organizers with the Migrant Sex Worker Project—Tings Chak, Brianna Greaves, Chelsie Mckee, and Renee Dumaresque.

We have hundreds of allies and cannot include them all here, but we want to mention the Migrant Rights Network, Asian Canadian Labour Alliance, No One Is Illegal–Toronto, No Pride in Policing Coalition, Barbra Schlifer Legal Clinic, Parkdale Community Legal Services, Showing Up for Racial Justice–Toronto, Friends of Chinatown, Toronto Chinatown Land Trust, the Community Justice Collective, the Women's Legal Education and Action Fund (LEAF), St. Stephen's Community House, TNG Community Services, HAMSMaRT, OHIP for All, South Asian Legal Clinic, Chinese and Southeast Asian Legal clinic, Migrant Workers Alliance for Change, Uninsured Health Network Clients, Rittenhouse, Santé Travesti(e)s et Transexuel(le)s du Québec (ASTT[e]Q), and many more organizations. You have given us so much to help us build and grow a powerful movement.

To Robyn Maynard and Harsha Walia—our comradeship and friendship with you over the years has deeply informed our work, our analysis, our strategy—and also our joy! It's with you that we dream bigger. We are honored to have your words in this book and to be building a shared analysis and movement with you both.

Thank you to Candida Hadley for your initial editorial support when this book was still a pile of ideas, and to the Haymarket Books team of Charlotte Heltai, Dao X. Tran, Jameka Williams, Anne Rumberger, and Julie Fain. Your support and feedback helped to make this book much clearer, more powerful. Thank you for nurturing it into existence. Thank you for everything you do to get grassroots movement analysis and organizing into print. We may never have written this if it weren't for your invitation.

We also want to appreciate two mentors whom we lost during the writing of this book—Carol Leigh and Liz Hilton. Carol Leigh created the term *sex work* in the late 1970s to push back on the stigma around sex work, and for over four decades, she used art, humor, and film to make multiple sex worker truths visible and to document and mentor sex worker movements. Liz Hilton was an Australian woman who worked with sex workers in Thailand for many decades as well. So many people go to Asia to observe and appropriate others' knowledge. But Liz, who was fluent in English and Thai, used her sense of humor, creativity, and language skills to bring the voices of Thai and migrant sex workers to the world, where they could speak for themselves. She was a force for solidarity who believed in the wisdom and power of the workers, saying, "Even if it takes a hundred years to advance decriminalization, we move forward one day at a time."

Elene: Thank you to Chanelle for your unwavering dedication and persistent efforts—day and night—in making this happen. Your role as a strong activist has significantly contributed to the growth of Butterfly and the migrant sex workers' movement.

I want to extend my heartfelt thanks to all the sex workers, organizers, activists, and mentors across the globe who have courageously shared their stories, inspired us, educated us, and continue to fight alongside us. Your strength, resilience, and dedication are a beacon of hope and change. You've shown us that together, we can challenge injustice and build a different world.

Special thanks are extended to the Butterfly team members and interns who have provided endless care and support to the migrant sex workers community: Alvis Choi, Anna Long, Arnie Li, Cici, Fian Poon, Garmen Chung, Hogan Lam, Jaden Peng, Keidan, Li Li, Lisa, Lorraine Chuen, Mary Lei, Mina Dao, Ming, Ping Tan, Princess Tauf, Ringo Chiu, Roxanne Chen, Starus Chan, Vanessa Wu, Veromi Arsiradam, Yan Chen, YY, and all of the interns and volunteers who have supported Butterfly.

A special acknowledgement to Nancy Sun, who was the first person to start outreach to migrant sex workers and has supported the development of Butterfly in Canada. I would also like to thank all the workers for their contributions to *Not Your Rescue Project*, including Su, Blue, Daisy, DM, Lisa, Linda, Mi, Niki, Sean, and Yi, who shared their important and powerful stories with us.

Chanelle: Thank you, Elene, for being such a brilliant organizer and friend. It has been a joy to make trouble with you as you built a movement by and for migrant sex workers in North America.

My gratitude to all the brazen, brilliant, and world-changing organizers, activists, movement scholars, and whores of all genders who have shaped my vision of liberation for over two decades.

I've been mentored and developed by more people than I could name, but let me at least shout out Empower Foundation–Thailand for taking me in as a volunteer so many years ago; the Catalyst Project for helping me to transform what I was learning on the ground into organizing; Critical Resistance for turning me into an abolitionist; revolutionary sex workers all over the world who radicalized me and taught me solidarity; and my comrades with Showing Up for Racial Justice, who have expanded my scope while tightening my strategy.

To the Butterfly community: your ability to organize under conditions of authoritarian state repression, through creativity, community, and care, is fucking phenomenal. It is an honor to have journeyed alongside you and helped bring your strategy and stories to the world.

Thank you to the friends and comrades who have talked through the ideas in this book with me (in alphabetical order): Grace Aheron, Dahlia Alé-Ferlito, Ivette Alé-Ferlito, Blyth Barnow, Ava Bynum, Alex Cafarelli, Leah Jo Carnine, Woods Ervin, Monica Forrester, Brianna Greaves, Joss Greene, Audrey Huntley, Rahula Janowski, Elisabeth Long, Jon McPhedran-Waitzer, Hilary Moore, Shannon Perez-Darby, Arti Mehta, kiran nigam, Kathryn Payne, Kai Cheng Thom, Jennifer Maldonado Tooley, Carla Wallace, Donna Willmott & Rob McBride, Kate Zen and to everyone who has invited us to speak in their classrooms, on their podcasts, published our ideas in magazines, and shared your insights and analysis with us. Thank you to Turner Willman for being such a believer in this book, providing practical support at its every stage and championing migrant sex workers justice in abolitionist spaces. To my family—the first people to teach me about sex working moms, the dangers of criminalization and the why of abolition. To my beloved Sunny Drake, my co-adventurer in everything, for keeping me alive, loved, and in my purpose.

APPENDIX

STOP BILL 251 PETITION

APRIL 2021

STOPPING FORD'S COVERT EXPANSION OF POLICING

Ontarians watched in disbelief and horror as Premier Doug Ford exploited the deadly third wave of COVID-19 to reinstate the racist and reprehensible practice of carding. Many have sprung into action to resist. But outside of public scrutiny, Premier Ford continues to expand policing powers in Ontario in other ways.

Ontario's Bill 251 is named the Combating Human Trafficking Act, but this law will do nothing to prevent human trafficking. Bill 251 will only expand police powers to racially profile all residents while targeting sex workers. Because the law is framed as being about "protection" and "combating human trafficking," Bill 251 has thus far escaped scrutiny despite its dangerous and far-reaching consequences.

Bill 251 gives unchecked power to police and a new cadre of "inspectors"—including the ability to conduct sweeping surveillance with no oversight. This will put more Black, Indigenous, and racialized communities, especially migrants, youth, women, and sex workers, at risk. These powers include:

1. The power of the government to appoint provincial inspectors for the purposes of this law, who "may, without a warrant or notice, and at any time, enter and inspect any place" to determine compliance with the law and

its regulations (regulations will be created once the law has passed).

2. Unfettered powers for these inspectors to examine, demand, remove, or copy any "thing that is or may be relevant to the inspection."

3. The power to "question a person on any matter that is or may be relevant to the inspection, including questioning a person separate from others." Noncompliance is a punishable offense, subject to a fine of $50,000 or $100,000 for an individual or corporation, respectively, violating protections against self-incrimination.

4. Hotels and other rentals (including possibly AirBnBs) are required to record all guest information. This information must be shared with the police if demanded, potentially without any court order.

5. Expanded power for law enforcement and child protection workers to detain youth under the age of eighteen (including sixteen to seventeen-year-olds) under this Act "for their protection" and force them to receive social services.

6. Sex workers are being targeted by law enforcement, making it more difficult to work safely.

These additional law enforcement powers reinforce the conflation of sex work and human trafficking, and in doing so, allow police to further criminalize sex workers and surveil and harass communities associated with sex work. Our communities have spoken out against the harms of criminalization and demand the decriminalization of our work. In Ontario and across the country, people increasingly support the call to #DefundThePolice and #AbolishingPolice, yet this bill does exactly the opposite, expanding the budget as well as the scope of policing. This bill is a step in the wrong direction and allows police, inspectors, and social workers to target, surveil, and forcibly detain us under the guise of claiming to "protect" and "rescue" us.

We call on all Ontario provincial political parties and Members of Provincial Parliament to reject Bill 251. We call on Ontario to stop

the expansion of policing, defund police services, and redirect resources toward marginalized communities. We further call on Ontario to adopt a human rights–based approach to human trafficking
that centers labor rights, migrant rights, and sex workers' rights, addressing numerous structural barriers including poverty, precarious
immigration status, and lack of access to affordable housing, health,
and social services that contribute to the risks of human trafficking.

NOTES

FOREWORD

1. Kate Zen, "In Defense of Sex Worker Rights," Medium, August 13, 2020, https://medium.com/@katezenjoy/dear-esperanza-5aa7db4d501a.
2. *Money for Prostitutes Is Money for Black Women* (Black Women for Wages for Housework, New York: 1975), https://freedomarchives. org/Documents/Finder/DOC46_scans/46.GenderAndSexuality. MoneyforProstitutes.Web.pdf.

INTRODUCTION: A RADICAL REFRAMING OF SEX WORK, MIGRATION, AND JUSTICE

1. Elene Lam and Starus Chan, "Letter: Bylaw 'Taking Terrible Toll' on Asian Massage Workers," *NewmarketToday*, August 13, 2022, www. newmarkettoday.ca/letters-to-the-editor/letter-bylaw-taking-unbearable-toll-on-asian-massage-workers-5692790.
2. We use the terms *sex trafficking* and *modern slavery* interchangeably. Some scholars have argued that there should be a more theoretically clear distinction between them—or to drop the term *modern slavery*. But we believe that neither concept is useful. Both terms falsely conflate sex work and migration with exploitation and violence, and thus harm migrant sex workers.
3. We define the carceral state as "the governing and legal institutions, as well as the policies and practices that organize and enact capture, punishment, and policing. The carceral state normalizes gendered antiblackness and racial-colonial violence while simultaneously maintaining these as the foundational conditions required for social order and racial capitalism. The contemporary carceral state shapes dominant notions of peace and safety through 'law and order' rhetoric and policy. This makes things like the weaponization of the law, the asymmetrical violence of policing, and cultures of gendered racial criminalization not exceptions, but fundamental functions of the state. The carceral state maintains order by isolating

and immobilizing targeted people and communities. This 'carceral' incapacitation includes but is not limited to: jails, prisons, detention centers, psychiatric facilities, parole, probation, electronic monitoring, public registries, and databases. The contemporary carceral state is deeply historical; it inherits, updates, and deploys the carceral structures of the slave ship, plantation, frontier, and apartheid order as part of its current approaches to captivity." *Resource Guide for Teaching and Learning Resistance*, Critical Resistance, August 2021, https://criticalresistance.org/wp-content/uploads/2021/08/CR_GuideforTeachingLearningAbolition-1.pdf.

4. When we say "leftist," we mean organizations and individual activists that support economic, racial, gender, migrant, and climate justice and an end to hierarchies of dominance and exploitation. This includes those working to end policing and prisons, to redistribute wealth, and to end labor exploitation (including socialist, labor, and union organizations). We also mean movements for Indigenous sovereignty working to end colonization and imperialism.

5. For example, in February 2023, police in Kentucky announced that they had laid human trafficking charges against three people ages forty-eight to sixty-nine associated with migrant massage spas after a yearlong surveillance campaign, initiated by a letter from a "concerned community member." Police described how one spa worker's use of a hot plate to cook and the fact that they had slept on the floor as evidence of human trafficking. "Bardstown Massage Parlor Busts: Police Describe 'Deplorable' Conditions for Trafficked Victims," WLKY, February 9, 2023, www.wlky.com/article/bardstown-kentucky-spa-massage-trafficking-prostitution/42814103. As we discuss later in this book, many nonprofits and government agencies train the public and service-sector workers on the "red flags" to watch out for as indicators of human trafficking, which are actually indicators of low-income migrants living where they work, such as using a hot plate to cook (instead of a full-sized kitchen) and sleeping without a bedframe. This has led to increased civilian reports of migrant sex work to the police. The risk of being reported to the police drives migrant sex workers further underground and away from support, and it increases their exposure to arrest, detention, deportation, and police abuse. See SWAN Vancouver, "Re-thinking Red Flags in Anti-trafficking Campaigns," 2022, https://swanvancouver.ca/wp-content/uploads/2023/11/Rethinking-Red-Flags-1.pdf.

6. For more information on SB 1718, which criminalized assisting

undocumented migrants in Florida, see: Florida Farm Workers, "FWAF Statement: Passing of Immigration Bill SB1718–HB1617," May 11, 2023, https://floridafarmworkers.org/articles/fwaf-statement-passing-of-immigration-bill-sb1718-hb1617/. For more information on the ongoing criminalization of abortion and the aiding of abortion in the US, see "Self-Care, Criminalized: Preliminary Findings," If/When/How, www.ifwhenhow.org/resources/self-care-criminalized-august-2022-preliminary-findings/.

7. "Groups File Motion in Lawsuit to Block Florida's Anti-Immigrant Law SB 1718," American Immigration Council, June 7, 2023, https://www.americanimmigrationcouncil.org/news/groups-file-motion-lawsuit-block-florida%E2%80%99s-anti-immigrant-law-sb-1718; "The Authoritarian Agenda Behind the Scheme to Attack Democracy and Abortion in Ohio," American Civil Liberties Union, July 12, 2023, https://www.aclu.org/news/reproductive-freedom/the-scheme-to-attack-democracy-and-abortion-in-ohio.

8. The inadmissibility prohibitions in the US specific to prostitution read: "Any person coming to the United States to engage in prostitution, or any person who has engaged in prostitution within ten years of his or her application for a visa, adjustment of status, or entry into the United States, is inadmissible. This section also applies to those who have made a profit from prostitution." US Citizenship and Immigration Services, "Inadmissibility and Waivers," www.uscis.gov/sites/default/files/document/foia/Inadmissibillity_and_Waivers.pdf. For more on the history of anti–sex work travel bans in the US and Canada, see Julie Kaye, *Responding to Human Trafficking: Dispossession, Colonial Violence and Resistance among Indigenous and Racialized Women* (Toronto: University of Toronto Press, 2017); Kamala Kempadoo and Elena Shih, eds., *White Supremacy, Racism and the Coloniality of Anti-trafficking* (New York: Routledge, 2023).

9. Denise Brennan, "Securing Rights and Seeking Justice in the US Deportation Regime," *S&F Online* 11, nos. 1–2 (Fall 2012 and Spring 2013), https://sfonline.barnard.edu/securing-rights-and-seeking-justice-in-the-us-deportation-regime/; Elena Shih, "The Trafficking Deportation Pipeline: Asian Body Work and the Auxiliary Policing of Racialized Poverty," *Feminist Formations* 33, no. 1 (Spring 2021): 56–73.

10. Red Canary Song, Massage Parlor Outreach Project, and Butterfly, with Bowen Public Affairs and Brown University Center for the Study of Slavery and Justice, *Un-licensed: Asian Migrant Massage Licensure*

and the Racialized Policing of Poverty, February 2022, https://static1. squarespace.com/static/61b809cc1599c2368549b018/t/622001964c0 ea93d1649303c/1646264732351/2022_Un-Licensed.pdf. *Un-licensed* was a collaboration between Butterfly, Red Canary Song, and Massage Parlor Outreach Project, coordinated by Professor Elena Shih at Brown University's Simmon's Center for the Study of Slavery and Justice.

11. Wilfred Chan, "The Police See Us as Disposable: What Life's Really Like in New York's Maligned 'Red Light District,'" *Guardian*, August 3, 2023; Elizabeth Nolan Brown, "Sex Work and Civil Asset Forfeiture Increasingly Go Hand in Hand," *Reason*, August 28, 2015, https:// reason.com/2015/08/28/asset-forfeiture-for-sex-workers/.

12. In the US, communication for the purposes of prostitution—or which aids and abets prostitution—is criminalized under many statutes including SESTA / FOSTA (Stop Enabling Sex Traffickers Act and Fight Online Sex Trafficking Act). In Canada, such communication is criminalized through PCEPA (Protection of Communities and Exploited Persons Act).

13. Judy Fudge et al., *Caught in the Carceral Web: Anti-trafficking Laws and Policies and Their Impact on Migrant Sex Workers*, Butterfly: Asian and Migrant Sex Workers Support Network, 2021, www.butterflysw. org/_files/ugd/5bd754_71be1154f6ff4bbb94a03ed7931a32df.pdf. For example, police in a city close to Toronto (Hamilton, Ontario) collaborated with border control and municipal licensing to ticket Asian workers in immigrant massage businesses, who were then deported. "Project Orchid Takes Aim at Illegal Massage Parlours," Hamilton Police Service, June 3, 2019, https://hamiltonpolice.on.ca/ news/project-orchid-takes-aim-at-illegal-massage-parlours/.

14. For a brief summary of "third party" laws, see Canadian Alliance for Sex Work Reform, *Criminalizing Third Parties in the Sex Industry: Impacts and Consequences*, June 2015, https://sexworklawreform.com/wp-content/uploads/2017/05/Third-Parties.pdf; and Global Network of Sex Work Projects, "Policy Brief: The Decriminalisation of Third Parties," 2016, www.nswp.org/resource/nswp-policy-briefs/policy-brief-the-decriminalisation-third-parties.

15. See Jenn Clamen, Kara Gillies, and Trish Salah, "Working for Change: Sex Workers in the Union Struggle," in *Selling Sex: Experience, Advocacy and Research on Sex Work in Canada*, ed., Emily van der Meulen, Elya M. Durisin, and Victoria Love (Vancouver: University of British Columbia Press, 2013), chapter 8.

16. See, for example, the ways that migrant sex workers were excluded from

government COVID supports: Elene Lam et al., "The Double-Edged Sword of Health and Safety: COVID-19 and the Policing and Exclusion of Migrant Asian Massage Workers in North America," *Social Sciences* 10, no. 5 (2021): 157; and Cecilia Benoit and Róisín Unsworth, "COVID-19, Stigma, and the Ongoing Marginalization of Sex Workers and Their Support Organizations," *Archives of Sexual Behavior* 51 (2022): 331–42, https://link.springer.com/article/10.1007/s10508-021-02124-3.

17. Red Canary Song, "Red Canary Song Responds to Shooting at Gold Massage Spa, Young's Asian Massage, and Aroma Therapy Spa," March 2021, https://docs.google.com/document/d/1_Q0mFJnivTZL5fcCS7eUZn9EhOJ1XHtFBGOGqVaUY_8/edit.

18. "Remarks by President Trump in Meeting on Human Trafficking on the Southern Border," White House, January 11, 2019, https://trumpwhitehouse.archives.gov/briefings-statements/remarks-president-trump-meeting-human-trafficking-southern-border/.

19. Jaco Booyens, "We Need Cops to Catch Sex Traffickers," *Newsweek*, June 23, 2020, www.newsweek.com/we-needs-cops-catch-sex-traffickers-opinion-1512638.

20. Sara Jean Greene, "Major Prostitution Bust: Seattle Police Raid 11 Massage Parlors, Freeing 26 Women," *Seattle Times*, March 7, 2019.

21. MPOP and Chinatown International District Coalition, "Solidarity with Massage Parlor Workers Means Ending Police Raids and Patrols in the CID," Coalition for Rights and Safety, March 2021, http://rightsandsafety.org/solidarity-with-massage-parlor-workers-means-ending-police-raids-and-patrols-in-the-cid.

22. Interview between Chanelle Gallant and community member, October 2023. They have asked to remain anonymous.

23. Shantae Rodrigues, "Sex Trafficking and Abortion: The Silent Public Health Crisis," Focus on the Family, August 30, 2021, www.focusonthefamily.com/pro-life/sex-trafficking-and-abortion-the-silent-public-health-crisis/.

24. Alison Bass, "Group That Opposes Sex Work Gave Money to Prosecutors' Offices—and Got Stings against Johns in Return," *Intercept*, March 24, 2018, https://theintercept.com/2018/03/24/demand-abolition-sex-work-nonprofit-prosecutors-king-county/.

25. To learn more about the harms of anti-trafficking measures on sex workers around the world, see *The Impact of Anti-trafficking Legislation and Initiatives on Sex Workers Policy Brief,* Global Network of Sex Work Projects. https://www.nswp.org/sites/default/files/impact_of_anti-

trafficking_laws_pb_nswp_-_2018.pdf. Or visit the Global Network of Sex Workers Projects website (nswp.org) and search under any country or region for reports from sex work organizations in that area.

26. For the impacts of the US led war on women in Afghanistan, and the organizing of Revolutionary Association of the Women of Afghanistan, see *Afghan Feminists Told Us War Wouldn't Free Them,* Sonali Kolhatkar, Yes! Magazine, August 24, 2021, https://www.yesmagazine.org/opinion/2021/08/24/afghanistan-taliban-women-feminists.

CHAPTER 1: WHO ARE MIGRANT SEX WORKERS?

1. See World Migration Report 2022, by the International Organization for Migration, https://publications.iom.int/books/world-migration-report-2022

2. Global Network of Sex Work Projects, "Policy Brief: Sex Work and Gender Equality," 2017, www.nswp.org/sites/default/files/policy_brief_sex_work_and_gender_equality_nswp_-_2017.pdf.

3. Our definition of motherhood includes transgender women who care for and protect chosen families comprising younger trans people. Parenthood includes all those who help young people to survive and thrive.

4. This is consistent with research showing that sex workers in general are more likely to be chronically ill or disabled. In the 2020 report *Erased: The Impact of FOSTA-SESTA*, 50 percent of sex workers surveyed reported having a disability or chronic illness, most commonly "invisible disabilities" such as chronic pain and autoimmune conditions. Danielle Blunt, Ariel Wolf, and Naomi Laren, *Erased: The Impact of FOSTA-SESTA*, hacking//hustling, 2020, https://hackinghustling.org/erased-the-impact-of-fosta-sesta-2020/. See also *Sex Work as Resistance to Marginalization—Lessons from Black Feminist Theory, Disability Justice and Black-Led Sex Worker Organizing.* Zee Xaymaca, *Disability Studies Quarterly* 42, no. 2 (Spring 2022).

5. Siobhan Brooks, "Innocent White Victims and Fallen Black Girls: Race, Sex Work, and the Limits of Anti–sex Trafficking Laws," *Signs: Feminist Frictions,* July 6, 2020, http://signsjournal.org/feminist-frictions-innocent-white-victims-and-fallen-black-girls/. Jasmine Sankofa, "From Margin to Center: Sex Work Decriminalization Is a Racial Justice Issue." Amnesty International USA, December 12, 2016, www.amnestyusa.org/frommargin-to-center-sex-work-

decriminalization-isa-racial-justiceissue/.

6. Quoted in Empower Foundation, *Hit and Run: The Impact of Anti-trafficking Policy and Practice on Sex Workers' Human Rights in Thailand* (Nonthaburi: Empower University Press, 2012).

7. Collected by Butterfly: Asian Migrant Sex Workers Support Network in 2018.

8. Collected by Butterfly: Asian Migrant Sex Workers Support Network in 2018.

9. This story was first published in Butterfly Asian and Migrant Sex Workers Support Network, "Four Asian Massage Parlour Workers Speak Out to Stop the Town of Newmarket Shut Down the Asian Massage Parlours," June 2021, www.butterflysw.org/_files/ugd/5bd754_96f07f41bc71421ba60c24718f28f9af.pdf.

CHAPTER 2: WHY MIGRANTS SELL SEX

1. Pluma Sumaq, "A Disgrace Reserved for Prostitutes: Complicity and the Beloved Community," *Lies* 2 (August 2015): 11–24, www.liesjournal.net/pluma-sumaq.html.

2. Harsha Walia, "'Perfected in Canada': The Racist Exploitation of Migrants; an Interview with Harsha Walia on Border Imperialism in Canada," *Breach*, October 28, 2021, https://breachmedia.ca/perfected-in-canada-the-racist-exploitation-of-migrants/; Fay Faraday, *Profiting from the Precarious: How Recruitment Practices Exploit Migrant Workers*, Metcalf Foundations, April 2014, https://metcalffoundation.com/publication/profiting-from-the-precarious-how-recruitment-practices-exploit-migrant-workers/.

3. "Temporary Foreign Workers: Your Rights Are Protected," Employment and Social Development Canada, Government of Canada, www.canada.ca/en/employment-social-development/services/foreign-workers/protected-rights.html.

4. Harsha Walia, *Border and Rule: Global Migration, Capitalism, and the Rise of Racist Nationalism* (Chicago: Haymarket Books, 2021); Ali Raza, "Jamaican Migrant Workers in Ontario Pen Open Letter Likening Conditions to 'Systemic Slavery,'" CBC News, August 20, 2022, https://www.cbc.ca/news/canada/toronto/jamaican-migrant-workers-open-letter-1.6557678.

5. "Globally, most cisgender women who sell sex (commonly referred to as female sex workers, or FSW) are also mothers," from Danielle Friedman Nestadt, Ju Nyeong Park, Noya Galai, S. W. Beckham,

Michele R. Decker, Jessica Zemlak, and Susan G. Sherman, "Sex Workers as Mothers: Correlates of Engagement in Sex Work to Support Children," *Global Social Welfare* 8, no. 3 (September 2021): 251–261, https://www.ncbi.nlm.nih.gov/pmc/articles/PMC10019358/. A reminder that we include transgender women in our understanding of motherhood. More research is required on the number of transgender sex workers who are informal adoptive caregivers to younger transgender people. For more details on sex workers and disability, see chapter 1: "Who Are Migrant Sex Workers?"

6.   In exchange for their cut of the sex workers' wages, business owners typically pay for the cost of the workplace and utilities (water, heat, phones, lights), housekeeping and janitorial services, advertising, reception, security, city licenses, insurance, and any building maintenance and repairs. Some anti–sex work interests consider this arrangement inherently exploitative. But in our experience, sex workers do not consider businesses inherently exploitative and instead differentiate between bad workplaces, where owners provide little in exchange (such as not keeping the building in good shape or offering good security), and good workplaces, where owners provide adequate support in exchange for their cut.

7.   Lin Lean Lim, ed., *The Sex Sector: The Economic and Social Bases of Prostitution in Southeast Asia* (Geneva: International Labour Office, 1998).

8.   "25 percent of live-in workers had responsibilities that prevented them from getting at least five hours of uninterrupted sleep at night during the week prior to being interviewed." Linda Burnham and Nik Theodore, *Home Economics: The Invisible and Unregulated World of Domestic Work*, National Domestic Workers Alliance, 2012, www.domesticworkers.org/wp-content/uploads/2021/06/HomeEconomicsReport.pdf.

9.   Lienne Dagger, "I'm Reclaiming My Power in a Violent World," JoySauce, March 16, 2022, https://joysauce.com/atlanta-shooting-asian-dominatrix-power-violent-world/.

10. We use the term "massage business" as an umbrella term that includes a range of businesses where workers provide hands-on massage. Some massage workers also provide sexual services, but most do not. The workers in massage businesses are usually not formally registered massage therapists, though some have extensive experience, training, and credentials from another country. Some massage businesses use a name that reflects the wording of their government license, such as "spa," "holistic center," "body rub parlor," "personal wellness center,"

or other terms.

11. We say "sexuality" here instead of "sex work" because people use their sexuality to meet their needs in many ways outside of the sex industry, such as marrying for economic security.

12. See, for example, the explosion in online sex work early in the COVID-19 pandemic. *The Year Sex Came Home,* Gabrielle Drolet, *New York Times*, April 10, 2020, https://www.nytimes.com/2020/04/10/style/camsoda-onlyfans-streaming-sex-coronavirus.html.

13. This is where we get the phrase "gay for pay." A man's decision to trade or sell sex to men does not require desiring them in his personal life.

14. Collected by Butterfly: Asian and Migrant Sex Workers Support Network in 2018.

15. Quoted from Elene Lam, *Behind the Rescue: How Anti-trafficking Investigations and Policies Harm Migrant Sex Workers*, Butterfly: Asian and Migrant Sex Workers Support Network, April 2018, https://www.butterflysw.org/_files/ugd/5bd754_bbd71c0235c740e3a7d444956d95236b.pdf.

16. Quoted from Lam, *Behind the Rescue.*

17. In the Canadian immigration system, a bondperson for someone in detention is an individual who is responsible for the detained person until their immigration case has concluded (usually through another arrest, a deportation order, or when the detained person gets legal residency). The bondsperson must be known to the detained person and is usually a family member or friend. Paid bondsmen are not legal in Canada.

CHAPTER 3: MIGRANT SEX WORKERS AND STATE VIOLENCE

1. Red Canary Song et al., *Un-licensed.*

2. Mandatory medical examinations of sex workers (or those who are profiled as sex workers) are another example of the kind of coercive public policies that many in the public think might be helpful to sex workers, but that actually *decrease* the health and safety of sex workers, their clients, and the public. Coerced medical examinations are not rooted in evidence, but in stigma. They rely on state surveillance and force, expanding criminalization by punishing workers who fail to comply with discriminatory regulations, especially those who are already criminalized for their immigration status. Migrant sex workers' health and safety is advanced when they have more power over their lives and work, not less. For more information on sex workers' sexual and reproductive health, see Global Network of Sex Work Projects, *Briefing Paper: Sex Workers'*

Access to Comprehensive Sexual and Reproductive Health Services, 2018; Ania Shapiro and Putu Duff, "Sexual and Reproductive Health and Rights Inequities among Sex Workers across the Life Course," in Sex Work, Health and Human Rights: Global Inequities, Challenges and Opportunities for Action, ed. S. M. Goldenberg, Thomas R. Morgan, A. Forbes, et al. (Cham, CH: Springer; 2021).

3.   This is described in "Fly in Power," directed by Yin Q and Grace Ra, YouTube video, https://www.youtube.com/watch?v=eTOE1pjdPME.

4.   Ivan Pereira, "Inside the Hunt into Border Patrol Agent Who Targeted Sex Workers," ABC News, November 17, 2023, https://abcnews.go.com/US/inside-hunt-border-patrol-agent-targeted-sex-workers/story?id=103833936.

5.   "Stories of Migrant Sex Workers," Butterfly: Asian and Migrant Sex Workers Support Network, 2019, www.butterflysw.org/_files/ugd/5bd754_b8357a1ec3b7482b9255294e85fa0a84.pdf.

6.   "HIV and Sex Work," *Lancet*, July 23, 2014, www.thelancet.com/series/HIV-and-sex-workers.

7.   "The Journey of Butterflies," Butterfly Asian and Migrant Sex Workers Support Network, 2016, https://www.butterflysw.org/_files/ugd/5bd754_6d9ddaec30e947efbef4e94b7e7ee828.pdf.

8.   Lam, *Behind the Rescue*.

9.   Chan, "'The Police See Us as Disposable'. . .".

10.   Jacob Geanous, Tina Moore, and Georgia Worrell, "This NYC Avenue Is Overrun by Brazen Brothels Operating in Broad Daylight, *New York Post*, July 29, 2023.

11.   Judith Levine, "Yes, Blame Christian Fundamentalism for the Atlanta Murders," *Intercept*, March 23, 2021, https://theintercept.com/2021/03/23/atlanta-shooting-sex-addiction-religion-morality/.

12.   Melissa Gira Grant, "Saying Never Again to the Violence in Atlanta Means Saying No to More Policing," *New Republic*, March 24, 2021, https://newrepublic.com/article/161792/atlanta-shooter-sex-worker-red-canary-song.

13.   Shanifa Nasser, "Toronto Spa Killer Pleads Guilty to Murder in Deadly Sword Attack, Cites Van Attacker as 'Inspiration,'" CBC News, September 14, 2022, www.cbc.ca/news/canada/toronto/incel-massage-parlour-guilty-1.6582534.

14.   Colin Freeze, "Toronto Man Pleads Guilty in 2020 Massage Parlour Attack," *Globe and Mail*, September 14, 2022, www.theglobeandmail.com/canada/toronto/article-toronto-man-pleads-guilty-in-2020-massage-parlour-attack/.

15.   Thank you to Joss Greene, PhD, for his helpful insights on this section

and extensive research on trans women, criminalization, and labor.

16. "In 2008, Cambodia introduced anti-trafficking legislation ostensibly designed to suppress human trafficking and sexual exploitation. The new law led to police crackdowns and brothel closures, prompting an exodus of female sex workers from brothels to entertainment and street-based sex work. While justified by Cambodian authorities as meeting international legal obligations to tackle sexual exploitation under the Palermo Protocol, the anti-trafficking law's effect was to infringe sex workers' right to health." Lisa Maher et al., "Conflicting Rights: How the Prohibition of Human Trafficking and Sexual Exploitation Infringes the Right to Health of Female Sex Workers in Phnom Penh, Cambodia," *Health and Human Rights* 17, no. 1 (2015): E102–E113, www.ncbi.nlm.nih.gov/pmc/articles/PMC6915836/.

17. H.R.1298–United States Leadership Against HIV/AIDS, Tuberculosis, and Malaria Act of 2003, Statute 734, May 27, 2003, https://www.congress.gov/bill/108th-congress/house-bill/1298/text, accessed December 1, 2023.

18. Sebastian Krueger, "A Striking Defeat for U.S. Government's Anti-Prostitution Pledge," February 24, 2015, https://www.opensocietyfoundations.org/voices/striking-defeat-us-government-s-anti-prostitution-pledge.

19. "The Economic Impact of the Fashion Industry," Joint Economic Committee, Democrats, February 22, 2019, https://www.jec.senate.gov/public/index.cfm/democrats/2019/2/the-economic-impact-of-the-fashion-industry.

20. Louise Voller, "Mass Faintings Afflict the Women Who Sew Our Clothes," Danwatch, June 25, 2017, https://danwatch.dk/en/undersoegelse/mass-faintings-afflict-the-women-who-sew-our-clothes-2/.

21. "'Work Faster or Get Out': Labor Rights Abuses in Cambodia's Garment Industry," Human Rights Watch, 2015, www.hrw.org/sites/default/files/reports/cambodia0315_ForUpload.pdf.

22. International Labour Organization, "How Is Cambodia's Minimum Wage Adjusted?," *Cambodian Garment and Footwear Sector Bulletin* 3, March 2016, www.ilo.org/wcmsp5/groups/public/---asia/---ro-bangkok/documents/publication/wcms_463849.pdf.

23. Maya Schenwar, "'Fast Fashion': Anne Elizabeth Moore on the Global Garment and Sex Trades," *Truthout*, July 17, 2016, https://truthout.org/articles/anne-elizabeth-moore-on-the-global-garment-and-sex-trades/.

24. Women's Network for Unity, www.wnu.unitedsisterhood.org/whoweare.php. This phrase has also been used by the Asia Pacific Network of Sex Workers.

CHAPTER 4: "WHITE SLAVERY" AND THE ROOTS
OF THE "MODERN SLAVERY" PANIC

1. Jean Turner Zimmermann, *Social Menace of the Orient: White or Yellow*,
    vol. 2 (n.p., 1921).
2. Quoted in Lorelei Lee, "The Roots of 'Modern Day Slavery': The Page Act
    and the Mann Act," *Columbia Human Rights Law Review* 52, no. 3
    (2021): 1199–1239.
3. Laura Lammasniemi, "'White Slavery': The Origins of the Antitrafficking
    Movement," openDemocracy, November 16, 2017, https://www.
    opendemocracy.net/en/beyond-trafficking-and-slavery/white-
    slaveryorigins-of-anti-trafficking-movement/; Mia Brett, "'Ten
    Thousand Bigamists in New York': The Criminalization of Jewish
    Immigrants Using White Slavery Panics," Gotham Center for New
    York City History, October 27, 2020, https://www.gothamcenter.org/
    blog/ten-thousand-bigamists-in-new-york.
4. Elizabeth Wheeler Andrew and Katharine C. Bushnell, *Heathen Slaves and
    Christian Rulers* (1907; repr., Teddington, UK: The Echo Library, 2006).
5. Mary Ting Yi Lui, "Saving Young Girls from Chinatown: White Slavery
    and Woman Suffrage, 1910–1920," *Journal of the History of Sexuality*
    18, no. 3 (2009): 393–417.
6. Eithne Luibhéid, *Entry Denied: Controlling Sexuality at the Border*
    (Minneapolis: University of Minnesota Press, 2002).
7. George Anthony Peffer, "Forbidden Families: Emigration Experiences of
    Chinese Women under the Page Act, 1875–1882," *Journal of American
    Ethnic History* 6, no. 1 (Fall 1986): 28–46.
8. Diana Lu, "Yang Song and the Long History of Targeting Asian American
    Sex Workers," *Hyphen*, August 28, 2019, https://hyphenmagazine.com/
    blog/2019/08/yang-song-and-long-history-targeting-asian-american-
    sex-workers.
9. Among the first people to be prosecuted under the White Slavery Traffic
    Act was Black boxing champion Jack Johnson, who was convicted
    for moving across a state border with a white sex worker. Historians
    describe this as retaliation for Johnson's open relationships with white
    women (he married white women) and his athletic superiority over
    white boxers. See Jessica R. Pliley, *Policing Sexuality: The Mann Act and
    the Making of the FBI* (Cambridge, MA: Harvard University Press, 2016).
10. Brian Donovan, *White Slave Crusades: Race, Gender, and Anti-vice
    Activism, 1887–1917* (Chicago: University of Illinois Press, 2006);
    Elizabeth Bernstein, *Brokered Subjects: Sex, Trafficking, and the Politics
    of Freedom* (Chicago: University of Chicago Press, 2018).

11. Kathleen Barry, "Female Sexual Slavery: Understanding the International Dimensions of Women's Oppression," *Human Rights Quarterly* 3, no. 2 (Spring 1981): 44–52.

12. Judy Klemesrud, "A Personal Crusade against Prostitution," *New York Times*, June 24, 1985, www.nytimes.com/1985/06/24/style/a-personal-crusade-against-prostitution.html.

13. Clyde Farnsworth, "200 Prostitutes of Lyons in Siege at Church," *New York Times*, June 7, 1975, www.nytimes.com/1975/06/07/archives/200-prostitutes-of-lyons-in-siege-at-church.html.

14. Kathleen Berry, *Female Sexual Slavery* (New York University Press, 1979), 3–4.

15. Donna M. Hughes, "The 'Natasha' Trade: Transnational Sex Trafficking." *NIJ Journal*, January 2001. https://www.ojp.gov/pdffiles1/jr000246c.pdf.

16. Elya Durisin and Robert Heynen, "Producing the 'Trafficked Woman': Canadian Newspaper Reporting on Eastern European Exotic Dancers during the 1990s," *Atlantis* 37, no. 2 (2015/2016): 8–24, https://journals.msvu.ca/index.php/atlantis/article/view/3907/pdf_19.

CHAPTER 5: "RED FLAGS": HOW THE ANTI-TRAFFICKING INDUSTRY SUPPORTS STATE VIOLENCE AGAINST MIGRANT SEX WORKERS

1. We want to lift up the small but important number of anti-trafficking organizations that support migrant sex workers' legal, labor, and migration rights, most notably the Global Alliance Against the Trafficking of Women. GAATW "sees the phenomenon of human trafficking intrinsically embedded in the context of migration for the purpose of labour." They do not exceptionalize migrant sex work as uniquely harmful, instead positioning the work within the broader context of migrant labor, stating that "GAATW therefore promotes and defends the human rights of all migrants and their families against the threat of an increasingly globalised labour market and calls for safety standards for migrant workers in the process of migration and in the formal and informal work sectors—garment and food processing, agriculture and farming, domestic work, sex work—where slavery-like conditions and practices exist." In our international advocacy, we have worked with and alongside GAATW and strongly value their work. However, the concept of "trafficking" is inherently problematic as it cannot be separated from an association with sex workers. This is why GAATW is so unique. We estimate that its members represent less than 1 percent of the anti-trafficking industry, which overwhelmingly

opposes the legal, labor, and migration rights of sex workers and migrant sex workers. For that reason, we call on anti-trafficking organizations that actually support sex workers to abandon the language and framework of "human trafficking" in favor of the frameworks that pursue labor rights, migrant rights, and sex worker rights.

2. Gregory Mitchell, *Panics without Borders: How Global Sporting Events Drive Myths about Sex Trafficking* (Oakland: University of California Press, 2022).

3. International Justice Mission, *Year in Review: Building a Safer World Together*, 2021, https://ijmstoragelive.blob.core.windows.net/ijmna/documents/22-IJM-YIR.pdf.

4. Annual Report, Polaris, 2021, https://polarisproject.org/wp-content/uploads/2022/10/Polaris-2021-Annual-Report.pdf; Erin Taylor, "Sex Workers Are at the Forefront of the Fight against Mass Surveillance and Big Tech," *Observer*, December 11, 2019, https://observer.com/2019/11/sex-workers-mass-surveillance-big-tech/.

5. "Alabama Drive-Thru Sex Toy Business on the Rise," CBS News, December 30, 2010, www.cbsnews.com/news/alabama-sex-toy-drive-thru-business-on-the-rise/; David Corn, "Gay Marriage Leads to Mass Murder?," *Mother Jones*, April 9, 2009, www.motherjones.com/politics/2009/04/gay-marriage-leads-mass-murder/.

6. "Patrick A. Truman, President," End Sexual Exploitation, https://endsexualexploitation.org/about/staff/patrick-trueman/5/; "Board of Directors," End Sexual Exploitation; https://endsexualexploitation.org/about/board/; Colleen Flaherty, "At Odds with Her University over Gender Identity," *Inside Higher Ed*, March 25, 2021, www.insidehighered.com/news/2021/03/25/professor-odds-her-university-over-gender-identity.

7. See WWE list of member organizations: https://www.worldwithoutexploitation.org/about; Benjamin Nolot, founder of Exodus Cry, https://www.opendemocracy.net/en/5050/revealed-christian-group-netflix-spring-break-sex/

8. Janice Raymond, *The Transsexual Empire: The Making of the She-Male* (Boston: Beacon Press, 1979, reissued in 1994 by Teachers College Press), 104, 178, https://janiceraymond.com/wp-content/uploads/2017/08/The%20Transsexual%20Empire.pdf.

9. In one of many such instances, a Christian anti-trafficking organization in Sangli, India, collaborated with the police on a brothel raid where officers assaulted ten sex workers who they dragged out by the hair. In their newsletter, the anti-trafficking organization described the raid as

a rescue of "minor girls" and featured a photo of a girl who appeared about four or five years old. Described in *We Have the Right Not to Be Rescued: When Anti-Trafficking Programmes Undermine the Health and Well-Being of Sex Workers,* Aziza Ahmed and Meena Seshu, Anti-Trafficking Review, https://doi.org/10.14197/atr.201219, Accessed May 19 2024.

10. "Human Trafficking Near Public Schools: How Close Is Human Trafficking to Your Child's School?," Children At Risk, April 2018, https://childrenatrisk.org/human_trafficking_near_schools/.

11. "Illicit Massage Business Toolkit," Children At Risk, March 8, 2022, https://childrenatrisk.org/imb-toolkit/.

12. "Human Trafficking Corridors in Canada," Canadian Centre to End Human Trafficking, February 2021, www.canadiancentretoendhumantrafficking.ca/wp-content/uploads/2021/02/Human-Trafficking-Corridors-in-Canada-Report.pdf.

13. "We Won't Stop until We End the Business of Modern Slavery for Good," International Justice Mission, www.ijm.org/our-work/trafficking-slavery.

14. For discussion about where the myth about the age of entry emerged and how it has been used to oppose human and labor rights for sex workers, see Chris Hall, "Is One of the Most Cited Statistics about Sex Work Wrong?," *Atlantic,* September 5, 2014, www.theatlantic.com/business/archive/2014/09/is-one-of-the-most-cited-statistics-about-sex-work-wrong/379662/; Fiona J. Trend-Cunningham and Kristine Jacquin, "Age of Entry into Sex Work Is a Myth," poster presented at the American College of Forensic Psychology conference, April 2018, www.researchgate.net/publication/324755230_Age_of_Entry_into_Sex_Work_is_a_Myth. There is extensive documentation of the pseudoscience of the anti-trafficking industry. We recommend Jennifer K. Lobasz, *Constructing Human Trafficking* (Cham: Palgrave Macmillan, 2019); Lyndsey P. Beutin, "Deceptive Empiricism," in *Trafficking in Antiblackness: Modern-Day Slavery, White Indemnity, and Racial Justice* (Durham, NC: Duke University Press, 2023); Kamala Kempadoo, Jyoti Sanghera, and Bandana Pattanaik, *Trafficking and Prostitution Reconsidered: New Perspectives on Migration, Sex Work and Human Rights* (New York: Routledge, 2012).

15. Beutin, *Trafficking in Antiblackness.*

16. Taina Bien-Aimé, "CATW ED Responds to the New York Times Article on Soros," Coalition Against Trafficking in Women, October 17, 2017, https://catwinternational.org/press/catw-ed-responds-to-the-new-

56 **NOT YOUR RESCUE PROJECT**

17. Tim Ballard, the founder of OUR, who was appointed by Donald Trump to a federal anti-trafficking council, is being sued by five former employees who describe how Ballard sexually assaulted them during OUR's operations. Biran Schott, "Allegations against Tim Ballard 'Ought to be Taken Seriously,' Utah A.G. Sean Reyes Says," *Salt Lake Tribune*, October 10, 2023, www.sltrib.com/news/politics/2023/10/10/allegations-against-tim-ballard/.

18. Dr. Elena Shih also brought our attention to another anti-trafficking organization founded by a white Christian woman called Truckers Against Trafficking, which created what they call the "Harriet Tubman Award," given to a trucker who contacts police about suspected sex trafficking. Truckers Against Trafficking promotes the criminalization of sex work and partners with multinational corporations like Amazon and Walmart, who have extensive records of labor exploitation, abuse, and union-busting.

19. "Polaris CEO, Catherine Chen, Appointed by DHS Secretary Mayorkas to Homeland Security Advisory Council," press release, Polaris, March 18, 2022, https://polarisproject.org/press-releases/polaris-ceo-catherine-chen-appointed-by-dhs-secretary-mayorkas-to-homeland-security-advisory-council/; Purple Rose (@PurpleRose0666), "Don't believe that National Human Trafficking hotline is a surveillance line that reports to ICE? Listen to an ICE agent explain it herself and how they use tips from the hotline for their investigations," X, June 24, 2021, https://x.com/purplerose0666/status/1407930051585208328?s=46.

20. Rita Trichur, "Sex Traffickers Are Using Shell Companies to Launder Illicit Profits in Canada, *Globe and Mail*, March 10, 2023, www.theglobeandmail.com/business/article-human-trafficking-shell-companies-money-laundering/.

21. Brittany Anthony, Jennifer Kimball Penrose, and Sarah Jakiel, "The Typology of Modern Day Slavery: Defining Sex and Labor Trafficking in the United States," Polaris, March 1, 2017, https://polarisproject.org/the-typology-of-modern-slavery/.

22. Polaris has since taken the report down, but its list of indicators can still be accessed at Stephanie Ebbert, "Signs of Illicit Massage Parlors, and What You Can Do," *Boston Globe*, April 27, 2019, www.bostonglobe.com/metro/2019/04/27/signs-trouble-and-what-about/z8pIHTrEbaM6XLzy6nf19K/story.html.

23. "For Law Enforcement," Canadian Centre to End Human Trafficking, www.canadiancentretoendhumantrafficking.ca/for-law-enforcement/.

24. Former CEO of the Canadian Centre to End Human Trafficking claimed that the organization was conducting its *own* investigation into the finances of the massage sector "to do a network analysis on the ownership of every holistic center in Toronto to uncover evidence of possible criminal intent and collusion amongst owners." Barbara Gosse, "Comments for Toronto Municipal Licensing and Standards Committee," Canadian Centre to End Human Trafficking, April 10, 2018, www.toronto.ca/legdocs/mmis/2018/ls/comm/communicationfile-79532.pdf.

25. Collected by Butterfly: Asian and Migrant Sex Workers Support Network in 2020.

26. As told to Chanelle Gallant in 2022.

CHAPTER 6: "CONSENT IS NOT RELEVANT": CRIMINALIZING MIGRANT SEX WORKERS

1. The conflation of sex work with violence continues to expand. For example, the US Department of Homeland Security is even starting to characterize "raising awareness about sex trafficking" as part of their counterterrorism efforts. Given that "sex trafficking" is a code for sex work (especially racialized sex work), this conflation could bring even more intense racialized surveillance and punishment to sex workers. See: *DHS Works with NFL, Nevada, and Las Vegas Partners to Secure Super Bowl LVIII*, February 7, 2024, https://www.dhs.gov/news/2024/02/07/dhs-works-nfl-nevada-and-las-vegas-partners-secure-super-bowl-lviii.

2. "7101: Purposes and Findings," in United States Code, Title 22–Foreign Relations and Intercourse, Chapter 78–Trafficking Victims Protection (US Government Publications Office, 2020), www.govinfo.gov/content/pkg/USCODE-2020-title22/html/USCODE-2020-title22-chap78-sec7101.htm.

3. Jo Doezema, "Who Gets to Choose? Coercion, Consent and the UN Trafficking Protocol," *Trafficking and Slavery* 10, no. 1 (March 2020): 20–27.

4. "Canada's Prostitution Laws," YouTube video, 5:02, posted June 15, 2011, https://www.youtube.com/watch?v=b3WlpN1Kdaw.

5. *An Analysis of Human Trafficking in the District of Columbia 2016*, page 4. https://cjcc.dc.gov/sites/default/files/dc/sites/cjcc/page_content/attachments/An%20Analysis%20of%20Human%20Trafficking%20in%20the%20District%20of%20Columbia%20%282016%29.pdf.

6. *Criminal, Victim or Worker? The Effects of New York's Human Trafficking Intervention Courts on Adults Charged with Prostitution Related Offenses,* Red Umbrella Project, October 2014, page 15. https://nyf.issuelab.org/resources/19277/19277.pdf.

7. Global Health Justice Partnership of the Yale Law School and Yale School of Public Health, Sex Workers Project of the Urban Justice Center, 2018, *Un-Meetable Promises: Rhetoric and Reality and New York City's Human Trafficking Intervention Courts.*

8. Collected by Butterfly: Asian and Migrant Sex Workers Support Network in 2020.

CHAPTER 7: THE POLICE ARE THE PREDATORS

1. Shree Paradkar, "Moral Panic over Sex Work Has Created Suffocating Prostitution Law," *Star,* October 6, 2022, www.thestar.com/opinion/star-columnists/moral-panic-over-sex-work-has-created-suffocating-prostitution-law/article_cc2bb837-a5bc-53a2-a5e6-11a2daa72a96.html.

2. Lam, *Behind the Rescue.*

3. Elizabeth Nolan Brown, "Sex Work and Civil Asset Forfeiture Increasingly Go Hand in Hand," *Reason,* August 28, 2015, https://reason.com/2015/08/28/asset-forfeiture-for-sex-workers/.

4. Richard L. Smith, "Edison Police Enforcement Action to Clean Up Route 27, Address Illegal Massage Parlors," RLS Media, December 15, 2022, www.rlsmedia.com/article/edison-police-enforcement-action-clean-route-27-address-illegal-massage-parlors.

5. Elena Shih, "The Racialized Policing of Human Trafficking in RI," *The Providence Journal,* June 24, 2021. https://www.providencejournal.com/story/opinion/columns/2021/06/24/opinion-shih-racialized-policing-human-trafficking-ri/7774233002/.

6. Lisa Duggan, "What the Pathetic Case against Rentboy.com Says about Sex Work," *The Nation,* January 7, 2016. https://www.thenation.com/article/archive/what-the-pathetic-case-against-rentboy-com-says-about-sex-work/.

7. Madison Pauly, "Massage Parlor Workers Say Policing Isn't the Answer to the Violence They Face," *Mother Jones,* March 19, 2021.

8. Henry Hess, "Toronto Sex Ring Not Alone," *Globe and Mail,* September 12, 1997, https://walnet.org/csis/news/toronto_97/gandm-970912.html.

9. Noulmook Suthibhasilp, Lillian Petroff, and Dora Nipp, *Trafficking in Women Including Thai Migrant Sex Workers in Canada,* Multicultural History Society of Ontario, June 2020,

www.mhso.ca/mhso/Trafficking_women.pdf.

10. Jamison Liang, "Atlanta Asian Massage Parlor Murders Are a Warning to the Anti-trafficking Sector," Open Democracy, March 29, 2021, www. opendemocracy.net/en/beyond-trafficking-and-slavery/atlanta-asian-massage-parlor-murders-are-warning-anti-trafficking-sector/.

11. Massage businesses that were investigated were more likely to be staffed by nonregistered, monolingual, working-class migrant women masseuses. Registered massage therapists—who are members of the Registered Massage Therapists' Association of Ontario, which is predominantly white—were not subject to investigations.

12. Elene Lam, *Survey on Toronto Holistic Practitioners' Experiences with Bylaw Enforcement and Police*, Butterfly: Asian and Migrant Sex Workers Support Network, May 2018, https://www.butterflysw.org/_files/ugd/5bd754_6d780ceba3cb4f6c85de4d3e9e0b7475.pdf.

13. Interview with Butterfly, 2018.

14. Lam, *Survey on Toronto Holistic Practitioners Experiences*.

15. Story collected by Butterfly: Asian and Migrant Sex Workers Support Network in May 2021.

16. "Safety for All, Respect for All: Protecting the Safety of Workers in Holistic Centres and Body Rub Parlours by Allowing Them to Lock Their Doors," Butterfly: Asian and Migrant Sex Workers Support Network, https://576a91ec-4a76-459b-8d05-4ebbf42a0a7e.filesusr.com/ugd/5bd754_50b08bb810734d928a0ead40faf0dca1.pdf.

17. "The Journey of Butterflies," Butterfly: Asian and Migrant Sex Workers Support Network, 2016.

18. "Stories of Migrant Sex Workers," Butterfly: Asian and Migrant Sex Workers Support Network, 2019, https://www.butterflysw.org/_files/ugd/5bd754_b8357a1ec3b7482b9255294e85fa0a84.pdf. One of the many discriminatory regulations facing massage workers in Toronto (and in other jurisdictions) are broad and discriminatory regulations regarding the clothing they are permitted to wear. In Toronto, some types of massage licenses specify that workers' clothing must be "professional," but what this means is open to interpretation by municipal officers and the courts. And there is no rationale for why massage workers are subjected to this rule but registered massage therapists (who are mostly white) are not. In practice, this regulation grants municipal officers with another tool they can use to harass and sexually abuse massage workers by ordering them to undress during investigations so they can "inspect" the workers' underwear for its "professionalism." In some cases, like with Niki, officers will issue

citations to massage workers for their clothing, even when they have just survived an attempted rape.

19. Meredith Dank et al., *Surviving the Streets of New York: Experiences of LGBTQ Youth, YMSM, and YWSW Engaged in Survival Sex*, Urban Institute, February 25, 2015, www.urban.org/research/publication/surviving-streets-new-york-experiences-lgbtq-youth-ymsm-and-ywsw-engaged-survival-sex.

20. https://www.cbsnews.com/sanfrancisco/news/kpix-exclusive-teenage-woman-oakland-police-sex-scandal-speaks/.

21. Shira Hassan, *Saving Our Own Lives: A Liberatory Practice of Harm Reduction* (Chicago: Haymarket Books, 2022), 20.

CHAPTER 8: THE LEFT AND MIGRANT SEX WORKERS

1. Purple Rose (@purplerose0666), "AF3IRM LITERALLY PAINTED TARGETS on Century Center's Asian Massage Parlors that employed undocumented workers who were targets of ICE raids," X, June 19, 2021, https://x.com/PurpleRose0666/status/1406371832119320576?s=20.

2. Rick Daysog, "Condoms, Other Personal Items Found in Waikiki Massage Parlor Raid," *Hawaii News Now*, May 10, 2020, www.hawaiinewsnow.com/2020/05/09/condoms-other-personal-items-found-waikiki-massage-parlor-raid/; Rick Daysog, "Honolulu Prosecutors Raid Another Century Center Massage Parlor," *Hawaii News Now*, May 25, 2020, www.hawaiinewsnow.com/2020/05/25/honolulu-prosecutors-raid-another-century-center-massage-parlor/.

3. Lynn Kawano, "Honolulu's New City Prosecutor Stops Massage Parlor, Prostitution Raids," *Hawaii News Now*, May 28, 2021, https://www.hawaiinewsnow.com/2021/05/29/honolulus-new-prosecutor-stops-massage-parlor-prostitution-raids/.

4. Melissa Farley and Vanessa Kelly, "Prostitution: A Critical Review of the Medical and Social Sciences Literature," *Women and Criminal Justice* 11, no. 4 (2000): 29–64, www.prostitutionresearch.com/Farley_Kelly%20Prostitution_A%20Critical%20Review%20of%20the%20Medical%20and%20Social%20Sciences%20Literature.pdf.

5. Kate Zen, "In Defense of Sex Worker Rights," Medium, August 13, 2020, https://medium.com/@katezenjoy/dear-esperanza-5aa7db4d501a.

6. Ted Cruz, "Modern Laws for the Fight against Human Trafficking," *TribTalk*, April 17, 2018, www.tribtalk.org/2018/04/17/modern-laws-for-the-fight-against-human-trafficking/?_

ga=2.4510515.1432496242.1523972028-965238643.1515448277.

7. See "Updates: Instagram Amplifying & Public Law No. 115–
    164," Survivors Against SESTA, March 15, 2019, https://
    survivorsagainstsesta.org/; "U.S.A. FOSTA/SESTA Legislation,"
    Global Network of Sex Work Projects, May 14, 2018, https://nswp.
    org/resource/nswp-briefing-notes/usa-fostasesta-legislation; Melissa
    Gira Grant, "Anti-Online Trafficking Bills Advance in Congress
    Despite Opposition from Survivors Themselves," *The Appeal*,
    March 14, 2018, https://theappeal.org/anti-online-trafficking-bills-
    advance-in-congress-despite-opposition-from-survivors-themselves-
    e741ea300307/.

8. Melissa Gira Grant, "The Real Story of the Bipartisan Anti–Sex
    Trafficking Bill That Failed Miserably on Its Own Terms," *New
    Republic*, June 23, 2021, https://newrepublic.com/article/162823/sex-
    trafficking-sex-work-sesta-fosta?ref=liberalcurrents.com.

9. Danielle Blunt, Ariel Wolf, and Naomi Laren, *Erased: The Impact of
    FOSTA-SESTA*, Hacking/Hustling, 2020, https://hackinghustling.
    org/erased-the-impact-of-fosta-sesta-2020/; Magali Lerman, "Impacts
    of SESTA on US Sex Workers' Vulnerability to Infectious Disease,"
    SWOP USA, 2018; Zhou Shuxuan, "The Real Lives of America's
    Chinese Masseuses," *Sixth Tone*, April 3, 2021, www.sixthtone.com/
    news/1007131; David Eichert, "'It Ruined My Life': FOSTA, Male
    Escorts, and the Construction of Sexual Victimhood in American
    Politics," *Virginia Journal of Social Policy and the Law* 26, no. 3 (January
    2020): 202, https://www.researchgate.net/publication/342903447_It_
    Ruined_My_Life_FOSTA_Male_Escorts_and_the_Construction_of_
    Sexual_Victimhood_in_American_Politics.

10. *Largest Sex Worker Conference in the USA Is Cancelled Due to Threat
    from FOSTA-SESTA*, Global Network of Sex Worker Projects, June 22,
    2018, https://www.nswp.org/news/largest-sex-worker-conference-the-
    usa-cancelled-due-threat-fosta-sesta.

11. See the work of Sins Invalid at www.sinsinvalid.org.

12. Emily Arismendy, "The Truth about Human Trafficking: Exposing
    Common Misconceptions," Safe Austin, www.safeaustin.org/the-
    truth-about-human-trafficking-exposing-common-misconceptions/.

13. See Andrea Ritchie, *Invisible No More: Police Violence against Black
    Women and Women of Colo*r (Boston: Beacon Press, 2017). Regarding
    the violent impact of sex offender registries on Black women in
    the sex industry, see the campaign work of Women With a Vision
    New Orleans and its long fight to have sex workers removed from

Louisiana's sex offender registry in Laura McTighe and Deon Haywood's *Fire Dreams, Making Black Feminist Liberation in the South* (Durham: Duke University Press, 2024). See also LeeAnn Adkins, "Labels, Supervision, and Surveillance: Motherhood and Sex Offender Status," S&F Online 15, no. 3 (2019), https://sfonline.barnard.edu/labels-supervision-surveillance-motherhood-sex-offender-status/.

14. "Stop Bill 251," Butterfly: Asian and Migrant Sex Workers Support Network, 2021, www.butterflysw.org/stop-bill-251; "Joint Submission on Bill 251, Combating Human Trafficking Act, 2021," HIV Legal Network, April 8, 2021, www.hivlegalnetwork.ca/site/joint-submission-on-bill-251-combating-human-trafficking-act-2021/?lang=en.

15. We have included the petition in the appendix.

16. Personal communication with Chanelle Gallant and Elene Lam, July 2023.

CHAPTER 9: WHAT IS MIGRANT SEX WORKER JUSTICE?

1. Personal communication with Chanelle Gallant and Elene Lam, July 2023.

2. For more information on the New Zealand model of sex work decriminalization, see: https://www.opendemocracy.net/en/beyond-trafficking-and-slavery/decriminalising-sex-work-in-new-zealand-its-history-and-impact/.

3. For more information about the harms of legalization to sex workers, listen to *Nevada Brothels and the Truth about Legalized Prostitution*, https://oldprosonline.org/nevada-brothels/.

AFTERWORD

1. On Britain's colonization of India, see Dylan Sullivan and Jason Hickel, "Capitalism and Extreme Poverty: A Global Analysis of Real Wages, Human Height, and Mortality since the Long 16th Century," *World Development* 161 (January 2023). On the Gayatri Spivak quote, see "Can the Subaltern Speak?"

2. "Human Costs," Costs of War Project, Brown University, Watson Institute for International and Public Affairs, page updated August 2023, https://watson.brown.edu/costsofwar/costs/human.

INDEX

abortion, 7–8, 20, 107, 117, 243n6
Adams, Eric, 87
AF³IRM, 183–86
Afghanistan, 21, 117, 225
AFL-CIO, 108
Alm, Steve, 184
Amazon, 52, 117, 256
Andrew, Elizabeth Wheeler, 101
Anti-Prostitution Pledge, 94
Arzaga, Ashley, 88
Asia, 67, 70, 102
ASTT(e)Q, 207
Atlanta, xi, 54, 88, 124

Barry, Kathleen, 107–8
Bedford, Terri-Jean, 223
Berlin, 137
Beutin, Lyndsey P., 123
Bill 251, 196-197
Black Women for Wages for House-
    work, xii
Boeing, 117
Britain, 224
Burke, Nora Butler, 89
Bush, George W., 94
Bushnell, Katharine C., 101
Butterfly: Asian and Migrant Sex
    Workers Support Network,
    ix, 2, 22, 33, 125, 169, 173, 207,
    217–221, 225, 229
  Bill 251 and, 199
  interludes on, 38, 40, 65, 71–72,
    136, 160–61
  research by, 84, 171, 178

Cambodia, 94–96, 251
Canada, ix, 9, 16, 124, 130, 165–66,
    199, 211, 223, 249n17
  anti–sex work laws in, 75–78, 87,
    96, 145, 147, 153–55, 160,
    198–200, 246n12
  decriminalization in, 223
  End Demand in, 146
  federal funding of anti-trafficking
    nonprofit in, 132
  "human trafficking" definition
    in, 14
  Human Trafficking Units in, 157
  interludes on, 38–44, 64, 66–74,
    134, 160
  migrant labor sectors in, 46–48
  right wing in, 17, 20
  trafficking myths in, 5, 99–100, 126
  travel bans in, 7, 40–41, 154, 210
Canadian Association of Elizabeth
    Fry Societies, 199
Canadian Border Services Agency,
    172
Canadian Centre to End Human
    Trafficking, 121, 131, 257n24
Can Do Bar, 208
Center to End the Trafficking and
    Exploitation of Children, 121
Central Europe, 110
Century Center, 183-184
Cherokee County Sheriff Depart-
    ment, 88
China, 81, 102, 104, 106
Chinatown Community for Equita-

263

ABOUT THE AUTHORS

ELENE LAM is an activist, artist, community organizer, educator, and human rights defender. She has fought for sex worker, migrant, gender, labor, and racial justice for over twenty years. She is the founder of Butterfly: Asian and Migrant Sex Worker Support Network and the co-founder of Migrant Sex Workers Project. She has used diverse and innovative approaches to advocate social justice for migrant sex workers, such as leadership building and community mobilization. She holds a master's of law and master's of social work. She is a PhD candidate at McMaster University (School of Social Work) and is studying the harm of the anti-trafficking movement. She was awarded the Constance E. Hamilton Award for Women's Equality by the City of Toronto.

CHANELLE GALLANT is the eldest daughter of a poor single mother. She has been building movements that can protect the lives and liberation of poor and working class women and queers for 25 years. Chanelle is a movement writer, organizer, strategist and consultant whose writing has appeared in over a dozen books and publications. She co-founded the Migrant Sex Workers Project, SURJ-Toronto and has provided training and advocacy on sex work and racial justice, from city hall to the United Nations. Chanelle sits on the national board for Showing Up for Racial Justice and Catalyst Project and has helped to move millions into organizing through donor advising and grassroots fundraising. She holds an MA in Sociology and was a Lambda Literary Fellow. Find her at chanellegallant.com

HARSHA WALIA is the award-winning author of *Undoing Border Imperialism* (2013) and *Border and Rule* (2021). Trained in the law, she is a community organizer and campaigner in migrant justice, anti-capitalist, feminist, and anti-imperialist movements, including No One Is Illegal and Women's Memorial March Committee.

ROBYN MAYNARD is an award-winning Black feminist scholar-activist based in Toronto and the author of *Policing Black Lives: State Violence in Canada from Slavery to the Present* and coauthor of *Rehearsals for Living*. She is an assistant professor at the University of Toronto and her writings on policing, feminism, abolition, and Black liberation are taught widely across North America and Europe.